A LIFE AT THE CHALKFACE

A Memoir Of A London Headteacher

by

Mike Kent

PRAISE FOR MIKE KENT'S BOOKS

I opened *Tales From The Head's Room* and then could not put it down! Mike Kent's stories are hilarious but also convey the hard work, effort and dedication that teachers put into our young people to give them a great education.

'Stupot', Teacher at The Blue Elephant Theatre, London.

Encouraging children to learn is what education is about and Mike doesn't let the nonsense get in his way. You'll be thoroughly entertained by *'Tales From The Head's Room'.*

'KimmyKool', Lecturer, Goldsmiths University, London.

Humour, heroism, common sense and inspiring humanity shine through Mike Kent's TES columns. His most recent books *'The Rabbit's Laid An Egg, Miss!'* and *'Tales From The Head's Room'* demonstrate how, against all the odds, it is possible to create a centre of educational excellence, where both children and staff actively enjoy the learning process. There is still hope for our children while the Mike Kents of this world exist!

Emma Davis, Trainee Headteacher

The collection of Mike Kent's popular columns in *'The Rabbit's Laid An Egg Miss!'* is addictive, giving tantalising glimpses of life as a primary school headteacher. I became totally engrossed in his humour, poignancy, frustration and joys. It will remind parents of the sort of education they really want for their children. Keep writing, Mike Kent.....the educational world needs you!

Emily Smith, primary school teacher

I loved *'The Rabbit's Laid An Egg Miss!'* I am a parent who was looking for insights into how schools work and how teachers think. It made me wish my children could go to his school!

M.S.Hunt, parent

This book, *'Tales from The Head's Room'* is one which teachers can return to again and again in delight and recognition.

Norna Moses, Adviser, Southwark Education.

PRAISE FOR MIKE KENT'S TES COLUMN

Your writing has a humanity that renders your columns pertinent, funny and extremely readable.

Gerard Kelly, Former Editor, Times Educational Supplement

Just wanted to let you know I've have just read your piece in the TES and thought it was wonderful. It brought a tear to my eye.

Sue Husband, Education Manager, McDonald's Restaurants

I love your gentle down-to earth humour and I couldn't agree more when you puncture the pomposity of so much educational thinking. You really do brighten up our Fridays!

Richard Marsden, Ofsted Inspector

My daughter has just graduated from the University of Sheffield with a first in Journalism Studies and the broadcasting award from ITV News. She got such a great start at your primary school!

Caroline Richardson, General Manager, Norwich Playhouse

I wanted to thank you for your sane and amusing columns, which I thoroughly enjoy.

David Percival, Formerly Principal, Northbrook College, Sussex

Just thought I'd drop you a line to thank you for your column. Sometimes I think I'm going mental and it must be me. Then I read your current piece and realise that, no, it isn't me. It's them.

Ian McNeilly, Director, National Association for the Teaching of English

Thank you for yet another excellent article on Friday. Just like you, my philosophy of administration was that if it didn't add anything to children's learning, it should go in the bin!

Mick Brookes, Former General Secretary, National Association Of Head Teachers.

I have seen for myself how high expectations at your school, coupled with genuine care and concern for the well-being of every child and adult are at the heart of your success.

Diane Conway, School Improvement Partner.

Thanks for reminding me every week of how primary schools could, and should, be run.

Peter Newsam, Former Education Officer, ILEA

As always, you were spot on this week. Best wishes to a true voice of the teaching profession.

Antony Lishak, Children's Author

You have been truly inspirational for children and other education professionals. You are a 'one-off' and will be impossible to replace.

Paul Morgan, School Inspector, Southwark Education

Just to say that I was moved to tears when I read the exceptional piece you wrote last Friday.

Alison Atkinson, Educational Consultant

An organisation I belong to needed someone to contact you and I said 'Me, me, he's wonderful!

Sue Palmer, author of 'Toxic Childhood'

Dedication

For Mark and John

Not saints… just lifelong friends

All the proceeds from this book will go to the Cancer Unit
at Guys Hospital, London

FOREWORD BY SIR TIM BRIGHOUSE,
FORMERLY COMMISSIONER FOR LONDON SCHOOLS

Autobiographies can vary so much. Authors may have a lot to say but can't say it and of course the reverse, sadly, is also true. But just occasionally, along comes an autobiography with lots to say and an enviable way of saying it. This is one of those books.

Mike Kent is a rare talent. He writes beautifully and has spent most of his life in schools, first as a pupil, then as a teacher and finally for thirty years as a headteacher in South London. So here is a rich tale, full of revealing insights into many aspects of education, and much riveting anecdote… all set against the backdrop of school life.

All successful teachers know they have to be good storytellers and the stories of the very best relate brilliantly to the thinking and understanding they are hoping to promote for those they are teaching… whether children or adults. Essentially, great autobiographies do the same thing and Mike Kent's deserves to be ranked among them for that very reason.

Take the early chapter on the local inspector. Vividly drawn, the cameo of the newly arrived inspector from Berkshire can be read in so many ways. For me it raises the issue of just how difficult it is to find the right people to become successful 'advisers' or 'inspectors' of schools. They can easily fall into the category of 'hostile witnesses'. Through their high profile role in accountability, inspectors are already set up to be the archetypical 'hostile witness'. As another of the chapters so clearly shows, they often live up to that expectation and in the process cause immense human and organisational damage.

All headteachers need something to turn to from time to time that will make them chuckle and see the funny side of the sometimes absurd and surreal dilemmas they find themselves in. Mike's book does just that. But his book isn't just for school leaders. His reflections on every aspect of primary school life will be enjoyed by anybody with the slightest interest in education. It will also help all those already leading schools, as well as anybody aspiring to leadership… and the many governors who are now expected to play a role never remotely contemplated when Mike first became a head. Oh…and there's a very amusing chapter on them too!

Throughout the book – and I suspect his career – Mike has punctured self-importance, mocked unnecessary bureaucracy and fought tirelessly for better chances for his pupils and the teachers who worked for him. He has walked endless extra miles for others. His ability to come up smiling in any circumstances has been a lifeline for him and since the humour is extremely contagious, empowering for others too.

Read on, and enjoy his story.
Tim Brighouse

First Published 2015
Text Copyright © Mike Kent 2015
Bretwalda Books, Unit 8, Fir Tree Close, Epsom, Surrey KT17 3LD
info@BretwaldaBooks.com
www.BretwaldaBooks.com
ISBN 978-1-910440-01-8

A LIFE AT THE CHALKFACE

INTRODUCTION

There's a bundle bee in our classroom, Miss. He shouldn't be in here. He should be out in the air, doin' honey.' Emily, age 5

I was a six year old at my Church of England infant school when I was first introduced to a headteacher.

It wasn't the most auspicious of occasions. Teresa Wilkinson's friend had dared her to push my reading book off the desk, and I had retaliated by pinching her bottom. Teresa had then put on a solemn face, complained about me to Mrs Reece the class teacher, and stood behind her grinning mischievously while Mrs Reece wagged her finger at me. This caused me to grin back, and thinking that I was not only sexually deviant but thoroughly insolent as well, Mrs Reece felt the most appropriate course of action would be to take me along to Miss Rayment, the headteacher, for a word or two that might return me to the path of righteousness. Miss Rayment, a devout Christian spinster in her mid fifties, peered at me distastefully over her spectacles, informed me that if I didn't mend my ways she'd be having a strong word with my mother, and then placed me cross-legged in the corridor outside her room, where she promptly forgot about me until lunchtime.

When I moved to the Junior department, Mr Chandler, the headmaster, was the only male in the building and because I was generally well behaved, I rarely saw him. He took occasional assemblies, though he didn't seem to get much pleasure from doing so, and once a month he came into the classrooms with a handful of paper strips, one of which he gave to the teacher, who instantly stopped whatever she was doing and checked it from end to end. I realised later on that these strips were the teachers' monthly salary slips. He would ask our teacher what we were doing, smile at us briefly, and then retreat to his office. Other than that, I spent four years at the school without coming into any kind of contact with him, although I was aware that he was pretty nifty with a cane. On one occasion, I remember five boys coming tearfully out into the playground looking very sorry for themselves, having just been caned by him. I had no idea what they'd done... they were older than me and I didn't dare ask... although it was rumoured that they'd been setting off fireworks at the back of the air raid shelter.

Although Mr Chandler rarely spoke to a child, I assume he must have gained at least a little pleasure from his job, because the memory of his tears during the assembly on the day he retired still stays vividly with me. Although he'd lasted until he was sixty two, his progressive deafness had made his position at school increasingly untenable, although he was determined to continue as choirmaster to the Mother's Union choir. My mother belonged to the choir and invariably came home from rehearsals in an irritable mood, since she and everybody else could hear perfectly well when something was out of tune, but Mr Chandler couldn't.

Apart from the occasional blip, primary school proved a very pleasurable experience for me. I enjoyed gathering knowledge and the company and friendship of the other children. I loved writing stories and poetry, I was fascinated by history and the sciences, and taking part in school or class plays was great fun. By the time I reached the final year, I was expected to do well in the eleven plus examination, and my parents hoped that I would attend the local grammar school.

But it wasn't to be. Shortly before the exams I contracted chicken pox and was deliriously ill with it, although I had recovered sufficiently when the time came to sit the exams, which lasted for three days. I remember writing in a haze, uncomfortable and still itching from the gradually disappearing spots, and although I felt I'd made a reasonable attempt at the papers, I didn't feel I'd done as well as I'd hoped. Waiting for the result was a tense time for my parents, and when the letter arrived on a Saturday morning my mother's expression immediately told me the worst. I had failed the eleven plus, and I would have to attend the local secondary modern school, a grim building with ancient teachers, a fearsome reputation and, it was rumoured, extremely unpleasant initiation rites for newbies. I remember my mother being so depressed about it she absentmindedly boiled a saucepan dry.

But then a reprieve. A new, young headteacher had taken over from Mr Chandler, and he called my parents in for a chat. It appeared that I'd done extremely well in the English and intelligence tests, and had failed the mathematics paper by just one mark. Although it wouldn't be possible to get me into the grammar school, there was a place available at a new comprehensive school and it was mine if my parents wanted it. The head explained that comprehensive schools were a very new idea, and if I chose to go I would receive a very similar education to the one offered at the grammar school. There was only one downside... the school was nine miles away. I'd have to be up very early. We didn't see this as a problem and I gladly accepted. Anything rather than the humility of having my head thrust down the toilet on my first day at the secondary modern school.

Unfortunately, the rosy picture that had been painted didn't match reality. The building, although relatively new, was drab and dull. Endless stone corridors leading to classrooms which all looked the same; great expanses of grey and grubby cream, a blackboard which stretched right across the room, and furniture with a battered, worn appearance, a look echoed by the teaching staff, many of whom seemed unable to make a lesson even remotely interesting. On my second morning, a newly made friend and I couldn't find the classroom we were supposed to go to for our first French lesson, and after being gleefully misdirected by several older children, we eventually arrived twenty five minutes late. The teacher, rather than showing a little sympathy, immediately gave us a detention. It was the start of a steady decline in my affection for the school.

Although I had begun my secondary school career bright-eyed and full of enthusiasm, it had rapidly waned by the end of my first year. By the time I'd endured three years at the school I couldn't wait to leave the building each day and get home to pursue all the other activities I enjoyed; camping, belonging to the scouts, going to the pictures, playing table tennis, cycling at weekends and burying my head in books of chemistry experiments. I'd also discovered girls, and found they were a lot more interesting than homework.

A school can only be as successful as the headteacher makes it. Looking back on my secondary education, I'm certain the headmaster, Mr Watson, had a great deal to do with its failure to give me the education I wanted. He was certainly an imposing figure, a commanding academic who strode swiftly along the corridors like God, his black gown flowing behind him and his mind eternally on higher things. Children and teachers stepped aside for him and I was pretty certain he brooked no dissent, or even discussion, from his teachers or anybody else in the building. The school was his domain, and he ruled it ruthlessly. Classes stood up when he entered to speak to a teacher, and he immediately ushered them down again. This seemed to me an irritatingly pointless activity, especially as he entered classrooms regularly, presumably to check on whether the lessons being offered were academic enough. While there, he would regale us with tales of his activities at public school, which bored us rigid and hadn't the slightest relevance to our teenage lives.

But although we feared him, he had little idea of how to deal effectively with misbehaviour. When a pupil had broken wind with remarkable velocity in a private study class he was supervising, he expected the culprit to own up immediately. When he didn't, Mr Watson lined up the whole group of boys in the corridor outside his room after the lesson and told them they'd spend every breaktime there until the little fool who'd disrupted the lesson so rudely had announced himself. Before long, bored witless and to his greater annoyance, the boys were fooling around in the corridor. After two days, he'd had enough. His door was flung open and he roared at the children to clear off.

Nevertheless, I muddled my way through the next five years, not working especially hard but always doing enough to get by, particularly in the subjects I enjoyed and which were taught well. Then, when I entered the sixth form and had to start thinking about a job, I discovered that the career guidance being offered left much to be desired. When the local careers officer came to speak to us, he seemed to have little of interest to say, other than that there were lots of opportunities at the huge EMI factory nearby. Worried by this, and feeling that my life ought to be taking some sort of purposeful direction, my parents attempted to make an appointment with Mr Watson to discuss my future. He wasn't particularly interested, since he didn't know me from Adam, but my parents insisted and achieved a fruitless half hour with him, where he looked at the mismatched subjects I was studying and hastily scribbled out a revised schedule of options which seemed worse than the one I already had. My mother said she'd have a chat with me about all this and get back to him if things didn't work out.

Obviously rattled by her determination, Mr Watson called me in to see him the next morning and asked what sort of career I had in mind. I explained that I loved going to the pictures and since Ealing Studios were just down the road from my house, I quite fancied the idea of applying for a job as a tea boy and then working my way up to becoming a world famous director. He didn't seem overly impressed with that, so I said another thought was journalism. Since I'd had several letters published in the local paper, it occurred to me that I could start as a novice reporter covering local robberies and weddings and progress eventually to Fleet Street, where I could become editor of a national newspaper. It was admirable that I was aiming high, said Mr Watson, but had I anything else in mind? There were, for example, plenty of promising jobs available at the EMI factory down the road.

I explained that I did have one other idea. My scoutmaster, a lively 28 year old who made our meetings and camping holidays enormous fun and for whom I had the greatest respect and affection, was also a primary school teacher. He thought it was a marvellous career, he was loving every minute of it, and he had suggested I should give it strong consideration.

Mr Watson nodded vigorously. It was obvious he thought this an eminently sensible choice, even if teaching small children wasn't something he would even remotely consider. Since getting into a training college required only five GCEs, he felt that even I might be able to manage that, despite my rather scruffy academic achievement to date. Furthermore, he was on first name terms with the principal of a training college in central London, and if I put my head down and worked extremely hard until I took my exams, he would put in a personal recommendation for me when the time came to apply.

This seemed an excellent arrangement to me. I duly passed my exams, Mr Watson did his bit, and I was accepted for training at a college in Westminster. I looked forward with great anticipation to becoming a primary school teacher; I'd start at the bottom as a class teacher, move steadily up the career ladder, and maybe at some point even become a deputy head. So long as I still had lots of contact with the children, because that's what I knew I'd enjoy most about the job.

But there was one thing I was particularly clear about. Based on my experience of them to date, I certainly didn't want to become a headteacher.

CHAPTER 1
A SCHOOL OF MY OWN

In the 1920s, Chicago was a danjerus place, full of bullits and broffles. Mark, Age 10

Storm clouds had been gathering through grey skies for the last two hours, and as I eased the car through the Camberwell evening traffic and into Comber Grove the rain began to lash down on the bonnet. Half way down the deserted street, clouds hurried ominously above the gaunt, three decker Victorian building that was Comber Grove primary school. It stood like a fortress for imprisoning children rather than a place in which to educate them. Built at the turn of the century when educational practice was vastly different, it had survived two world wars, a succession of working class children and a change of name. A woman carrying three shopping bags, looking much older than she was, hurried past the iron car park gates, calling in a language I didn't recognise to the small child trailing behind her. A dog rummaged in the fast food remains that somebody had tossed at the street bin and missed.

I eased the car through the gate and into the tiny staff car park... when the school had been built teachers would have been thought lucky if they owned bicycles... and I sat back in the seat mentally rehearsing answers to the questions I thought I might be asked. The interview was at eight o'clock, and I had twenty minutes to spare.

The rain suddenly eased and I hurried to the main entrance. As I walked into the brightly lit corridor, a stocky middle aged man with early evening stubble and trousers loosely supported by green braces paused from locking a classroom door and motioned me towards a staircase.

'Come for an interview? I'm Fred. Premises Officer. Up there, first right, 'alfway along the corridor, sit yerself down on a chair in the Viewing Room and wait for the Clerk. What time's yer interview?'

'Hello Fred. It's at eight o'clock.'

'You're early then. Rotten night to come out. They're runnin' a bit late. One of the governor's cars wouldn't start. You'll probably have to wait for a while. Are you at a local school?'

'The Grange. In Bermondsey. I've been deputy head there for eleven years. Have you been here long?'

He gave a deep throaty chuckle. 'Too long, mate. Not a barrel of laughs, this school. That's why Mr Andrews is retirin', though he ain't been well for years. Kids are always getting up to somethin'. They flooded the toilets again today. Infants, it was. Stuffed tissues into a sink and it went through three floors. Mind you, everything's different now. Kids seem to do as they like. There's no discipline these days. I blame the parents, personally.' He looked at his watch and took a rolled-up cigarette from behind his ear.

'Oh well, good luck. They're not a bad set of governors. I reckon you'll be in there about half an hour.'

I knew where to go. I'd visited the school as soon as I'd received the letter telling me I'd been shortlisted for the headship. The interview was being held in the staffroom directly opposite the Viewing Room, so called because it contained a television, a screen, and a 16mm projector. Inside, a row of wooden chairs had been arranged against a wall. Never particularly comfortable in a suit, I straightened my tie, flicked the raindrops from my jacket and sat down to gather my thoughts. Across the corridor, I could hear the current candidate answering questions in a surprisingly loud voice, although I couldn't make out what he was saying, or what questions were being asked. It occurred to me that if he got the job he wouldn't have any difficulty being heard at the back of a school assembly.

Teaching primary school children had brought me intense satisfaction. After three years at training college, I'd opted to teach in Islington, at that time an extremely challenging area of London for a young teacher. Although I'd progressed quickly and steadily up the career ladder, working in three socially deprived areas of London, I'd had no desire to try for the ultimate goal.. a headship and a school of my own. I'd been perfectly happy with a deputy headship throughout the seventies, because I felt I'd achieved the best of both worlds. I loved class teaching and the pleasure of being with young children, but as a senior manager, I'd also had considerable responsibility for shaping the direction and ethos of the school. I had an excellent relationship with my headteacher, I enjoyed the banter and humour of the staffroom, and there was great pleasure to be had from helping resolve issues and problems experienced by everybody within the school society... the children, their parents, the school governors, the teachers, the head and the local education authority. It was an invigorating and rewarding job, and one that I loved.

And then, one July morning, my headteacher brought a newly qualified teacher into my classroom to meet me. This was Miriam, she said, and she'd be joining the staff permanently in September, but as she'd finished her training she was keen to help out until the end of term. As our eyes met, some kind of intense chemistry took place and within days we were going out together. Months later we were married and realising that my small bachelor flat would have to be exchanged for a three bed semi and a fat mortgage. And preferably sooner rather than later, as my new wife already had a six year old daughter. It was time to raise the stakes, earn more money, and become a headteacher.

The promotional route in London during the early eighties was straightforward. If you were successful and worked hard, you would be rewarded with additional money and a special post of responsibility for a curriculum area. If you wanted to go further, you tried hard to get your work noticed by the local inspectors, who'd visit your school several times a year. Then, with suitable references and a nod from the inspectors, you'd apply for a deputy headship, usually in a nearby school, because inspectors talked to each other and by that time you'd have earned a certain reputation. If you were successful, there you'd stay, particularly as teaching at that time tended to be a career that lasted a lifetime. Unless, of course, you eventually fancied the far more challenging role of running your own school.

The route to a London headship was equally straightforward. Often, if the local inspector thought you were ready, he'd tell you of local vacancies that were coming up, and suggest you applied. Since you were a known quantity, it would be beneficial for him if you were appointed to a school under his responsibility, and he would usually be on the interviewing panel. You could also scan the advertisements in the educational press, and if you found something suitable you'd send for the application pack and keep your fingers crossed. If you were shortlisted, you'd be invited to look around the school and meet everybody before the interview.

And now, here I sat, on a rainy Friday night, with a miserable head cold, waiting to be interviewed by a panel of school governors. As usual, six applicants had been shortlisted, and three would eventually be selected for the final interview at London's County Hall, the hub of the Inner London Education Authority, a body that had responsibility for every primary and secondary school in London until the early nineties, when the Thatcher government disbanded it.

Twenty minutes later, I heard the staffroom door open, voices saying goodbye to the candidate and footsteps as he strode off down the corridor. For a moment I'd hoped he might come into the Viewing Room so that I could ask him how things had gone, but almost immediately the door opened and a tall, smartly dressed gentleman carrying a clipboard walked over and shook my hand. He consulted the clipboard and smiled.

'Ah, Mr Kent, I think? Last one to be interviewed. I'm Godfrey, the Clerk to the Governors. I'll be taking notes, and I'll let you know the outcome of the interview in a few days. If you'd like to follow me, I'll take you in.'

Some large tables in the staffroom had been arranged as three sides of a square. A chair had been placed in the centre of the fourth side and I sat on it tentatively. I glanced swiftly round the room, crossed my legs and smiled, hoping that my body language seemed positive. There were three or four people sitting behind each table and several of them were scribbling notes on pieces of paper. Some smiled back at me, some didn't. The man at the centre of the table opposite me pushed his fierce black spectacles to the end of his nose and looked cautiously over them.

'Good evening, Mr Kent. Thank you for coming. My name is Alan Warren and I'm the Chair of Governors. I'll be asking you some questions first. Then the governors will introduce themselves and everyone will ask you a question in turn. So, tell us why you would like to be the headteacher of our school.'

It was an easy question and one I'd prepared thoroughly for. I talked about the achievements in my career so far, the pleasure I'd had from my deputy headship, and the reasons why I now felt ready for the ultimate challenge. For a fleeting moment I considered raising a smile by mentioning my large mortgage and then immediately dismissed the idea. If they didn't laugh I'd have wrecked my chances from the start. The Chairman seemed satisfied with what I'd said and he turned to the elderly gentleman sitting on his left, whose arm was in plaster. He saw me glance at it.

'I fell off my bike,' he said. 'Getting too old for it, I suppose. Roads are getting more dangerous every day. Far too many cars in my view. Would you have far to come to get here?'

This didn't seem particularly relevant to primary education, but I explained that I only lived twenty five minutes away by car, so the journey would be very straightforward.

'Important for the Headmaster to be in before everybody else,' he said. 'Traffic can be terrible. Ever thought about getting a bike? Keeps me fit and trim. How old do you think I am?'

I hadn't the slightest idea, but I thought it would be prudent to err on the side of flattery.

'Not a day over thirty, I'd say.' There was a ripple of amusement.

'No. Try again.'

'Um.. Fifty eight? Or thereabouts?'

'Seventy nine. Would have come here on my bike tonight if I hadn't fallen off it.'

The chairman coughed gently and motioned towards a slim, attractive woman on his left.

'Mrs Peters, your question I think?'

She smiled brightly at me and read her question from a piece of paper. 'Hello Mr Kent. I'm a parent governor. Do you think parents have an important role in the life of a school?'

I felt my body relax into the chair. Another question I'd expected and prepared carefully for. I explained how crucial it was for the school to win the support and help of the parents, and how they could work alongside the teachers to make children's education a fully rounded experience, as well as helping out at all the functions and concerts I hoped the school would organise. She nodded vigorously at everything I said and then thanked me. I turned to the person next to her for his question. He was a man in his fifties with thick, bushy white eyebrows that shot up and down as he spoke.

'Discipline, Mr Kent, discipline. What are your thoughts on that?'

'It's the essential starting point. If children aren't well behaved then you certainly won't have effective learning.'

'Well, obviously,' he replied, with a ferocity that surprised me. 'The thing is, what are you going to do about it? It's all very well saying you need it, but you've got to have a plan.'

'Of course. It's something I'd want to sort out at my first staff meeting. It's essential that each teacher has the same expectation of good behaviour, and…'

He waved his arm. 'Yes, yes, they might have the same expectations, but some teachers can do it and some can't. And half our intake come from homes which are a shambles. Mr McGinley tells me the toilets have been flooded yet again. If they carry on like this we won't be teaching 'em maths, we'll be building a bloody ark.'

My voice rose a little as I explained firmly that it didn't have to be like that. There were lots of techniques for cultivating good behaviour in children and I'd happily expound my theories if he wanted me too.

'Not really enough time,' the Chairman said. 'And anyway, your references would seem to indicate that you've got that sort of thing under control. It's just a case of whether you can get everybody else to do it as well. Mr Gambi, your question.' I'd noticed that Mr Gambi was the only black governor on the panel. He too read his question from a slip of paper.

'Many schools take part in Black History Month. Is Black History Month something that you would support in your school, and if so, how do you see it being used and what are the benefits?'

I was aware that Camberwell, like many areas of inner London, had a rising black population, and that this had caused problems in some of its schools. Poor housing, resentment from white families, discipline problems, racial abuse and accusations of institutionalised racism in schools had created uncomfortable tensions and resentment, although I was aware that the ILEA was doing a great deal more than most authorities to counter this negativity. Nevertheless, I thought carefully before answering.

'I'm not really in favour of it. I think it can highlight differences rather than promote harmony.'

'So you don't believe in celebrating black culture?'

'Of course I do. I believe in celebrating all cultures and their achievements. Especially through the arts. But I don't think it's necessary to have a Black History Month to do that. We should be enjoying every culture all the year round.'

'So you wouldn't do Black History Month?'

'I would need to be persuaded that it's the best way to appreciate black achievement.'

'So Black History Month isn't something you'd introduce here? I see. Thank you.' He scribbled on his paper and seemed decidedly unimpressed. The Chair turned to a trim, elderly lady in a plum coloured suit who leaned forward, folded her arms and looked at me quizzically.

'We're in interesting times, educationally, Mr Kent, don't you think? When I was a little girl at primary school we all sat in rows doing the same thing at the same time. Lady Plowden certainly turned all that on its head in the sixties, didn't she?'

'By and large I think it was a very positive move,' I said. 'After all, every child is different and the Plowden Report made all teachers look at children as individuals with differing needs. It gave schools far more freedom with the curriculum.'

'Far too much in my view,' interrupted the governor with bushy eyebrows. 'If you've got thirty kids, all wandering round doing a painting whenever they feel like it, you've got a recipe for chaos. Be like a bloody wet playtime all day.'

It was a view I was familiar with. Primary schools across the country were still coming to terms with the massive changes in education and the new ways their classrooms were being organised, and many teachers were struggling with them.

'It doesn't have to be like that,' I said. 'Children learn best when they're interested and enthused. A classroom should be organised for their benefit, not the teacher's. If it's well run, you can have several different activities going on and children will learn at their own speed and their own ability level.'

'Still sounds like a recipe for chaos to me,' he said. 'How can one teacher cater for thirty children all doing different things? I'd be interested to see you make it work.'

'Hopefully you'll be giving me the chance to,' I countered, a little weakly.

Fred had been wrong. We'd already used up a lot of time and I certainly wasn't going to be out in half an hour. But despite the head cold, I was beginning to enjoy myself, especially as the questions became more probing. I was asked about dealing with a difficult staff member, what provisions I'd make for children with special needs, what I felt about reading schemes, and whether I considered nursery education to be important. Then I was questioned closely about the latest reports on education, how I would assess the progress of children in my school, and how I'd handle an emergency such as a broken boiler in the middle of winter. By the time the chairman thanked me and said the interview had come to an end, I felt the governors had had their money's worth. I drove home wondering whether I'd answered the questions sensibly, or merely irritated people. The line between showing that you're able and confident yet not arrogant and overbearing is a thin one.

The next seven days were an agony of waiting. I felt the school could be the right one for me and I wanted the headship. There was plenty I could do there and it would prove a suitable challenge. I ran the questions over and over in my mind. Some I felt I'd answered well, although I felt I'd been too hesitant and non-committal with others. But then, what the hell, I had my own views about the way things should be done and if they didn't like them they wouldn't put me through.

Then, on Saturday morning, the official envelope dropped through the front door. The governors were pleased to tell me that I was now in the short list of three final candidates, and would I please attend an interview at County Hall the following Thursday.

This was exciting. I spent the next few evenings feverishly reading everything about current educational practice I could lay my hands on. My wife and friends asked me mock interview questions and I talked to my current headteacher about the next interview. It wouldn't be easy, she said, but the local inspector would be on the panel and he knew my dedication to the job, so the omens were good.

On the day of the interview, I was surprised at how nervous I was. My wife hugged me, assured me I'd be fine, and added that even if I wasn't, more headships would come up and this interview would be good practice. Leaving in plenty of time, I drove through the crowded midday traffic, over Westminster Bridge and down into County Hall's massive parking area. For a moment I panicked. The car park seemed full. Should I try and find a side street somewhere? But if I did that, and couldn't find a space, I would be late for the interview and that would ruin my chances.

With a sigh of relief, I noticed a car reversing out and I carefully manoeuvred into the vacant slot. The next job was to find the room where the interview was being held. County Hall was a vast building with endless corridors, and although the letter had told me that I should report to room 103, actually finding the room took another twenty minutes. I was relieved that I had left home so early. Room 103 was at the end of a long corridor, and when I reached it there was a woman sitting on a bench by the wall. She smiled as I approached. I recognised her face from a recent meeting I'd attended.

'I'm Eileen,' she said. 'I'm the deputy at St Michael's. I heard you were going for the job too. David's in there now. This'll be his fifth headship interview. He deserves to get a school but he hates interviews.'

'Me too,' I said, 'But the first one didn't seem too bad.'

'It's difficult to know what the governors are looking for. Comber Grove is a tough school. I think half the governors want a progressive head and the other half want to get the kids sitting back in straight rows. Oh well, we'll see.'

She began flipping through the pages of her magazine and I looked blankly at the wall opposite, once again rehearsing the answers to possible questions in my mind. Would I be asked the same ones again, or would they have compiled a different set? Eventually the door opened, David came out and sat down, and Eileen was called in.

'How was it?' I asked him.

'Absolute bastard,' he said. 'The worst yet. Don't think I'll be getting this one.'

I grimaced and commiserated, although secretly thinking that if he'd fluffed things, it would be a contest between Eileen and me. I could hear her voice in the distance, confidently answering the question she'd been asked. She'd been a deputy for longer than me, she was well known in the authority, and she'd been tipped for a headship for some time. Perhaps this one was destined to be hers. Eventually the door opened again and Eileen walked out, smiling and confident.

'Not too bad at all,' she said. 'Much better than the last one. At least the committee seemed human.'

After several minutes, Godfrey appeared at the door. 'Mr Kent,' he smiled. 'Nice to see you again. Please come through.'

I walked into the room. It seemed enormous, and although

it had two large windows, its wood panelled walls and vast oak table made it seem very dark. Seven people sat behind the table, and in front of it a small table and chair had been provided for the candidates. There was a carafe of water and a glass on the table, although I knew if I poured a drink my hand would probably shake and I'd spill it. Looking round, I recognised the local inspector, the Chair of Governors, and the teacher governor who'd been present at the previous interview. The other three people were representatives from the authority, one of whom spoke warmly to me.

'Well, congratulations on getting through the first interview, Mr Kent,' she said. 'I gather the governors were very impressed, and your inspector has given you an excellent reference. Now this is the tough part...'

Everyone smiled sympathetically and I leaned forward ready for the onslaught, but although the interview was searching it was conducted in a relaxed and friendly manner. It seemed that I had already proved myself at the first interview and the panel simply wanted to reassure themselves that I was ready to run one of their primary schools. At last, the chairwoman looked at her watch and smiled.

'Well that's it, Mr Kent. Thank you very much. We've asked you a lot of questions. Is there anything you'd like to ask us?'

'Well, just one thing,' I said. 'I'd like to ask you to give me the chance to show you what I can do.'

'We're going to consider whether we should do that right now. Please sit outside.'

I felt I'd done a pretty good job, though a glance at Eileen reminded me that she had, too. 'About ten minutes and we'll know,' said David. 'It'll be one of you two. Don't know whether it's even worth me staying.'

'Cheer up,' Eileen said, 'You'll get one eventually. Most deputies do.'

We fell silent and sat with our hands in our laps. I realised how exhausting the whole process had been, and it wasn't something I relished repeating as many times as David had. Perhaps I should have just been satisfied with deputy headship.

And then I heard the words that made my heart leap. The door opened and a voice in the room said 'Godfrey, can you ask Mr Kent to come back in please.'

'Well done!' said Eileen warmly. 'It's yours. Oh well, back to the drawing board for us.'

I sat down in front of the panel once more, hardly believing my luck.

'It's been a pleasure interviewing you, Mr Kent', said the lady who'd introduced the panel. 'We want to give you that chance to show what you can do. We hope you'll be very happy.'

As I drove home, my mind was racing. This was very exciting. I'd been given my own school and I was going to be responsible for shaping the education of a whole generation of children.

'Well?' said Miriam, as I walked through the door.

'Fluffed it, love. Still a deputy I'm afraid. Don't know how we're going to pay the mortgage.'

She looked surprised and disappointed. 'Never mind. There'll be plenty of others. And we'll manage.'

'Not really,' I grinned. 'The mortgage is safe. I got it!'

'Oh you are a sod! That's brilliant! I love you!'

We celebrated that night with champagne and a meal we couldn't afford. It was a delicious moment and I had almost half a term to prepare for my new job. Life was indeed a bowl of cherries.

Unfortunately, it wouldn't be long before I was grinding my teeth on the stones...

CHAPTER 2
FINDING MY FEET

The sun is a living orgasm. Andrew, Age 10

Alan Green was the local schools inspector attached to the ILEA division in which I was going to work. Shortly after my interview, he telephoned and asked me to come and chat to him about my appointment. This was an important meeting, because he knew the school and its staff extremely well, and he could give me valuable insight on how I might approach my first few weeks. He motioned me to a chair in his tiny office and took a file from his desk.

'The roll has fallen steadily over the last few years,' he said. 'It's certainly not a failing school, but it's not a particularly popular one either. Quite a few parents choose to send their children to the neighbouring primary schools. By and large the staff are competent, and there are a couple of very good ones, but they don't have a good leader, and it shows. The head has retired now. He'd been off sick for some time.'

'So the deputy is running the school at the moment?'

'Yes, and unfortunately she's not very popular with the staff. It'll be your only real problem, but it's a big one, simply because she is your second in command. I'm not quite sure how you're going to deal with that. Your big advantage is that the classes are relatively small because of the falling roll. The children aren't easy though, so you'll have your work cut out. And there could be a problem with the budget.'

'How much of a problem?'

'Oh, your staff will get paid, but there's quite a lot that needs to be done to the building. The roof is leaking in places and some of the windows are dangerous. The deputy is always complaining about it, but the authority doesn't have the money for big repairs at the moment. And I gather there was a bit of a mess with the accounting last year, so you'll have to be a bit cautious with your spending.'

He opened his folder and handed me a set of documents on different coloured papers.

'You might find these helpful. The authority has produced them as a guide for new heads. Each one deals with a different aspect of leadership and there are lists of things you need to consider early in your headship. They should serve as a useful prompt for all the things you'll need to get done.'

'It all seems a bit overwhelming... having the ultimate responsibility for everything.'

'You'll be fine. Don't rush around changing lots of things straightaway though. Nobody likes sudden change, especially teachers. Give yourself time to settle in. Get to know your staff and the children. Find out who the saints and the sinners are. Then make changes gradually. And when you do make a big decision about something, try to carry the staff with you. Discuss it thoroughly first. If you've got most of the staff with you, the others will follow, even if a bit reluctantly.'

'What about the school governors? Are they likely to be supportive when I want to change things?'

'I don't know them that well, but they're a fairly amiable bunch. The usual thing... mostly local people with an interest in education. A couple of aspiring councillors and politicians, a couple of parents. The chairman works for the Home Office. He strongly recommended you for this job, so he'll certainly be on your side.'

'And how do they feel about current educational practice?'

'Most of them probably won't know much about it. After all, legally they only have to turn up for three meetings a year. Meetings are in the evenings, so unless they bother to come and visit you during the day most of them will probably think the children are still sitting in straight rows chanting tables. You'll get used to governor's meetings. They can be quite bizarre. And because anybody can become a school governor, you sometimes end up with a privately educated dotty old girl with time on her hands who wants to do a bit of good in the community. Which is all very well in theory, but a time-wasting pain in practice.'

'It might be helpful to attend a governors' meeting before I start in September. Is that possible?'

'Of course. Have a word with the deputy. You'll be alright for a bit because you're an unknown quantity to her. And have a word with Godfrey. He's the clerk you met at the interviews. He knows them all well and he's a great diplomat. Meantime, I wish you the very best of luck. I'll be popping in a couple of times in your first term, but then I'm retiring, so you'll have a new, younger version of me checking up on you.'

By the end of the afternoon, my mind was reeling. I had the possibility of a difficult deputy head, a falling school roll, children who were likely to prove challenging, a staff that hadn't been effectively led for over a year, budget difficulties, a new local inspector and possibly unsafe premises. Added to which, I'd only taught seven to eleven year olds in my career so far. I'd rarely encountered an Infant, and I hadn't the slightest knowledge of what teaching a nursery aged child involved. And since my youngest daughter was just months old, there were nights when we didn't have much sleep. It was going to be the steepest of learning curves, and I wondered if I'd chosen the right point in my career to take on a school of my own.

It seemed essential to learn as much as I could about the school before I joined it in September. A staff meeting would be a vital first step, so I set a date, drafted a brief agenda, and posted it to my new deputy, asking if she would duplicate and circulate it. Then I telephoned the clerk to the governors, asking if I could join them at their next meeting. He readily agreed, and said he'd been going to invite me anyway. Then I took each item on my staff meeting agenda and wrote down everything I wanted to mention. First impressions are important, and I didn't want to make a mess of it. I needed to sound confident, even if I didn't feel it.

Annoyingly, my first meeting with the staff proved far more difficult than I had anticipated. Since there were only seven classes and a nursery, the turnout seemed very small, although the part-time teaching staff had come along as well. Most of the staff had only been teaching for a short while, apart from Brenda, a vivacious auburn-haired woman in her late thirties who was in charge of the Infant department and who had been particularly welcoming on my initial visit, Clarissa who ran the Nursery and who would be retiring during the coming year, Briony who taught the oldest children, and Teresa my new deputy.

I'd not met her before, as she'd been at a meeting during my first visit to the school before the interview. A tall, slim woman in her mid fifties, efficiently dressed and purposeful, she had shaken my hand firmly when I arrived for the staff meeting and briefly introduced me to everyone. She seemed helpful and friendly and, although it was early days, I wondered why Alan Green had warned me to be so cautious. Every teacher seemed to have brought a notepad and pen. I wondered whether it was to make notes, or hold me to account if something I said at the meeting didn't tally with what I did once September arrived. Since I only knew one or two people, I asked everybody to write their names on a paper label, and pin the label to their clothing.

I smiled, told them how pleased I was to have the job, and explained that I would be spending the first couple of months getting to know the staff, the children and the general routines of the school. Then I outlined my philosophy of primary education, stating my view that a primary school, especially in a socially deprived area like Camberwell, should be a bright and colourful place, filled with displays of the children's work. Almost immediately there was an interruption by Gerry, the only male teacher on the staff.

'A lot of children here can't read or write very well,' he said. 'The fashion these days seems to be to let children do what they like, whenever they like. We need to know how far you go down that route...'

'Well, I certainly believe that children should learn at their own pace, and that the best learning takes place when they're interested and involved.'

'So you're not keen on formal education? There's a lot of talk about learning through play these days and we don't think that works well with these children. Well, some of us don't, anyway.'

I sensed that not everybody in the room supported his view, but they were keen to see how this dialogue would develop. I felt I needed to step cautiously and try to satisfy both camps for the time being.

'Yes, I know all about the current fashions. Let me just say that in my own classroom the mornings are relatively formal, and then in the afternoons there are lots of individual and group activities for my children to get into. Provided it is carefully planned , I think that system works well. It does for me, anyway,' I added lamely.

'What about the children's behaviour?' asked Wanda, a teacher with a chubby, questioning face who had been watching me intently over her spectacles from the corner of the room.

'In what respect?' I asked.

'It's not always dealt with properly here,' said Gerry. The deputy shot a distasteful glance at him.

'What, exactly, do you mean by that?' she said.

'You know very well. The other day Wanda called me to fetch Robert Flood because he was trying to hit Andrew Miles over the head with a chair. I had to sit on him to stop him punching me. And you were at a meeting.'

'It was an important meeting. And when I came back I excluded Robert for a day.'

'But that didn't work, did it? Some of the children are getting more and more outrageous with their behaviour. Which is hardly surprising because we aren't dealing with the underlying causes…'

'And what, in your opinion, are the underlying causes?'

I had the feeling this was likely to develop into a very difficult dialogue, and the developing tension was tangible. I needed to seize control very quickly. There were obviously issues that the staff felt very strongly about, but opinions were divided.

'There's no point in discussing this further at the moment,' I said quickly. 'I don't know you, and I don't know the children you're talking about, or the problems you're experiencing. As I said, I need a little time to make myself familiar with everything. Then we can discuss how we're going to deal with them.' I sensed relief amongst the quieter members of staff.

'Can I ask if you're going to continue with clubs?' asked Brenda. 'On Fridays we break the whole school into groups and the children choose activities to do. It's nice because the infant children get to work with the juniors and do things they wouldn't normally do in their classrooms.'

'Certainly for the time being,' I said. 'It's a good idea.'

'Well, it is if it works,' said Gerry immediately. 'The trouble is, it often doesn't. I seem to end up organising hundreds of kids in the playground with footballs while one or two people have things like sewing groups with five girls.'

'Is that another dig at me?' said the deputy. 'I can't help it if fifty boys don't want to do sewing. And anyway, I thought this was supposed to be an opportunity for children to do things they particularly liked.'

'It's something else we can look at early on,' I said, beginning to feel I was refereeing this staff meeting rather than running it. A young teacher sitting upright on a chair by the wall tentatively raised her hand and I smiled at her, inviting her to speak. Unfortunately, she had a strong Scottish brogue and I had difficulty understanding her. She repeated her question and I was still hesitant. Fortunately Brenda sensed my discomfort and interpreted quickly.

'Annette's asking about the curriculum. There are so many things that need doing here,' she said. 'We haven't got proper policies on anything, there's no syllabus, the lateness is awful, the only maths equipment we seem to have is a set of rulers, two of the toilets are permanently locked because the schoolkeeper can't be bothered to repair them, the behaviour is deteriorating...'

'And the tea urn keeps breaking down,' said Susan, a teacher sitting close to me who hadn't spoken yet. 'I haven't had a cup of tea for days. You wait for the urn to boil, then the fuse goes and before you can fix it the whistle's blown.'

'What about the nursery?' asked Clarissa. 'How do you feel about nursery education? I suppose we're still going to have our own budget allowance?'

'I think it's essential,' I said, pleased to say something positive. 'Trouble is, I don't know a great deal about teaching four year olds. As you know, I'm a deputy at a school with seven to elevens only. But I'm sure I'll learn quickly,' I added hopefully.

'The nursery children are lovely. I do hope you'll be coming down to do some activities with them. We've got some difficult parents though. We've had a couple of nasty racist incidents recently. We're hoping you can deal with all that.'

There was a sudden loud whirring noise to my left. Briony had taken a large asthma pump out of her bag and was inhaling deeply. Then she rummaged in her bag again, took out a packet of cigarettes, and lit one. 'We'll need to start thinking about Christmas, soon,' she said.

For a moment I was lost for words. I couldn't believe that somebody with asthma would be inhaling tobacco smoke, and since we weren't yet at the end of the summer term, Christmas seemed the last thing we should be thinking about. She noted my bemused expression.

'The Christmas play,' she explained. 'I always start it in October, so I'll need to chat to you about some ideas I've got.'

'Ah, I have some thoughts on that too,' I said. 'I'm very keen on music and drama. It's not on our agenda today, but I'll be wanting each teacher to do something for the concert we'll have at Christmas.'

'But not everybody's a drama specialist, and I always do the Christmas show.'

'Maybe, but I think most teachers would enjoy producing a little concert item with their classes...'

'Then you'll end up with a substandard concert, and the parents will be very disappointed.' She took a long draw on her cigarette and looked to everybody for a supportive nod. Several teachers looked down at their feet. The meeting was becoming more uncomfortable by the moment.

'Again, it's something we can discuss in September. We need to finish now. Is there anything I need to know urgently? You can always give me a ring at my school.'

'Mrs Jessop,' said Briony.

'Sorry? Who's that?'

'One of the school helpers. We'd all like you to do something about her early on.'

'So what's the problem? What does she do?'

'That's the problem. She doesn't do anything. She spends her time avoiding work.'

'I think that comment is very unfair,' said the deputy. 'I find her perfectly agreeable. She does lots of jobs for me.'

'Yes, she knows just how to please people high in the pecking order,' said Gerry.

Once again we were approaching tension point, and I looked at my watch. 'We really must stop,' I said. 'I'll look into all these things in due course.'

If every staff meeting was going to be like this, things were going to be very difficult indeed, and there were still some teachers I hadn't yet met. There would be so much to do in the first few weeks and I would need to be thoroughly prepared. The first step seemed to be the creation of a strong sense of direction, so that everybody knew what my aims were and how I wanted things to be. Unless I could achieve reasonable agreement amongst the teachers, the children would quickly sense the restlessness and tension. Indeed, they probably already had, and almost certainly it was the reason for much of the poor behaviour in the school. I also needed to remember the school had been without a headteacher for well over a year, a very long time in the life of a challenging inner city primary.

Meantime, my last term as a deputy was tinged with sadness, because I was leaving a thriving, happy and successful school. During the final week, the school organised a special concert for me and I was presented with many gifts, among them an electric typewriter... ideal, I thought, for typing tightly controlled staff meeting agendas at my new school.

On the last day of term, I filled my car with boxes of equipment, books and lesson plans I had collected during my years as a class teacher and drove them to my new school, piling everything in a corner of the room that would be my office for the foreseeable future. I was determined not to become an office bound head, and to teach whenever I could. Being with children was, for me, one of the most exciting and enjoyable aspects of the job.

A fortnight's holiday on the Isle of Wight in August with our family refreshed me completely, and as summer ended I went into my new school for the last two weeks of the school holiday. Fred was surprised... he couldn't understand why anybody would choose to work during a holiday period, but since he'd decided he ought to get somebody in to repair the toilets before the start of term, he was happy to let me in as well. The playground and bottom corridor were filled with children, as the local authority hired out the premises as a play centre during school holidays, although the idea didn't endear itself to Fred.

'Bleedin' waste of time mendin' these toilets,' he said. 'They'll only get broken again before September. Be a bloody sight better if we didn't have these play centres.'

'It gives the children somewhere to go,' I said. 'At least they're not on the streets.'

'Be better if they were. Most of 'em aren't our kids anyway, so they don't care what they break.'

'We'll have a think about it in September,' I said.

There was an awful lot I'd need to be thinking about in September, I realised. But at least I felt rested and refreshed, and ready for the difficulties I was likely to encounter during my first term as a headteacher.

Or at least, I thought I was.

CHAPTER 3
FIRST DAY AT THE CHALKFACE

*On School Journey I watched lambs gambling on the grass. Sarah,
age 9*

Monday morning, September 4th, 1981, and I was in school
by 7.30 am.

I steered my car carefully around the skip full of broken
furniture in the car park, which Fred had said was being collected
before the children arrived. Despite what some of the staff seemed
to feel about him, he and his cleaners had obviously worked hard
during the holiday and the corridors and classrooms seemed
clean, polished and tidy.

During the weekend, he'd let me come in again and I'd
finished sorting my office out. Now I wandered round my school
expectantly, enjoying the lull before the children and teachers
arrived and familiarising myself once more with the layout of the
rooms. It was an interesting building, on three spacious floors with
several mezzanine rooms reached by tiny twisting staircases off
the main corridors. Store cupboards and wash rooms, filled with
cleaner's buckets and brooms, were at the end of each corridor.

During the late sixties, when outside toilets for schools
became unacceptable, the cloakrooms on each corridor had
been converted into toilets at considerable expense. After the
conversion there was nowhere for the children to hang their
coats, so wooden battens with hooks had been screwed to the
walls outside the classrooms. It wasn't a very satisfactory solution;
I noticed that most of them seemed to be sagging, and the end
of one had come away from the wall completely. Fred obviously
hadn't got around to screwing it back during the six week break.

There were twenty classrooms and the nursery department.
Because the school roll had fallen drastically, only eight classrooms
were in use, creating barren areas in the school which looked

extremely drab. Some of the empty rooms had been used for dumping furniture and equipment nobody else wanted or needed. Another thing I'd need to sort out quickly. Most classrooms were fairly small, and I wondered how the staff managed to cope with modern teaching techniques in them, where a range of activities needed to be going on at the same time. Perhaps, I thought, it was fortunate that the school roll had fallen. At least the rooms wouldn't be stuffed full of children. The high ceilings were a bonus too, giving every room a feeling of spaciousness, and it was obvious from the piles of new exercise books, pens, paint, carefully written notices and name cards that most of the teachers had been in school during the holidays to prepare their rooms for the new term.

The building contained three halls, one on each floor. They were dull, barren areas that needed redecorating. The ground floor hall was close to the kitchen and used as a dining area, and tables and chairs were stacked at one end of it. The middle hall had gymnastics climbing equipment screwed to one wall, and the hall on the top floor contained nothing at all, other than a few drama blocks and a piano with a torn cloth cover. The ceiling was badly stained, where rain had seeped through faulty roof slates.

Although the building was generally sound, I discovered that many of the windows were either jammed slightly open, or had small panes of glass missing. Most were in a poor state of repair. This wouldn't be a problem at the moment, as the early September weather was extremely warm, but it would soon become a priority as winter arrived, especially as the heating system was ancient and unlikely to be very effective at the top of the school. The lighting in the school was also very elderly, making the corridors in particular seem very dismal. I shuddered to think how much time Fred spent climbing up a ladder to change the bulbs.

On three sides of the building were playgrounds, poorly maintained and uninteresting. Fine for kicking a football around, but not a scrap of grass or a sign of nature anywhere, other than leaves which had fallen from the few trees in the street overhanging the high brick walls. There were separate playgrounds for infants and juniors, with small covered areas under which the children could stand if it was raining, and the infant playground had climbing logs in one corner. They were in poor condition, there was no safety surface, and I wondered how many children had gone home with splinters or minor injuries during the last year or two. The nursery playground was much smaller than the others and contained a sandpit, although it looked as if foxes had used it as a handy defecation area during the long holiday. The car park ran along the shortest side of the building, and faced the road where the main entrance was.

I walked back to the staffroom to make myself a mug of coffee. Steam was pouring from the urn by the sink, causing the lid to rattle, and I turned the temperature down. It wasn't surprising that the urn's performance was erratic if it was left to boil away like this, I thought, and I assumed Fred must switch it on each morning as he did his door-opening rounds. I had no idea what the arrangements for staff refreshments were, so I'd brought my own coffee and powdered milk, and as I stirred the drink Gerry walked into the room. Although he drove an ancient van he'd bought for a pittance, I'd learned that he was a cycling fanatic, owned an extremely expensive bicycle, and cycled to school at great speed each morning even if it was pouring with rain. This undoubtedly accounted for his lean, athletic appearance. Although I'd originally assumed he was a class teacher, he'd been appointed to the school as a full time remedial teacher, taking small groups of the least able children out of their classrooms for intensive basic skills work. Because so many of the children had poor reading and writing skills, he'd created a remedial department in one of the empty classrooms. A part time teacher and a teaching assistant had been employed to help him, although I hadn't met them yet.

'Morning,' he said, stroking his small black beard thoughtfully and heaping three spoonfuls of sugar into his very black coffee. 'Here we go again. Ready for it?'

'Hope so, but I've got a lot to learn. Really only just finding my way about the place. Did you have a good holiday?'

'Cycled around the Lake District. The sun didn't shine once. Still, that's past history, isn't it. Now it's back to the joys of Simon Fuller struggling with the printed word. Oh well, come up and visit me sometime. I think somebody famous said that, didn't they?'

'Yes, Mae West. In a film called 'She Done Him Wrong'.

'Wow, film buff are you? Well, I'm sure visiting me won't be as much fun as visiting Mae West, but you're very welcome.'

He picked up his mug and walked to the door, as Brenda, the teacher in charge of the Infant department walked in. She smiled warmly.

'Gerry doesn't believe in long conversations,' she said. 'Some people find him very abrupt, but he's passionate about these children learning to read and write properly. He's never been very happy about the whole child-centred thing. He thinks children need to be taught, not wander around learning by osmosis.'

'I can sympathise. A lot of teachers still feel that way. Current educational techniques probably work well in the shires where children are stimulated at home, but I know from experience it's much harder in areas like this. I think it's all a question of balance.'

'Well, we work very hard in the infant classes here to get most of them reading. It's the most important thing we can do. We use reading schemes, even though they're unfashionable these days. We're hoping you won't want to change that.'

'Rest assured. I believe in the importance of reading too. And I don't have a problem with reading schemes.'

'You'll have a problem with the younger inspectors,' said Wanda, the Year 4 teacher who'd just come into the room. 'They're not all like Alan Green. The government is pushing all this new stuff about teaching reading, and using reading schemes is definitely out. You'll be pressured to get rid of them.'

'I don't mind a bit of pressure,' I said. 'We'll do whatever we think works best.'

'We're certainly glad you're here,' said Brenda warmly. 'The last year hasn't been a particularly good one for the school. We're hoping you can bring a bit of enthusiasm and vitality back to the place.'

Other members of the staff were coming into the room, looking at their watches and queuing by the urn. I smiled at them, spoke briefly about their holidays, and then retreated to my small office. Lucy, the school secretary, was pouring mail from a sack onto my table. Although I'd opened some of it during the last days of the holiday, I was still amazed at the volume of post that a school could accumulate during the six week break. My office was next to Lucy's room, which seemed an excellent arrangement, as I'd be needing her help constantly during the first few weeks.

'Hello,' she said. 'Do you want me to open this lot, or will you do it?'

'I'll do it, but I'll probably need to ask you about most of it.'

'Well, two thirds of it will be advertising, so you'll probably find a lot of it can go in that great filing cabinet known as the waste bin. Anything you're not sure about, leave in a pile and I'll sort it.'

By ten to nine, I'd only opened fifteen letters. Just dealing with the mail seemed to be a job that might take me the rest of the day. At two minutes to nine my deputy put her head round the door. I'd been a little concerned as I hadn't seen her, and I'd expected her to be at school almost as early as me, although I knew she travelled a long distance.

'Sorry, the journey was awful this morning. Don't know if I can keep it up much longer. I'm just going down to blow the whistle,' she said. 'Is there anything urgent?'

'I don't think so. Everybody seems to be in. I haven't opened much of the mail yet. Perhaps we can have a chat at lunch time. I've made a list of things we need to discuss.'

'Okay. As long as I don't miss my lunch break. I'll meet you in here.'

The whistle blew, the classes were brought in by their teachers, and almost immediately a long line of parents and children had formed, stretching from Lucy's room to the end of the corridor. Some children had forgotten what classes they were supposed to be in, others began hunting through the lost property boxes searching for items of clothing they'd lost last term and a few had come to collect the dinner registers for their classes. One boy who'd left the school at the end of last term had returned because he still hadn't been allocated a secondary school and his mother hadn't bothered to take the matter up with the local authority. Instead, she'd sent a note asking if he could do another term at Comber Grove. I suspected that if I agreed, she wouldn't bother to find him a secondary school at all. There was little I could do other than send him home again.

Many parents in the queue were people who had recently moved into the area and wanted places for their children. Mostly from Asia or Africa, few could speak English well, and they relied on a friend or neighbour they'd brought along as an interpreter. Lucy spent a great deal of time trying to explain that now wasn't a good time to do this, as lots of information about the family needed to be taken and they'd have to come back when she was less busy. One English mother had no difficulty explaining forcefully what she wanted; her two boys, one junior, one infant, were scruffily dressed and very dirty and she said the older sibling had been expelled from his previous school and told not to come back in September. The mother, emaciated and drawn, obviously had a drug problem and had difficulty focusing. Although I knew our roll was low, I had no intention of accepting a child without knowing about his previous history. I explained that I'd only just arrived, and that she'd need to return in a week or so once I knew how many spare places we had. I never saw her again.

Other parents in the queue wanted to pay their children's dinner money. Some had put the money into an envelope, sealed it, and written the child's name and class on the front, others wanted to know how much they still owed from last term, and several just reached into their bags and pulled out handfuls of coins, inviting Lucy to take what she needed and put the rest back. I had no idea why the parents couldn't pay the dinner money directly to the teachers, but I assisted Lucy with writing down the children's names, the classes they were in, and how much was being paid. I was astonished at how quickly and effectively she dealt with the parents, even when they spoke little English. She seemed to have an almost intuitive understanding.

'Emma Chizzet,' said one father with an Australian twang. He was accompanied by his eight year old daughter.

'Hello Emma,' I said, welcoming her back to school. They both looked thoroughly bemused by my comment. 'Her names Lucy,' said the father. 'Emma Chizzet.'

'Sorry,' I apologised, 'Hello Lucy Emma Chizzet.'

Lucy quickly interrupted. 'He's asking you about the dinner money he has to pay. How much is it, he wants to know.'

As the queue rapidly shortened, a tall, exceptionally well endowed woman holding the hand of a pretty infant child with a shock of ginger curls grinned at me. I noticed that most of her teeth were missing.

'You the new 'eadmaster?' she asked. I agreed that I was.

'I'm Mrs Elson and this is Cheryl. You'll soon get to know me, because I'm always up here looking for Cheryl's coat. Bloody child loses everything, don't you, Cheryl?' Cheryl looked up at her mum, grinned and nodded.

'What do you think of me tee shirt?' Mrs Elson asked. My eyes drifted down to the legend printed on the front. 'Stop Staring At Me Tits', it read.

'It..um.. suits you,' I said.

'Got it in Margate at the weekend,' she said. 'Only three quid. Right, here's Cheryl's dinner money.'

Within half an hour the queue had shrunk to nothing. Obviously this was a regular feature of September's first day, and one that Lucy was well prepared for.

Leaving the mail for the time being, I walked around the school, popping into every classroom and saying hello to the teachers and children. Every class seemed quiet and purposeful, although I knew from experience the first day of the September term is always like that. For many children, the holiday seems too long. They miss their friends, they run out of things to do, and almost without exception they seemed pleased to be back. Each class has a different teacher from last year, and in each room the children are listening attentively as classroom rules and regulations are carefully explained. I ask all the children if they've had a pleasant holiday, and whether they know who I am. They all do. I tell them that I'll see them shortly in assembly, thank the teacher, and I move on to the next class.

Most primary schools have an assembly at some point in the day, but unless a school assembly has some value, there's little point in doing it. During my early career, I'd been astonished by some of the school assemblies I'd seen. My first headteacher's assemblies had consisted of a mandatory hymn and prayer, a couple of supportive words to the members of the football or netball team if they'd managed to thrash St Clements, and a rant at somebody who'd broken the school rules. It was an utterly pointless use of time and I've no idea why he bothered.

At my second school, the headteacher waited until the children had filed into the hall, and then made a grand entrance by flinging the hall door open, prayer book and bible tucked under his arm. Then he'd stride purposefully to the small lectern on the stage, where the staff sat behind him on chairs. There he would read an obscure text, attempt to explain it, and tell children off if he saw them shuffling with boredom. On one occasion, seeing two black children having a conversation, he shot a stern look at them. 'Sit still,' he ordered, 'You're not in the jungle squabbling over a bit of raw meat now.' Even though this was the early seventies, when racism could still be found in many schools, the mouths of every teacher dropped open with horror. These days, he would have been arrested.

A good headteacher will always make the most of an assembly. It's an opportunity to talk with the children, read to them, play them music, share activities, and discuss events happening in the world. Assemblies can be interactive, too. Children can show and explain work they've done, perform short plays or social situations, or talk about a particular project they've been undertaking in their classroom. I'd discovered that the assemblies led by Comber Grove's previous head had been rather dull affairs, making me even more determined to get mine properly organised and interesting from the start.

At ten o'clock, I rang the bell for the children to come into the hall. Before the holiday, in a document I'd sent to the teachers about changes I wanted to make from the beginning of term, I'd explained that I'd take junior assemblies every day and infant assemblies twice a week, to which I'd also invite the nursery. I wasn't certain I could keep this up, because I'd only taken one assembly a week when I'd been a deputy head, but it seemed an ideal way to have regular contact with all the children.

This morning the children sat quietly and attentively, because they were interested to see what their new headteacher was like, and what he was going to do. I talked about holidays, why they are important to us, and how people use their leisure breaks. I told them about my recent family holiday on the Isle of Wight, and I showed them pictures, photographs and artefacts, inviting children to come to the front and guess what some of them were. There was a wave of appreciative laughter when I showed them a photograph of my daughter's face smothered in ice cream.

The assembly seemed to have gone down well and two of the teachers complimented me on it as they left the hall. It was very encouraging, and I knew the rest of the week's assemblies would probably be successful too, as I'd chosen several different holiday themes and prepared them at home with great care.

The morning passed pleasantly. There were few interruptions because everybody was busy in the classrooms. Lucy typed industriously in her room, although I had no idea who she was writing to. I was brought coffee and a digestive biscuit by a school helper at eleven, and by twelve I'd sorted and organised all the mail. Everything outside my office seemed to be working normally and smoothly, nobody asked my advice about anything, and I had the vaguest feeling that I was slightly superfluous. At twelve fifteen, Mary, the school cook, knocked on the door. Another woman was with her, carrying a tray.

'Did you want your dinner up here, or are you coming down?' she asked.

'I've brought sandwiches today,' I said. 'I wasn't sure what the routine was. And I'm seeing my deputy at lunchtime, so I'll have to be up here anyway, but from tomorrow I'll be downstairs eating with the children.'

'I said to Doris, he'll probably eat up here today, didn't I Doris? Put the tray on the desk for him.'

Doris nodded and uncovered the plates on the tray. A roast, with lamb, nicely cooked vegetables, jelly and custard. It all looked very appetising.

'You'll have to come downstairs most days anyway,' Mary said. 'They play up something shocking if there's no teacher down there. Half the food ends up on the floor. We're hoping you can do something about that. And the infants always put their knives and forks in the scrapings bowl instead of the hot water, and I haven't got any spare staff to watch them, have I Doris?'

'No Cook, you haven't,' Doris agreed.

I wasn't sure whether Mary was angling for additional staff or wanting me to stand by the knife and fork bowl, but as with so many other things since I'd taken up this job, I promised to look into the matter.

As they left, Teresa came into the room with her sandwiches. I mentioned the dinner hall problem, but she said that since it wasn't mandatory for teachers to be on duty at lunchtimes, she preferred not to be there, feeling that the lunchtime supervisors should have been able to deal with any behaviour issues that arose. I was slightly taken aback, as lunchtimes are a social occasion and I'd always felt it important for teachers to eat with the children.

I took out the list of things I wanted to discuss with her, and started by asking her to tell me a little about the teachers, how long they'd been here and what experience they'd had. It seemed that she had little time for most of them, particularly Gerry, who'd apparently had a vigorous row with her in the staffroom just before the holiday. I asked her to tell me about the quality of teaching in the school, but she said she knew little about it because as a class teacher herself, she was unable to get round and see what was going on. It would be infinitely preferable, she intimated, for her to be out of the classroom, doing administrative work. As I'd been a teaching deputy myself, this wasn't something I wanted. As far as I was concerned, one important role of the deputy was to create a model classroom, which other teachers could admire and learn from.

I ran through a list of the things I wanted to change early in the term. We'd need regular staff meetings, partly to discuss the creation of a proper curriculum, and partly for teachers to air their concerns. We'd need to discuss how we dealt with poor behaviour, the systems for rewarding and encouraging children, our methods for meeting and talking with parents and how we'd keep them informed about the concerts and events we'd organise throughout the year. Even the method of handwriting we taught the children, which seemed haphazard throughout the school, would need very close attention.

I felt excited by the challenges, but Teresa didn't seem to share my enthusiasm. She thought it was better if parents were kept out of the way as much as possible, and she wasn't keen on evening events, because it would mean she'd be very late getting home. She also felt the children in her Year 6 class had the potential to be badly behaved, and that I needed to have a strong talk with them before they began to play up. This, she thought, would start happening within a fortnight. She felt that Briony, who'd taught them the previous year, had allowed them far too much freedom, even though she was a popular teacher. She finished by saying I also needed to have a very serious talk with Fred. He never kept an eye on his cleaners and two of them weren't doing their full time. She knew, because they often left school at the same time she did.

She screwed her sandwich packet into a tight ball, tossed it into my bin, smiled a tight little smile and left my room. I wasn't sure whether our talk had achieved anything at all, and after the enjoyment of the morning I felt apprehensive. In order to carry out any changes effectively, I needed to have the full support of my deputy, and from what I'd seen so far this was going to be hard to achieve. I busied myself making some colourful notices to put around the school, then I took Lucy a mug of tea and asked her about the past year.

'It's been pretty grim,' she said. 'I've been here for three years, but since Mr Andrews became ill things haven't really gone very well, especially with all the current changes in education.'

'It must have been hard for him.'

'He was never able to cope with the new freedom that primary schools have. When he started out, children sat in straight rows, chanted tables, and got caned if they didn't know them. He went on several courses, but when he tried out the things he'd learned the results were quite bizarre. He'd been told young children who are cooped up in cramped council flats needed to explore spatial awareness, so one day he let them crawl all over the stage blocks. The kids just climbed under them and he couldn't get them out.'

'So he eventually lost interest?'

'No, not really. He just found everything harder to handle, particularly as he became ill. And I don't think Teresa has much enthusiasm for the school. She spends a lot of time complaining. Now you're here, perhaps you can give it all a sense of direction and make the place a bit happier.'

The telephone rang and she turned to answer it. 'It's the inspector,' she said. 'Shall I tell him I'm not sure where you are?' I shook my head and took the receiver.

'Just checking that you've actually arrived,' Alan Green said cheerfully. 'How's your first day?'

'Interesting. Busy. Bewildering,' I said, struggling for adjectives. 'There's so much to do, but I'll get there eventually.'

'Of course you will. You'll be fine. I'll pop in and see you sometime next week. Call me if there are any problems.'

I did indeed have problems, though even if I'd mentioned them there was little he could do, apart from let me lean on his sympathy and greater experience. Even so, I appreciated him taking the trouble to call, and at least the day ended well. Just before hometime, a group of first year children came into my room with greeting cards they'd made, welcoming me to the school. The amusing portraits of me and their encouraging messages cheered me up enormously, and I pinned them around my room. I intended to display as much children's work in my office as I could. As I was buffeted by the personalities, problems and difficult situations that would emerge during the next few months, their cheerful pictures would help to keep me on course and remind me that a school is essentially about children.

CHAPTER 4
A TERM OF TRIAL

'Otters are well up the food channel. When they get there, they go dark.' Mark, 11, answering a SATs question on the food chain.

Everyone remembers their primary school headteacher. Unlike secondary heads, primary headteachers are far less remote, if only because a primary school is much smaller. Ask any member of the public what they think a primary headteacher's job entails and they won't have a problem telling you. Headteachers are smartly dressed, they have an office of their own and they spend a lot of time in it. They listen to the concerns of parents, receive visitors, appoint staff, and meet with the school governors, those seemingly important people most classroom teachers never see. They are also responsible for making sure the curriculum is properly implemented in their schools, and that every child makes steady progress. They'll also say the best heads always find time to spend with the children, or teach a class occasionally. In a small countryside school the reality may indeed resemble that, but leading a primary school in a big city was very different, as I was quickly discovering. My first year at Comber Grove was a roller coaster ride; exhilarating, exciting, amusing and nerve-wracking in just about equal measures.

Other than getting to know the names of the children and the abilities of the staff, the first priority was to make my drab, Victorian building a far more attractive place to learn in. When I'd been a teaching deputy head, I'd filled the walls of my classroom with children's work; paintings, stories, models were everywhere, and they provided a constantly growing reminder of everything the children had learned during the year. Then we spread out into the corridor, and visitors coming into the school were constantly awed by how bright and colourful it all was.

I wanted Comber Grove to be the same, but just decorating

classroom walls with children's work took up a lot of teacher's time, let alone finding enough additional material to display in the halls and corridors. Then I had an idea. Every Monday, in assembly, I set the children the task of illustrating a news event, poem or story that I read to them. They could illustrate the stories in any way they chose, in any size and with any materials… but they had to do it, and they had to complete it that week. The teachers were enthusiastic, and in a matter of weeks I had enough work to fill one of the halls. The transformation worked wonders; the hall had suddenly become a bright and attractive place to be, the children loved looking at the pictures produced by their peers, and visitors to the school were impressed by the standard of the children's creative work. Before long, we had decorated the other two halls with colourful, stimulating work displays as well.

During those first months, I worked tirelessly to make the school environment more exciting, often staying at school into the early evening. With Fred's help, I put up large display boards along the corridors and on the staircases, asking each class to be responsible for creating a work display on the board nearest their classroom. Then I broke up the boredom of the corridors with tables of science experiments and displays. On one, children could explore optical illusions as they passed. On another, an old radio had been taken to pieces, with labels describing what each part did and how it worked. A third showed how a film projector worked.

Since children love handling historical artefacts and learning about the past, I created the beginnings of a school museum on the middle corridor, outside my office. Parents often paused to look when they came to see Lucy or to talk with me, and before long they were bringing in items they thought might be of interest; an old bus conductor's ticket machine, a gas mask, an ancient camera, a wind-up gramophone, magazines that had been found under a carpet during house redecoration. This had an added bonus; it provided an ideal opportunity for me to get to know many parents, and to talk to them about my plans for the school. Before long, the museum area needed to be extended because we had so many items for visitors and children to enjoy. Children were now far less likely to hurtle along the corridors; they would walk and pause by the displays, looking to see what was new, and trying out some of the activities that were on offer.

The large number of empty classrooms were a negative aspect of the school, giving it a half used feel, and this was something I needed to change quickly. The teachers agreed that we should try to find a use for them, and I arranged a staff meeting to discuss what we could do. After a long discussion we decided to create an art workshop, a maths room with lots of activity and exploration facilities, and an infant library to store all our reading material.

Steel bands were fashionable at the time in inner London primary schools, partly as a nod towards racial integration, and partly because children can produce tunes on them very quickly. Comber Grove had a set of steel pans and a teacher who visited once a week. It seemed sensible to create a proper music room in which they could be permanently set out, and we constructed temporary shelving to store the other musical instruments the school owned. Not that there were many; a small set of percussion instruments, a box of recorders, some glockenspiels with several bars missing and five guitars, one of which had no strings at all. Nevertheless, I considered music to be a vital element of the primary curriculum, and I was determined that this area would grow rapidly. At least my enthusiasm and hard work reaped dividends with the staff. Most of the teachers volunteered to organise the various resource rooms and make sure they were kept useable and tidy.

It was obvious we couldn't make full use of these rooms without an extra injection of cash, and on Alan Green's first visit I showed him round the school and asked if he could find me some additional money.

'Well, there's a possibility,' he said. 'The authority realises that new heads usually need a bit of help. If I found some money for you, how would you use it?'

I outlined what I wanted to do, and showed him how I'd planned it all in detail, even down to the likely cost of shelving and materials. He seemed very impressed.

'Okay, I'll have some additional money transferred into your school account.' This was so encouraging I decided to press a little further.

'Music and drama are my particular things... do you think there's any possibility of having a few more stage blocks for the top hall? And maybe a bit of stage lighting...'

He shot a suspicious look at me. 'No promises. Money is always tight. But I know what it's like when you're a new head. I was the same. Get a few quotes and send them to me.'

I had the quotes to him within a week and he kept his word. With the new blocks, a stage was created at one end of the hall, a support structure was built for scenery, and a set of lights rigged onto a metal roof support above it. Our future concerts for parents were going to be well worth watching.

There was still lots to be done, and the playgrounds bothered me. The climbing logs in the infant playground simply had to go, and if I could show they were dangerous I might get funding for some better climbing apparatus. I phoned Alan Green again, and he said I should talk to Tom Smith, the resources officer at County Hall. He promised to have a word with him first, and within a week Tom had visited my school. I plied him with tea, decent biscuits, and boundless enthusiasm for making my school the best in London. He agreed that the logs were dangerous, and promised to send a team to remove them before the end of term. He'd also brought along some catalogues of playground equipment that he said was hard wearing and good value and he said that if I was interested, I could pay for whatever I chose over a period of three years. I decided to press my advantage.

'I wouldn't want a huge climbing structure for the children. The school roll is quite small,' I said. 'Just something creative and colourful. But I'd also like a school garden. When they come to remove the logs, do you think they could dig up a bit of the playground and put a brick border round it? Then I could fill it with earth and each class could have a little garden plot to grow flowers and vegetables.'

'You don't want much, do you?' he smiled. 'Still, if you don't ask, you won't get, and we're here to try and help. I'll see what I can do.'

Staff meetings became increasingly important. Things were changing rapidly, and teachers needed to be involved, informed and enthused. We were soon having at least one intensive meeting a week and often two. Teachers would report on their progress with the various resource rooms, and then we'd talk about aspects of the curriculum. Everything seemed to need money, and the lack of direction during the past couple of years had meant that much of the equipment had been lost, stolen or broken. We looked carefully at the way we were teaching the basic skills, and we devised new policies and methods for teaching them. We examined the way we taught reading and we re-organised all the class libraries. Behaviour was a problem in some of the classes with older children, and I told the staff that I was available at any time to help them with difficult children, although I stressed that children rarely misbehaved if they were interested and absorbed in what they were doing, and that it was up to us to make our lessons as fascinating as we possibly could.

Then we looked at the administrative systems in the school, everything from the way we collected dinner money and sent out newsletters, to the way we stored lost property and made sure children got to school punctually. I'd also begun ordering good quality materials for the children to use; colourful card and paper, bright drawing pens, a wide range of paint, art and modelling materials, and nicely bound exercise books and work folders. Although several teachers thought this was extravagant, I knew that children always produced their best work if they were given quality materials and taught how to use them wisely. I also knew things wouldn't be perfect for a long time, but at least we seemed to be making progress on all fronts, the school was looking attractive and welcoming, the children were settling well, and we were receiving extremely positive comments from the parents.

I'd even managed to solve the Friday afternoon clubs problem. The main difficulty seemed to be the lack of adults, meaning that some teachers, like Gerry, were trying to cope with impossibly large groups of children, while activities like embroidery with sewing machines could only be undertaken by very small groups, simply because the school only had five sewing machines. The answer was to provide more adults, and a greater range of activities. I persuaded Fred to do carpentry, Lucy to do calligraphy, and I offered video film making.

Then another idea; I telephoned a senior lecturer I knew at the local teacher training college, and asked her if she could lend me fifteen students on Friday afternoons to do some creative activities of their own choosing. She thought it was a great idea, because her students would be getting additional practical experience with children, but she said she might find it difficult to persuade other lecturers because alterations would need to be made to their timetables. Nevertheless, she was back on the phone three days later, and on Friday fifteen students arrived. Gerry no longer had a massive group just kicking a football around in the playground.

All this was very encouraging and exciting, but alongside our successes were the everyday incidents and situations that all headteachers have to deal with. Provided you are charismatic, knowledgeable and interesting, teaching young children is relatively easy. They will listen to you, generally do what you want them to, and respond to your greater knowledge and experience of life. Dealing with adults is an entirely different ball game, and a good manager or leader will tread sensitively, carefully and when necessary, firmly to keep everything on an even keel. This is vital in a school, because children are incredibly astute. From a very early age they have a great sense of fairness, and they quickly assess whether a teacher is worth listening to. They can also sense whether there is harmony amongst the staff, and if they form good relationships with their teachers, they will feel a fierce sense of pride and loyalty to their school.

From the start of my headship, there were staff problems I needed to tackle. The first had been mentioned to me almost as an aside, during the staff meeting before I'd joined the school. Mrs Jessop had been employed as a school helper years ago, but her role had never been clearly defined. She would mix paint for the classes, make coffee for the teachers on playground duty, sharpen pencils, and give out exercise books, pens and paper when teachers sent her their stock books. Her morning role, in the days before Mrs Thatcher banished school milk, was to carry crates of it around the school each morning, depositing one with each class, and then collecting the crates an hour later. It wasn't very demanding work, so she spent much of her time wandering into the kitchen, gossiping with the kitchen staff and having a smoke in their back room. Most of the staff knew what was going on, and Mrs Jessop's negative commitment contrasted strongly with the only other helper, Mrs Gander, who worked very hard indeed, often taking things home to finish. Understandably, she felt a measure of resentment towards her colleague who did so little.

I called both helpers into my room and explained that I was changing the way I wanted them to work. They'd be allocated sessions with each class. Mrs Gander would work with the junior classes, Mrs Jessop with the infants, and their tasks would be determined by the teachers. Since Mrs Gander was already working in this way, she was perfectly happy, but Mrs Jessop wasn't having any of it. Nor were the Infant teachers, who weren't keen on the idea of having her in their classrooms. What about the milk, Mrs Jessop asked. Who would give the crates out and collect them up again? The teachers were busy, and they were much too heavy for the children. And besides, giving out and collecting milk bottles was what she'd been employed to do. Anything else she did was a bonus, so I should consider myself very lucky.

It was my first encounter with an obstinate adult, and I was taken aback. Nevertheless, in order for any change to be successful it has to be done in a positive manner, and I knew it would take careful handling. I persuaded the infant staff to give it a try and they eventually agreed to allocate work for her, or give her children to read with, if she could do it in the corridor, where there were tables and plenty of room. Mrs Jessop eventually agreed to try the new timetable, provided she could do her milk bottle duties first.

I soon realised I'd bitten off plenty to chew. Mrs Jessop slowed down with the milk bottles, spent very little time listening to children read, and still found plenty of time to gossip with the cooks and have a smoke. It would have been easy to summon her to my room and demand that she did what I'd instructed, but I wanted to be subtler than that. Instead, I'd appear in the corridor, smile, and say that I'd got time to help her with the crates, dispatching them in record time. If she was with the cooks, I'd suddenly appear in the kitchen to discuss the day's menu. Eventually she reluctantly realised that I wasn't going to let this go, and she gradually did what I'd asked her to do, even finding after a few weeks that she was actually enjoying her day's work more than before.

Coming to terms with Gerry's views about education took a different approach. Although he'd been in the staffroom on my very first morning and he'd invited me up to see how he worked with the children who needed remedial help, I didn't get around to it for several weeks as there were too many other things to be done.

When I opened the door of his room, I was greeted by everything that was alien to my view of primary school practice. Apart from several tatty bookcases and some ancient oak tables, the room contained very little. There were no display boards, no pictures on the walls, no carpet on the floor, nor the slightest attempt to make the room into a welcoming place for children. Along one wall was a very long table surface constructed from lengths of chipboard, and above this was a set of wooden cubicles, each with a pair of headphones, so that children could sit without being distracted by whatever was going on around them. Two battered grey metal filing cabinets stood in the corner.

Gerry sat at one of the large tables, on which there were fifteen tobacco tins containing cards with letters, sounds, or parts of words on them and some reading books which would have been fashionable at the turn of the century. A small group of children sat around him, and the children called out the letters or sounds as he picked them from the tins. He praised them warmly when they got something right, but was almost aggressively insistent they kept trying when they were wrong. He demanded absolute concentration from everyone in the group, and since they were children who struggled, they found this difficult. Nevertheless, they seemed perfectly happy, and were eager to enjoy the individual attention they were receiving.

'So, you'll be wanting a carpet and some display boards in here,' I said, when the children had gone back to their classrooms. 'I didn't realise the room was so bare.'

'That's exactly how I like it,' he replied. 'Don't want to change a thing. I don't want anything getting in the way of their learning. I don't have them for long and it needs to be very intensive. My aim is to send these children out of this room able to read and write at least a little as quickly as possibly. If I don't achieve that, they'll probably continue being a nuisance in class, and waste the teacher's time and everybody else's.'

'You don't believe in making the room attractive to work in, then?'

'What's the point?'

'Well, you might as well say there's no point in decorating your lounge or filling it with nice things because it's possible to live without them. Personally, I prefer to be in comfortable surroundings because it makes me feel good. And I think it's the same for children.'

'No, it'll distract them. You have to remember that the children I teach are the ones who have the concentration of a gnat. I need to be on top of them all the time, and they need to be on task all the time. That's why I've got the cubicles and headphones for individual listening.'

'Well, I still think it's very drab.'

'Drab's my favourite colour.'

'Okay, for the time being we'll agree to disagree. Just prove to me your system works, and I won't interfere.'

And his system did work. Several months later, I checked up on the progress his children had made. All of them, without exception, had improved dramatically, and this had reaped positive benefits in the classroom. The behaviour of these children improved, too. They no longer felt inadequate and they could contribute to whatever was going on in their classrooms. Although I still felt the same progress could have been achieved in more enjoyable and comfortable surroundings, I kept my word and didn't interfere.

My deputy, however, was proving to be a nut I couldn't crack. She contributed little to staff meetings, arrived at school just before nine, and seldom stayed for very long after school. Her Year 6 class was not an easy one, for they were the oldest children in the school, but they were no example to the rest of the children. There were accusations of intimidation in the playground, arguments in the corridors, and one girl in particular, a beautiful Jamaican child named Jemima, well developed for her age and with deceptively good manners, seemed to control her friends and admirers with an almost religious discipline. In order to be accepted in the class, you had to be well in with Jemima. You lent her your coloured pencils when she asked for them, offered her sweets if you had any, and wore the right clothes to avoid ridicule. Teresa didn't seem to like her children very much, particularly Jemima, and they appeared to be doing their best to avoid doing much work, which was annoying for the several very able children in the class who wanted to do well. As we neared Christmas, all the other classes were working hard to produce a short play for our Christmas concert, especially as we now had a large stage, a good sound system and professional lighting, but Teresa's class seemed to be doing very little.

'Have you thought about what you're going to do?' I asked her one morning. 'There are only a few weeks to the concert.'

'Probably nothing, the way they're behaving,' she said acidly.

'Well, you need to do something. I can't have everybody else performing a play and the top class doing nothing.'

'I'll think about it. I'll probably do a Nativity.'

I couldn't think of anything less appropriate. Nativity plays are best performed with small children and watched by adoring parents. Perhaps, I thought, ever eager to look on the positive side, she intends to do a clever, modern interpretation. A few days later,

I popped into her room to see if anything was happening. Yes, they were preparing their play, Teresa said, and it was indeed going to be a Nativity. She'd found it in a magazine, and although it was for six year olds, it was simple enough for her class to understand, although they'd probably have to read their parts from a script as there wasn't much time left. And Jemima was going to play Mary.

I despaired. There was little I could do, but I determined to become more involved with her class the next time we organised a concert. This time, I thought, it would probably pass muster, but it was disappointing that the oldest children in the school didn't have something better to get their dramatic teeth into.

My optimism was misplaced. It was far worse than I could have imagined. The hall was crowded with parents, and each class in turn came onto the stage to perform their Christmas carol, poem or play. I had watched all the items at the dress rehearsal the day before, so I knew the concert would go down well with the parents, but Teresa's class hadn't taken part because they were still rehearsing in their classroom. Unfortunately, I hadn't timed the items very accurately, and as the concert went into its second half, I realised we were unlikely to finish before hometime. I'd packed the parents into the hall very tightly, and I knew there would be some disruption if we overran, because many of them would need to go and collect their infant and nursery offspring from the playground.

When Teresa's class took the stage, it was obvious the lead characters had had a few disagreements before the performance. One of the Wise Men refused to walk on the stage, Joseph constantly grimaced at Mary, the animals in the stable couldn't be heard through the masks they wore, and since they were carrying scripts anyway, they had a job maintaining a four legged position. For twenty very long minutes, I watched in agony, and just when I thought things couldn't get much worse the cast began throwing straw from the manger at each other. Meanwhile, parents of infant children were trying to weave their way out of the hall. Unable to tolerate any more, I hurried onto the stage, thanked the parents for coming and then turned to stare hard at the children. They sensed I was in no mood for a confrontation, and they came off the stage muttering at each other. I followed them into their classroom, told Teresa that I wanted to speak to them, and closed the door with a slam.

'Your behaviour out there was appalling,' I said. 'I can't imagine what the parents thought. And throwing hay at each other was the last straw.' I suddenly realised what I'd said, although none of the children had picked up the unintended pun. 'And your behaviour, Tony, was disgraceful.'

'I didn't start it,' he said bitterly. 'Jemima chucked a bit at me first.'

'No I never,' said Jemima.

'She didn't, Sir,' chorused the girls around her.

'Well I'm really disappointed. You spoiled the concert as far as I'm concerned. And you're the top class.'

'They will be suitably punished,' said Teresa. 'They won't have a Christmas party.' I wondered whether Teresa really wanted to punish them in this way, or whether she simply couldn't be bothered to organise a party.

That evening I collapsed into an armchair and fell asleep by seven o'clock. The half term leading up to the Christmas concert had been a fraught one and I was extremely tired. Every day had brought fresh problems and the children were excitable and distracted. I began to wonder if we'd made as much progress as I thought, but Brenda was a constantly cheerful support and it surprised me that she hadn't applied for the deputy headship.

'It's not for me,' she said when I asked her after school. 'I'm happy to run the infant department, and to spend my day with children. They're a lot easier than adults.'

'I just don't feel we're making enough progress.'

'Of course we are. The staff feel there's a sense of purpose about the place, there are lots of new things happening, the staff meetings are enjoyable and the children are a lot more interested. I'd say you've made quite an impact.'

'That's kind of you, but I shouldn't think the parents feel like that. Not after the straw throwing at the concert. God, I hope there weren't too many school governors at the show.'

'Oh, don't worry, the governors rarely come, unless it's an evening show, and the parents will have forgotten it by tomorrow. Now cheer up. And make sure you come down tomorrow for our infant Christmas party. You don't fancy dressing up as Father Christmas, do you?' Buoyed by her words, I decided to go home early, have a rest, and then sketch out a few ideas for a musical event I wanted to organise next term.

I suddenly realised that my car keys were missing from the container on my desk. They must be in my coat, I thought, and I hurried through the pockets. They weren't. Neither were they in the bag I carried to and from work. Perhaps Lucy had seen them on my desk and put them away safely... but she would have told me, and anyway she'd gone and probably wouldn't be home for another hour. I phoned my wife and said I might be late, which would delay us in picking up our daughter from the child minder. It had started snowing heavily and there was nothing for it but to catch a bus, fetch the spare keys and come back to school again. It was the first time I'd ever mislaid my car keys, and I was angry with myself for leaving them in a pot on my desk.

Then, with a lurching feeling in my stomach, I realised my car might have been stolen. The school security was poor, the car park was dimly lit, and the gates were always left open for deliveries. I ran downstairs and with enormous relief saw that my ancient Mini was still there. I told Fred what had happened and then hurried to the bus stop. The snow had caused the traffic to become congested and although I only had a short journey home, it took almost an hour and a half. Fortunately, my neighbour had collected our daughter and, too tired to play with her, I collapsed into an armchair and slept. In the morning, I sighed with relief again when I found that my car was still in the car park.

Two days later, the keys turned up. I was standing by the stairs welcoming the children as they went to their classrooms, when Tony from Teresa's class approached me.

'Sir, I found these. I don't know if they're yours, but I know you drive a Mini.' He held out a bunch of keys and smiled disarmingly.

'Yes, they are,' I said. 'Thank heavens. Where did you find them? I was really worried about those.'

'They were out in the road, Sir. I was just going home and I happened to look down and there they were, in the gutter. Must go now Sir, before Miss does the register.' He stared intently at me, and then ran off down the corridor.

And then, although I couldn't prove anything at all, everything suddenly clicked. I'd told Tony off after the concert, and he wasn't used to being told off. Because he was often a nuisance in the classroom, Teresa would let him take the dinner registers around the classes because it got him out of the way for half an hour, and the registers were kept in my room. From that day on, I kept my car keys in a box, on top of a tall cupboard, and I never lost them again.

But the term did end on a positive note for me, especially as the final week had been the most strenuous of the entire term. Annette, the Scottish infant teacher, who was never away from school, had eaten a take-away meal and contracted food poisoning. There were no supply teacher agencies in those days, the local education authority had nobody they could send, and I had to share the children amongst the other classes. Lucy's daughter had influenza, and she'd needed to stay at home to look after her. And somebody had sprayed deodorant heavily in the staff toilet, causing Briony to have a fit of asthma. As she puffed and wheezed, I wondered whether she'd make it through the holidays. She was no better the next day, which meant I had to teach her class and organise her Christmas party. And Teresa's class were being particularly disruptive, because they hadn't been allowed to have a party at all. Which may have been the reason she came to me after school on the last day of term, asked if she could speak to me, and closed the door quietly.

'I've had enough of all this,' she said. 'I don't see why I should put up with their behaviour any longer, so I'm going to take early retirement. I've just come down to let you know I shall be leaving at Easter.'

CHAPTER 5
A TEST OF MY LEADERSHIP

Centipedes have got loads of legs to walk with. Not like cows, with only one leg on each corner.' Gloria, age 6

At the start of the Spring term, the search for a new deputy head began in earnest.

I had no idea how long I intended to stay at Comber Grove, but it would be at least five years and this appointment was going to be crucial to the life of the school. I needed somebody who would share my enthusiasm, take away some of my massive workload, and set up a model classroom that would impress and enthuse other teachers. He or she would need to be good with people, talented with children, and be willing to work the same long hours I did. They'd have to be unflappable in a crisis… because it was becoming obvious we had many… be willing to help organise the curriculum and staff meetings, and relate well to our parents, some of whom were difficult and demanding. I also didn't want someone who'd be with me for a couple of years and then hurry off into a headship. It was going to be a tough call, and I talked to Alan Green about it.

'There's one very important thing,' he said. 'You've got to appoint the person that's right for you. Superficially it's a governor's appointment, of course, and I can't be there because I'm retiring at the end of the month, but you'll have to sway the votes when you sum up after the interviews.'

'So the appointment is theirs and not mine?'

'Theoretically, yes. But there's lots of ways round that. Once you've advertised, make sure you show all the applicants round your school personally. Talk to them all at length. Send them to the staffroom for a cup of tea so that the teachers can assess them too. You'll soon find out which ones they like. Then do your shortlisting. Six is ideal. And make sure you visit the school of the candidates you shortlist. You can tell an awful lot from that.'

'It'll mean I'm out of school a lot. I could get the Chair of Governors to visit some.'

'No, you do it. You're the one who's got to work with the person who gets the job. Governors are very easily impressed by the wrong things.'

'That's if I get six people to shortlist. I might not even get six applicants.'

'Oh, you will. Your school is becoming well known in the authority. You'll get at least a dozen. And there's a bright young teacher at one of my schools that I think would be just right for you. Her name is Denise Anderson.'

Incredibly, we received twenty three applications, and I invited all the teachers to visit the school. Inevitably, even though I'd written copious notes about the candidates after I'd met them, by the time I'd shown number five around I'd forgotten what number one looked like. I decided to take a photograph of the other nineteen. These days, with their agreement, I could have taken a snapshot on my mobile. In the pre-digital age I had to rely on a cumbersome polaroid instant, but at least looking at the photos brought back an instant mental image of what they'd said while they were with me.

Meeting all twenty three was exhausting, though I quickly realised things would be greatly simplified if I took them round the school in batches of three or four. Even so, it took three weeks to see everybody, as there were still many other things demanding my attention. The teachers, fortunately, were very patient about the disruption it caused. They understood how crucial the appointment was.

After talking with the staff, and then talking through the applications with the Chair of Governors, we whittled the list of candidates down to six, and at that point it did seem that our favourite was Denise Anderson. I trusted Mr Green's experience, and Denise's application was cleverly written, with a wry touch of humour and a good knowledge of everything that I considered important in primary education. She'd attended the right courses, contributed effectively to her current school, and her application had a freshness that I found very appealing.

But as Alan had intimated, it was the school visits that were revealing. Seeing the finalists working with children was always going to be the ultimate test, and watching them in their usual daily surroundings gave me an insight into strengths and weaknesses I couldn't have picked up on during their visits to my school.

Denise's classroom was well organised and interesting, but a little too neat and clinical, although she was popular with her class and other teachers spoke highly of her. I could understand why Alan thought she was ready for a leadership position. Two other candidates had obviously been preparing much too hard for my visit, and one displayed an almost manic enthusiasm. Even allowing for nerves, I found this disconcerting. Another two candidates were warm, welcoming and efficient, with highly organised classrooms and a skilful manner with children. Any of them would have probably made good deputies, and they were all ready for a career move upwards.

And then I visited Georgia's classroom.

Georgia had been one of the last teachers to apply. Brenda had met her on a professional development course, got to know her well, and suggested she apply for our vacancy. She wasn't interested. She loved being a class teacher, and that was as far as she wanted to go. But Brenda wasn't giving up, and after a couple of weeks intense badgering, she'd persuaded Georgia to come and see us. A well spoken, slim and extremely beautiful West Indian woman in her early forties, I'd liked her immediately when she'd visited, and she'd talked enthusiastically about primary education as we'd walked around the school. She was excited about the changes I was making to the school, and her philosophy seemed identical to mine. But then she'd submitted a very ordinary application, and the school governors had hesitated about including her in the shortlist.

But now, her classroom immediately dispelled any doubt. It was astonishing. Pictures, models, displays, collages, exciting curriculum corners… the classroom was a wonderland of learning that her children were obviously highly motivated by. Her manner with the children was delightful, and when the headteacher came into the classroom to give her some books, she motioned me into the corridor.

'Georgia is a much loved teacher,' she said, 'and incredibly talented, although you'll already have noticed that. I can't recommend her highly enough, but I have to tell you, I shall hate it when she goes.'

The next day I worked out a schedule, preparing letters of rejection for the unsuccessful applicants and letters telling the lucky ones what time to come for interview. Then I asked Lucy if she'd pop over to the letter box and post them. When she returned, there was a questioning look on her face.

'I thought you'd rejected Alan Stanley and Georgina Winton?'

'I did. Why?'

'Because I've just posted letters to them in brown envelopes. And the brown envelopes were for the successful ones.'

My stomach sank. This was awful. While I'd been sorting out the letters, many children had been coming into my room to ask me things, and I'd obviously slipped up. Now I was going to have two very excited applicants who shouldn't have been excited at all.

'I'll just have to write to them and tell them I've messed up,' I said. 'They won't be very happy, but I don't see what else I can do.'

'Look, leave it to me. I've got an idea.'

Thirty minutes later she was back with all the letters.

'How on earth did you manage that?' I asked.

'I've got a long arm,' she smiled. 'I reached in and pulled them out. No, actually, I waited until the postman came to collect them and I pleaded with him. Feminine charm. It's why you need a female secretary. Just don't appoint the wrong deputy at the interview, that's all.'

Even though a deputy headship is an important appointment and I'd circulated the application papers to all thirteen governors, only six turned up for the interview. I was quickly learning that although governors have a great deal of influence over a school, they could often show a disarming lack of interest. We'd allotted each candidate forty minutes, and all turned up at their appointed time trying to look as relaxed as possible. I was reminded of my own interview here, and what an unnerving experience being interviewed can be.

I tried extremely hard to make each person feel relaxed and comfortable, and the governor's questions were simple and to the point. All interviewed well, Denise in particular, but by this time I knew who I wanted. By nine o'clock we'd seen everybody, and the Chairman briefly summarised the strengths of each candidate. Then he looked at his watch and tapped the table.

'I think we're ready to make a decision if everybody's agreeable,' he said. 'All of them were very good, but my vote is for Denise Anderson. I'm told the authority's inspector favours her highly too.'

There was a murmur of agreement from everybody in the room.

'Good, that's settled then. We appoint Mrs Anderson. I gather that's okay with you too, Mr Kent?' I was surprised by the suddenness of his decision. I thought he might at least have asked who I favoured.

'Well no, it's not, actually,' I said. He seemed annoyed that I had questioned his decision.

'So you'd prefer someone else then? Personally, I didn't think anybody interviewed better than Mrs Anderson.'

'It's not only the interview that counts. Remember, you have only met these candidates this evening. I have spent a lot of time with all of them. And I'm certain that Mrs Faith is the right person for our school.'

'Really? I'd like to hear what other governors think.'

'Mrs Anderson is the best candidate,' said the elderly governor who'd asked me about discipline in my own interview. 'She seems to know how to keep the kids in line.' Once again most of the governors murmured and nodded. My annoyance at their decision was rising, and I was determined not to back down.

'Look, I shall be here for quite a few years. I am the one who has to work with the appointed person. Anyone on this governing body could leave at any time, but I have a strong commitment to this school and its children. And I'm sorry, but this really has to be my choice.'

'Well, I'm happy to go with Mr Kent's choice,' said the parent governor. 'I'm very happy with the way the school is being run, and so are my daughters.'

'I agree,' said the white haired gentleman who had asked me about travel during my interview. I sensed that he'd had enough, and was keen to get home.

'Very well, I'll stand by the governors' decision. Let's put it to the vote.'

Georgia was appointed, and as soon as the governors had left, I phoned her. She felt she hadn't interviewed well and was surprised and delighted. I knew this was going to be the real turning point for the school and that once she'd arrived we would be able to move forward rapidly. Unfortunately, this wasn't going to be as soon as I would have liked. Her school was reluctant to release her before July, and I could appreciate that she wanted to finish the school year with her class. Since Teresa was retiring at Easter, I'd have to make do without a deputy for a term, although this hardly seemed an insurmountable problem at the time.

Meanwhile, we were suddenly subjected to a spate of thefts. One morning in February, Fred was at the gate as I drove my car into school. As I'd got to know him better, I'd learned that he rather enjoyed a crisis, and I could tell from the look on his face that something serious had happened in the last twelve hours.

'You'd better come upstairs quick,' he announced gravely. 'We've had a burglary.'

I followed him up to Lucy's room. The door had been jemmied, and the contents of Lucy's cupboards were all over the floor. One of the filing cabinets had been forced open, and as soon as I looked inside I knew what was missing. A fortnight ago, the school photographer had visited, and Lucy had been collecting money from the parents. The lock on the school safe had broken, so she'd stored it overnight in her filing cabinet because it was being collected by the company this morning. The cabinet had been hammered open and several hundred pounds were missing.

'They got in down here,' said Fred. 'Probably kids. Look, I'll show you.'

He took me to the end of the corridor, where a window had been smashed. Bits of the frame were lying all over the floor in a pile of dust and grime.

'I didn't want to clear it up till you'd seen it,' Fred said. 'Cost you a bit of overtime, I'm afraid.'

'Leave it till we've phoned the police,' I said. 'We'll have to bring the children up the other staircase.'

My mind was racing. Our insurance would probably cover us, provided they accepted us storing the money in a flimsy filing cabinet, but the photography firm would need paying straight away. I'd have to use school money until we were re-imbursed. School burglaries weren't unheard of, especially in deprived inner city areas, but this one didn't make any sense. Lucy had taken care not to tell anybody where she'd put the money overnight. And how had anybody got in through such a small window? They could have climbed over the playground wall, and there was a drainpipe close to the window, but it would have been necessary to balance very precariously on the pipe to attack the window frame with any force. And wouldn't somebody have heard?

Three weeks later we had another serious theft. Mary, our cook, had been to the bank one lunchtime and withdrawn two hundred pounds. It was a gift for her daughter, who needed to buy a new washing machine. Mary had concealed the money in her handbag and put it under her coat in her office, but then she'd been called to the dinner hall to talk with a visiting supervisor. When she returned to the office, her handbag was open, the contents were all over the table, and the money had gone. Somebody had obviously noted that she'd left school and gone to the bank, but she'd only told the kitchen staff, and other than Fred's wife Betty, who was working in the kitchen temporarily, she'd known her kitchen assistants for years and she trusted them all implicitly.

There was little I could do, other than promise to buy her a small safe to keep in her office. I notified the police, more as an insurance procedure than in hope that they could do anything. The next morning Betty bought her a large bouquet of flowers which cheered her up a little, but Fred didn't have a great deal of sympathy.

'Fancy leaving her handbag on a table,' he said scornfully. 'That's just asking for trouble.'

Three weeks later, two handbags disappeared from the staffroom. A day after that, a purse was taken from a visiting attendance officer's handbag. She'd put the bag down in the library for five minutes while she went to the staffroom for a cup of tea. Once again the police were called. The officer merely said that as long as people left their belongings in unsafe places, there would always be temptation. Even in schools and hospitals, he was sorry to say. Especially hospitals. He'd known somebody nick the contents of an entire medical cabinet in broad daylight. The following day both handbags were found, minus money and credit cards, on the waste ground on the other side of the playground wall when Fred took his alsatian for a walk.

I called an urgent staff meeting and impressed on everybody the danger of leaving anything valuable lying around. I promised to buy a set of lockers for the staffroom, but said that in the meantime we would need to be particularly observant. It was possible for anybody to walk into the school virtually unchallenged, and it would be assumed they were parents, or visitors looking for the school office. I talked to the children in assembly, stressing that if they saw anybody they didn't know in the school, they should immediately tell a teacher or classroom helper.

Theft in a school is highly distressing. You simply don't expect it. You want to believe that everybody connected in any way with your school is honest, but it is for that very reason that schools are especially vulnerable. I wasn't certain that these burglaries had been committed by somebody from outside, but although I had suspicions, I hadn't the slightest evidence to go on. Nevertheless, I decided to try a little psychology. I put a dozen sheets of white paper in a very large brown envelope, wrote 'to be collected by the police officer' in large black letters on the front, and left it on Lucy's desk. During the next few days, lots of people asked about it, and I explained that it was some evidence that had been found which would incriminate the thief. Then, at the end of the week, I took the envelope home and threw it away.

From that moment, the burglaries stopped, possibly because everybody, including the children, now had a heightened awareness of the thefts. Possibly because police had been seen around the school and everybody knew the matter was being taken seriously. But I like to think my envelope might just have played a part.

Shortly after that we had to call the police again, though not because something had been taken from the school. On this occasion, we were given a gift we really didn't want. It was Monday morning, and Lucy had just finished adding up the dinner money and was about to give it to Fred for banking. A young black male walked into her office and said that he'd like to put his daughter on the school roll, and that he'd like her to start today. Lucy explained that we did have a few vacancies, and she asked which school his daughter was currently attending.

'She isn't,' he said, 'she's here.'

He pointed to the little bundle of blanket he was carrying and turned it round towards us. Tightly wrapped, and fast asleep, was a baby who couldn't have been more than a few months old.

'But she can't attend school,' said Lucy, 'she's far too young.'

'Well what about the Nursery? She could go in there.'

'She's much too young for that too. This is a primary school. You'll have to wait until she's at least three and a half.'

'That's no good. I've split up with my girlfriend and I've got to get to work.'

Lucy explained that he'd need to find a child minder, but that really she was too young even for that. Muttering that he didn't have time to look for child minders, he left the room and we assumed that was the end of the matter. Fifteen minutes later, at playtime, Jason from Class 5 walked into my room. He was a polite, friendly boy.

'I'm really sorry to trouble you, sir,' he said, 'but some bloke has just given me this.' In his arms was the tiny bundle of baby.

I jumped up from my seat. 'Well what did he say? And where did he go?'

'Dunno Sir. 'E jus' said could I look after it for a bit and he'd be back at hometime.'

The baby was awake now. Her dark, beautiful eyes looked blankly at Jason, and I realised how desperate the young father must have been. I carried the baby into Lucy's room, where teachers and helpers oohed and aahed at the little girl and were appalled that anybody could have dumped her in a child's arms and gone to work. Lucy phoned the police, explained the situation, and within half an hour a young policewoman arrived.

''I haven't worked this patch for long,' she said, 'but already nothing surprises me. I could take him to social services but I really need to contact the mother and father. And that's going to be a bit difficult, I think. Is there any chance that you could keep the little girl until this afternoon? I'll come back at two o'clock and wait for dad.'

The baby was so delightful it didn't take much persuading. Mrs Gander found a cradle that was used in the nursery, some musical toys were fetched from the Reception class, and a parent who'd been talking to Lucy ran home to fetch a spare bottle and teat to feed the baby with. At three o'clock, the father walked into the office. He was tired and distressed, and the police woman took him quietly into the library to talk about his situation. Then all three left the building, and I hoped that the mother would be back at home when they arrived. Having a tiny daughter myself, and never having encountered anything like this before, I found it extremely upsetting. Nevertheless, these recent setbacks were relatively minor compared with the test of my leadership that I was about to face.

At the end of the Spring term, Teresa said her farewells and left the school to head off into retirement. We'd managed to survive together without any major arguments, but I don't think either of us were sorry to say goodbye. Now I had to find a supply teacher who could teach her class through the summer term, and I phoned the local education office. The reply didn't surprise me.

'Sorry,' said the recruitment officer, 'We just don't have anybody available at the moment. Try us again next week.'

This seemed to be the response every time I phoned, and I was annoyed that nobody ever seemed to be available. I had learned that other schools near me didn't have too much trouble obtaining supply teachers, so I assumed that because I was a relatively new headteacher, people at the office knew that I wouldn't make much of a fuss.

Instead, I taught the class myself, once again relying on Lucy to run the office and abandoning everything else that I had to do. The class was very aware that they only had one term left at Comber Grove, and they decided that they might as well try me out, especially as they'd had an uncomfortable year with Teresa.

Although I was desperate to order modern furniture for all the classrooms, my friendly resources officer couldn't do it all at once, and the older children still sat at individual desks with lids. On my first morning with Class 5, they eyed me cautiously as I took the dinner register and explained that I would be with them until we were able to find an appropriate supply teacher.

'That's lovely, Sir,' said Jemima. 'You're a very nice man.' Her friends grinned and looked at her knowingly.

'Thank you, Jemima,' I said. 'I hope you'll still be saying that after I've given you some work to do.'

'I hope we do lots of paintin', said Peter, a small boy with a shock of ginger hair. 'We haven't done much of that this year.'

'It's writing first,' I said. 'I want to see how good you are at it. Can you take your pencils and books out please.'

With a deliberate action, Jemima lifted her desk lid and let it drop heavily. 'Oooh, sorry Sir,' she said, 'I didn't mean that to happen.'

Her friends immediately followed suit, dropping their desk lids noisily and apologising profusely.

'Those lids are awful,' aren't they,' I said, 'but they're great for cracking walnuts. Shame I wasn't teaching you before Christmas.'

Jemima smiled briefly and settled back into her chair, obviously deciding to give me a chance to prove myself. I took a book of ghost stories from my bag and read them one I knew they'd enjoy. Most of the class listened quietly, watching me carefully, and then I set them a writing task. After thirty minutes, I walked round to see what they had done. Jemima had written two pages and illustrated it with a colourful picture. Tony had written three words.

'Well Tony,' I said, 'it's a start. But I actually want a bit more than three words.'

'But that's all I ever write. Miss never used to ask me for any more.'

'Yes, but Miss isn't here now. And I'm like Oliver Twist. I'd like a little bit more.'

His face screwed into a question mark. 'But I have to go and do the dinner registers.'

'No, Jemima can do that. She's finished.'

Jemima and her friends grinned at Tony, which infuriated him. He threw his pencil on the floor, folded his arms and grimaced at me.

'Well I ain't doin' any more writin',' he said.

'That's up to you,' I said, 'but if you don't want to be part of the lesson you'd better sit outside.'

Somehow, we struggled through the day. The afternoon was much easier as Jemima seemed to have decided that my lessons might be worth listening to, and if she listened, her friends would follow suit. I'd planned some creative activities, and at the end of the day they enjoyed dramatising the story I'd read to them. I told them we'd show it in assembly the next day, which was exciting for them and helpful to me, as I wouldn't need to prepare an assembly as well as organise work for the class. By midweek, I was really enjoying myself, and they were too. They had been learning about the Tudors, a topic I took up with enthusiasm, and by Friday we'd created a superb wall display about Henry the Eighth and his wives.

When I returned to my room after school, there was an enormous amount of paperwork to catch up with, three parents had called to see me, a teacher needed to discuss a class outing, and Fred wanted me to know that an infant had loosened the pipe attached to the lavatory cistern, flooding unsuspecting youngsters with water when they pulled the chain. But there was one good piece of news. The education office was sending me a supply teacher on Monday.

On Monday morning, Mr Khamzi arrived five minutes before the whistle blew. He was a middle aged, softly spoken Indian gentleman, smartly dressed in a brown suit, a crisp white shirt and a carefully knotted tie. He said he'd had a difficult journey, but he would probably get used to it.

'I want a permanent job in a school,' he said. 'I have done supply teaching in many schools in this authority, but it is time they found me something permanent.'

'Well, at least you'll have a whole term here,' I said. 'My deputy's just retired, and you'll be taking her class.'

'I have a great deal of experience. It is time I too was given a deputy headship.'

This seemed an odd thing to say, but I smiled politely, gave him a timetable sheet, a whistle and a copy of the curriculum, and then I took him to his classroom.

I popped into the room several times during his first week. The children were uncomfortably quiet, and he seemed to resent my entrance. After four days, a group of parents came to see me, saying that their children were frightened of the new teacher, and found the work he was giving them to do very tedious and difficult. Tony's mother was particularly vociferous, since Mr Khamzi had threatened to sellotape his mouth if he didn't stop talking in class. Since Mr Khamzi had taken to leaving school promptly at hometime, I went up to his classroom immediately after school and looked through the children's desks. Their work seemed to consist of inappropriate worksheets, dull photocopied exercises and copying from the blackboard. The following day, I asked him to come and see me at lunchtime, and I took him around the other classrooms, showing him the learning environment I expected. He nodded respectfully, but I had the feeling he hadn't the slightest intention of taking any notice.

The next day, a child came to my room at playtime and told me that there was no teacher on playground duty. I looked at the rota, and realised Mr Khamzi should have been out there, especially as I'd told him on the day he arrived when his duties were. Once again, I asked him to come to my room. He said he'd forgotten, and added that he didn't think supply teachers should do playground duty or attend staff meetings. I told him that since he was here as a full time member of staff for a term, he was required to do both. It wasn't an option. I was becoming seriously worried. The children were unhappy, little real learning was taking place, parents were complaining, and Mr Khamzi seemed to be doing as little as he could get away with.

The following Monday he phoned in sick. A tummy bug, he said. I sympathised, and phoned for another supply. As usual, nobody was available, so once again I taught the class myself. The children seemed relieved to see me, and it was a thoroughly enjoyable day, but it meant taking all my office work home to do. I taught on Tuesday and Wednesday, too. The children's disappointment was tangible as he walked into the classroom on Thursday.

The following week, he was away again for the first three days. When he appeared on Thursday, he said the tummy bug was still causing him trouble, but he'd got a doctor's appointment, so would it be okay if he left school early? I was tempted to point out that he always did that anyway.

During the next month, he was absent at least twice a week. His condition was worsening, he said, and he was struggling with getting to school. I was now becoming very impatient indeed. Occasionally I was able to obtain a different supply teacher, but the children's work and behaviour was deteriorating rapidly. When Mr Khamzi returned, I stated firmly that things had to change. At this point I was seriously considering dividing the children amongst the other junior classes, but this was their final term at Comber Grove and I really didn't want to do that. I was also concerned that our annual Open Evening was approaching, and I wondered whether Mr Khamzi could be left alone with the parents of Class 5. It occurred to me that they might attempt to lynch him, and I'd certainly have to sit in the classroom with him when he spoke to the more aggressive mothers.

Other than the work I'd done with the class, there was little on the classroom walls and the room look dull and uninviting. I reminded him that he'd need to give the room some attention before Open Evening, and also check the children's books carefully to make sure his marking was up to date.

'Of course,' he said. 'But I shall need some extra time without the class in the room to do that.'

'That's something I am not able to give you,' I said. 'All the other teachers work before and after school on that sort of thing.'

'But you have given the other teachers non-contact time.'

'No, only one or two who have been ill or on courses.'

'I have been ill too, and I consider that you are treating me unfairly.'

'I'm sorry, but I don't share your view. You have had a great deal of time off and I am not prepared to give you additional non-contact time.' At this, he took a small notebook and pencil from his pocket and hurriedly wrote some notes. I told him that the conversation had ended, and he left my room.

And then he disappeared altogether. When I telephoned the authority to say that he hadn't arrived for school yet again and that I'd had enough, the officer didn't seem at all surprised. At eleven o'clock she phoned me back to say that they'd tried unsuccessfully to track down Mr Khamzi and assumed that he must be ill again. I was assured that he wouldn't be sent back to me, and they'd found another supply teacher who could join me the following day. Fortunately, this proved to be a delightful young Australian. The children took to her immediately and I breathed a sigh of relief.

But not for long. Two weeks later, I received a telephone call from one of the authority's solicitors. Mr Khamzi had been in discussion with his union and they had advised him to take legal advice. He felt he had been discriminated against while at my school. He also considered that I'd singled him out to criticise his teaching, and he had not been given proper support or respect. Furthermore, he had been treated unfairly and made to carry out inappropriate tasks.

He believed this was all due to his colour, and he intended taking me to a racial tribunal.

CHAPTER 6
WALKING WITH DINOSAURS

The class was asked to use 'benign' in a sentence. Nina wrote 'I am eight but I will soon benign'

September, and my second year as a headteacher. I had a dynamic new deputy head I was looking forward to working with, but any excitement I felt about this was overshadowed by the knowledge that soon I would be called to a tribunal.

Fortunately Andrew Brown, the authority's solicitor, had been helpful and positive, and I'd spent three hours in his company going over every detail of Mr Khamzi's brief stay at the school. I had supportive statements from parents, I had taken careful notes of what the children in Class 5 had said, and I also had evidence from the teachers, who were extremely concerned that I was being treated in this manner by a supply teacher who had taught badly and taken so much time off.

During the conversation with the solicitor, I discovered that Mr Khamzi had also taken a considerable amount of Gerry's time, since Gerry was the union representative for the staff. Gerry had been as irritated by Mr Khamzi's accusations as the rest of the staff, as he felt they were unfounded and unfair and he declined to give him any support. Mr Khamzi had therefore sought out the area representative instead. After the initial skirmishes we'd had when I joined the school, it did seem that Gerry was now firmly on my side.

'Take it from me, you really don't have anything to worry about,' Andrew said. 'I think what you did was perfectly reasonable. And after all, the man wasn't there half the time.'

'It's worrying, nevertheless,' I said. 'He could make up all sorts of things at the tribunal.'

'He could. But I don't think he will.'

Although Andrew's experience of these matters made me a

little less apprehensive, it was still a time of great anxiety for me and my family. The looming tribunal seldom left my mind, and I found it difficult to concentrate on my work. And then, several months later when the day of the hearing arrived, I discovered the reason for Andrew's confidence.

The tribunal was held in one of the large conference rooms at County Hall, and was presided over by an elderly gentlemen with a shock of snowy white hair and thick black spectacles. On the right hand side of the room, in the front row of a bank of chairs, sat Mr Khamzi with his union solicitor. As usual, he was dressed immaculately and it occurred to me that he'd probably never taught an art lesson with a class in his life in case he got a splash of paint on his suit. He stared straight ahead, while his solicitor shuffled through some notes. Although there were three rows of chairs, there was nobody else on that side of the room at all. It was several months since I'd seen Mr Khamzi, and I noticed that nearly all of his hair had turned grey.

In complete contrast, about fifteen people sat in the other half of the room, all with folders and documents on their laps. Andrew sat in the front row, with a pile of paperwork in front of him. To my surprise and delight, I recognised five other local headteachers, who nodded and smiled at me. They seemed surprised to see me, and each other. I assumed that Mr Khamzi had worked at their primary schools too… with the same results. It had obviously been necessary for Andrew to deal with each case, confidentially, on its own merits. The judge looked at his watch, and rapped his knuckles on the table in front of him.

'Good morning everyone. It's now ten o'clock and I would therefore like to make a start,' he said. 'We have a lot to get through and there are a number of people who will be making statements. Mr Jennings, would you make your introductory statement on behalf of Mr Khamzi, please.'

He looked towards Mr Jennings, who seemed to be in urgent conversation with Mr Khamzi and not to have heard. The judge tapped the bench again.

'Mr Jennings, would you…'

'I do apologise,' said Mr Jennings. 'I've been speaking to my client and I would be grateful if I could have a confidential word with you, please.'

Mr Khamzi's solicitor walked to the front bench and spoke in a low voice. The judge nodded, explained to everybody that the hearing would be delayed by five minutes, and then the solicitor led his client out of the door. When he returned, Mr Khamzi sat down wearily, and the solicitor spoke to the judge again. Then the judge turned to speak to us all.

'I am pleased to say that this hearing will not go ahead,' he said. 'Mr Khamzi has reached an agreement with his solicitor and with the authority, and I congratulate them on finding an amicable solution. Thank you for attending this hearing, which I now declare closed. You may all leave now.'

The headteachers turned to each other in bewilderment. What was going on? At the very least they wanted a chance to explain why they'd had so many problems with Mr Khamzi, and they were angry at being called to a tribunal which wasn't happening. Andrew ushered us all into a corner of the room and explained.

'He's made a deal with the authority,' he said. 'He will take early retirement if they give him a monetary settlement. And they're happy to do that because he's been a nightmare in this authority for over two years. The settlement will be a big one, so the poor old taxpayer forks out yet again. As you've all discovered to your cost, he's just been passed around the schools. Quite a few heads were warned off, but you wouldn't have known about him, Mr Kent, because you're relatively new. I just hope you get a letter of apology from the authority, but you probably won't.'

My experiences, it turned out, hadn't been as bad as the others. In one school, Mr Khamzi had attempted to fine children when they misbehaved. In another, he insisted that children brought money for a charity he said he was organising. In a third school, he'd got into a fierce argument with a parent which almost came to blows. In all the schools, he'd only attended for one or two days each week, claiming illness on the others. And now he was leaving the authority with a very tidy sum for the disruption he'd caused and the allegations he'd made. It made me very angry indeed.

But at least it was over, and a weight had been lifted from my mind. I could now enjoy the company of my new deputy, who was already proving her worth at school. She was quickly earning the confidence of the staff, and Fred was impressed by her polite and professional approach. So much so, he wasn't quite sure how to approach her when he discovered that a child had defecated on the toilet floor on a day when I was out at a meeting. Struggling to find suitable phraseology, he informed her that there was a tomtit on the toilet floor'. 'Really?' Georgia replied, assuming that he meant an injured bird had become trapped in the toilets, 'Well... slide a piece of card underneath it, get it to the door, and see if it flies away.'

I had allocated a class of eight year olds to Georgia, and within weeks she had enthused them with her fascinating approach to teaching. I'd already seen and admired what she could do in her previous school, and it wasn't long before she'd created a similar learning environment for her classroom at Comber Grove. The teachers admired her diligent organisation, they talked to her about the teaching techniques she was using, and they helped her create exciting displays of work for the corridors.

When I had outside meetings to attend, it was a relief to know that everything would run smoothly at school, and she often stayed late to share ideas about new things we could introduce to the school. She was a keen gardener, and by the end of her first half term she had arranged for each class to cultivate a section of the garden area that had replaced the dangerous climbing logs. She started a choir, shared the school assemblies with me, and re-organised the infant library and reading books. She was never absent, her wealth of experience was highly valued by the staff, and her friendly smile and infectious laughter first thing in the morning provided an ideal start to the day.

One day, after school, we were discussing how much the children loved model making. The conversation turned to dinosaurs, and Georgia suddenly had a flash of inspiration.

'Why don't we create a Dinosaur World?' she said. 'The children would love it. So would the parents.'

'Good idea,' I agreed. 'But where?'

'In the top hall. All seven classes could build a different kind of dinosaur. Gerry's great at art, so we'll put lining paper on the walls and get him to paint a background all round the hall with a group of children. If classes make their dinosaurs as big as possible, it'll be pretty impressive.'

It sounded a fascinating idea, and at the next staff meeting we discussed it with the teachers. We'd do it during the Spring term, which would give them plenty of time to plan what sort of dinosaurs they'd build, and it wouldn't interfere with their normal curriculum. The children would also produce informational writing and pictures about their dinosaurs to put on display boards around the hall, so that the exhibition would be a feast of colourful artwork, interesting facts, and lifelike models. If it all worked well, we'd invite other schools to visit our Dinosaur World, and no doubt representatives from the local authority would be pretty impressed too. It would all help to put our school even more firmly on the map.

All the teachers were enthusiastic, except one.

Annette, the Scottish teacher, had left recently and I'd been sent Laura Simpson, a young newly qualified teacher who had impressed me initially, but although she worked hard and was particularly good at teaching gymnastics and physical education, she disliked doing anything creative with her class of infants. She hated the mess it could cause. Paintings and models from her class tended to be unimaginative and sterile, and because children love creative activities, I felt that her children were missing out. I also determined to be more cautious with my next appointments and delve a little deeper into their talents and teaching techniques. While the other teachers enthused about the project, Laura sat quietly and seemed uninspired.

'My children won't be able to do that,' she said.

'Why not?' Georgia asked. 'They'll love it.'

'It's much too difficult for them. They're infants.'

'So are mine. And I know they'll be able to do it. You can at least give it a try.'

The other teachers agreed, and Laura reluctantly nodded. With so much enthusiasm from the rest of the staff, it would have been difficult for her to refuse.

But she dug her heels in, and when the time came to work on the project, progress in her classroom was extremely slow. She didn't know which dinosaur to build, she didn't know what materials to use, her classroom was small so there wouldn't be enough room to build one, and her children weren't showing much interest anyway. Couldn't she just get her children to do some writing and a few paintings? I knew as well as she did that children are fired by their teacher's enthusiasm, and since she wasn't showing much, her children were naturally following suit. I decided to make a bold move.

'Okay', I said, 'this is what we'll do. I want you to build a dinosaur, because every other class is doing one and it would hardly be fair if this class didn't. But we'll build two dinosaurs with your children. Let's split the class into two groups. I'll build a dinosaur with one group, and you can build a small one with the other.' Since she only had eighteen children in her class, it was an offer she couldn't refuse.

Once again, it was taking time away from all the administrative work that was piling up on my desk, but the education of the children was paramount, I didn't want Laura's class to miss out, and I was certain that her children would respond just like the others. I decided to go for broke… we'd build a massive brontosaurus as a centrepiece to our Dinosaur World, and if nothing else, it would show Laura that infants could build a dinosaur as well as anybody.

At the weekend, I drove to the local DIY store and bought lengths of wood, a roll of chicken wire, screws, nails and a set of castors. Then, on Monday morning I sent a note around the classes, asking if they could spare as many old newspapers, magazines, cartons and egg boxes as possible. Although I'd intended to build a simple wooden structure with the children, around which we'd fashion the body of our brontosaurus, I soon found something even better. In a corner of a disused washroom there was a broken vaulting box which hadn't been used for a long time. We could build our body around that. Carefully tipping the box over, I screwed a castor onto each corner.

On Tuesday and Thursday afternoons, I took my group to the art room and we began to cover the box with newspaper and old sugar paper which had lain in the stockroom for years. Then I screwed eight foot lengths of timber to each side of the box and joined the lengths at the top end. We now had the structure for our head and neck, and I did the same for the tail. I set to work winding chicken wire around the timber, and Sinjit, an eager little boy who'd brought dinosaur picture cards from home, climbed onto the vaulting box and carefully twisted the wire into the shape of a head. Then we covered it with layers of newspaper soaked in wallpaper paste.

'We never done anything like this before,' said Sinjit, standing back to admire the enormous beast taking shape in front of him. 'Its goin' to look so real. I like doin' this. It's good fun.' The rest of the group murmured their agreement.

'I think we'd better wheel it into the hall before it gets any bigger,' I said.

We carefully eased it through the art room door, along the corridor and into the hall. As the neck glided past a classroom window, I heard a child shout 'Wow! Look at that!'

After four more sessions, we were able to start painting and I drove to the DIY store again for some buckets and large brushes. I'd asked the children to bring one of their dad's old shirts for the painting sessions, but inevitably lots of grey paint went on the children's faces and hands as well as our brontosaurus. At hometime, I washed the children as best I could, and felt it might be best if I went to the playground to explain to their mothers why they were covered in grey.

'Well, I don't know what you're doin' up there,' said Andrew's mum, 'but he can't wait to get to school on Tuesdays. He thinks it's bleedin' marvellous.'

I thought it was bleedin' marvellous, too. By the time we'd finished and added the eyes, tongue and teeth, the brontosaurus looked so realistic it was quite unnerving.

'I'm glad you've moved that thing out of the washroom, Mr Kent. It was giving me the creeps,' said Ethel, the top floor cleaner. 'I don't even like it in here very much. I'm sure if I turn my back it'll bite my bum.'

News of the amazing brontosaurus in the top hall spread, and classes were excited about finishing their own dinosaurs. Each day the exhibition grew, and a new dinosaur regularly appeared in the hall, looking splendid against Gerry's landscape background. Teachers were staying for longer periods after school, bringing information to the hall that the children had written about their models. Several teachers had to dismantle heads, claws, arms and legs to get their dinosaurs up the stairs, but the only real problem occurred with Georgia's stegosaurus, which refused to stand up straight as the legs were too flimsy. Once again I went to the DIY shop to buy brackets and fixings that I could use to create a support. Even Laura's group had managed to create a pterodactyl, which we suspended on a cord from the ceiling.

During the last week of half term, we invited the parents, governors and classes from other local schools to view our exhibition. The adults were amazed that young children could create such stunning models, and frankly, so was I. Many parents took photographs of the dinosaurs their children had worked on, and Sanjit's mother was insistent that her entire family should be photographed standing proudly around the brontosaurus. The exhibition was a resounding success, and Georgia and I were soon planning another exhibition for the next year.

'There you are,' I said to Laura, 'I told you they could do it. Wait till you see what we've got planned for next year.' She never found out, because she applied for another job where she would be in charge of physical education throughout the school, and she left us at the end of the year.

Even though the school was rapidly acquiring a reputation in the neighbourhood and our numbers were rising, my staff was still a relatively small one. There were few problems and in general people worked hard, but I was rapidly learning that managing people wasn't as easy as I'd first thought. There could be sudden bursts of temperament, or staff meetings in which people would violently disagree with each other, or occasions when I was irritated by something that simply didn't seem to bother anybody else. Like washing tea and coffee cups.

The staffroom had a huge Butler sink, there was no shortage of water, and since I always washed my own mug up after I'd made a cup of coffee, I assumed that everybody else would do the same. When I'd been a classroom teacher, primary helpers like Mrs Jessop had been assigned to washing teachers' cups, but I wanted classroom helpers to be involved with children rather than teacups, and I didn't see why teachers couldn't wash a piece of crockery up. But they didn't, and the cups sat in the sink. Rather than wash one cup, teachers would just help themselves to a fresh one.

I mentioned the growing problem to Georgia, and she wrote a bold notice saying 'Please Wash Your Cup', which she stood at the back of the Butler. Two days later, it was apparent that the only thing getting wet was the notice. In no time at all the writing became smudged, so she made another one, and laminated it. The hot water curled it up. I put a polite note in the staff notice book, asking if people would be kind enough to wash their own cups. They didn't need to wash anybody else's. Just their own. Just the one. But still the Butler bulged.

And then the problem suddenly snowballed. A teacher who was leaving bought a dining set and cutlery for the staffroom as a present. It didn't stay there long; teachers would hurry in at lunchtime, fetch what they intended to eat, and wander off to mark books with one hand and eat with the other, taking the plate and utensils with them. Most plates were usually retrieved, some from the oddest places. I found one on the window ledge in the staff toilet. At least, I thought, my teachers are very busy people. The remaining plates were with the knives and forks in the Butler.

Then one morning I found the sink bleached and the crockery stacked and sparkling beside it. I thought new leaves had been well and truly turned. But no, the cleaner had looked at the state of the Butler every evening, couldn't stand the pile of unwashed crockery, and worked her way through the lot. Undoubtedly, I thought, the staff will be impressed and feel guilty. Two days later, I realised my optimism knew no bounds.

Once again I put hints in the notice book. Eventually I ran out of subtle quips and the Butler ran out of space. Georgia sighed despairingly, rolled her sleeves up, and set to work after school. I suggested we buy fifteen white mugs and write people's names on them. Then we'd catch the culprits. She pointed out, gently, that people would just use somebody else's.

We agreed it should become a major agenda item at the next staff meeting. The curriculum would have to stand aside while we debated this burning issue. Nobody, of course, owned up to not washing their cups, but there was a wide variety of alternative ideas. A dishwasher, someone suggested. Good idea, I said. The only problem is that somebody needs to stack it. And unstack it. And add rinsing fluid, and salt. Washing your cup isn't a gargantuan task, I said, just a target. Smart, and achievable. Could we try once again? Everybody agreed we could.

But we couldn't, and since the cleaner on that corridor was having family problems and was very short of money, I saved face to some extent by paying her to clear the Butler. She was happy to earn a little more, the staff were pleased, and I was relieved to do away with an itch I hadn't been able to scratch.

That term I discovered that even when you think you know somebody well, it's still very easy to make an unfortunate decision. Brenda was a member of staff I valued enormously, always friendly and cheerful, delightful with the children and their parents, and a shoulder I had often leaned upon when I didn't have an effective deputy. It seemed impossible to upset her, but I managed it quite spectacularly.

She needed to undergo some medical tests, and as I was unable to obtain a supply teacher once again, I taught the class on her first day in hospital. Looking at the ancient oak cupboards around the room I thought it would be really nice to buy her a brand new set of storage furniture, as a surprise for when she returned. After school, I scanned the catalogues carefully, and then phoned to make sure it could all be delivered before she came back. With Fred's help, I spent a few hours getting the old stuff shifted into a corridor and the new cupboard installed.

On the day Brenda returned, I waited up in my room, knowing it wouldn't be too long before she burst into my room in delight, thanking me profusely and saying what a kind and considerate headteacher I was. She certainly burst into my room... but with a face like thunder. 'Right', she demanded, 'I want the bugger who's nicked my furniture!' Humbled, I spent the rest of the day removing the new, tackier cupboards and re-installing the original oak, and I never made that sort of rash decision again.

Some incidents involving teachers can be very tricky to handle, particularly when the person involved denies what has happened. Although I was discovering that most of my staff had high professional standards, I was concerned about a part-time teacher, Rowena Best, who was working with Gerry in his special needs setting. A middle aged Yorkshire woman, Rowena had been employed just before I arrived at the school, and children who needed extra encouragement and sensitivity found her severe manner unnerving.

Word reached me that she was being unnecessarily strict with her groups, and that if a child wasn't working hard enough, or reading well, she would dig them in the ribs with her elbow. Although at this time mild punishment, even an occasional light slap, wasn't unheard of in primary schools, it certainly wasn't something I was prepared to tolerate in my school. And then, one morning, Mrs Eldridge came to see me.

'I'm really sorry to bother you Mr Kent,' she said uncomfortably. 'I don't like to complain, because Andrea loves coming to school, but she's terrified of going to Mrs Best's groups.'

'I'm really sorry to hear that,' I said. 'What's the problem?'

'Well, Andrea says that if she doesn't get a word right, Mrs Best pokes her in the chest with her finger. And then last night, Andrea came home and showed me a bruise on her thigh. She said that Mrs Best had pushed her off the chair.'

Since I'd learned that children sometimes made unfounded complaints, I listened carefully and promised to look into the matter. I'd always found Mrs Eldridge to be an extremely reasonable parent, anxious to support the work we were doing, and I suspected that in this case, the smoke indicated a fire. Nevertheless, my first duty was to support my teachers wherever possible, and I called Andrea to my room. It also seemed sensible to have Georgia there, particularly as I needed to look at the child's thigh.

'Mum says your leg is bruised,' Georgia said gently. ' Can you show us, and tell us how it happened?'

Andrea looked embarrassed. 'I couldn't read a hard word in my book,' she said. 'And then Mrs Best got really cross with me, and she pushed me off the chair.'

'And did anybody else see this?' I asked.

'No Sir, the rest of the group had gone and I had to stay behind to read a bit more. I don't really like going to Mrs Best's group, because she shouts.'

Shortly before hometime, I went up to Rowena's room. I knew that she'd be alone, preparing her work for the next day, and I explained what had happened. Rowena immediately became angry.

'That's absolute rubbish,' she said. 'You know what the child is like. She's a liar, and her mother always believes every word she says. I think you should have a strong word with Mrs Eldridge. Andrea probably fell over in the playground.'

I was taken aback by Rowena's abrupt manner, but I couldn't make a direct accusation as I had no first hand evidence. I hadn't seen the incident and neither had anybody else.

'Well, she's certainly got a nasty bruise on her thigh,' I said.

'So she might have, but I strongly resent the accusation that I might have done it,' she said testily.

'I'm not making an accusation,' I said firmly, worried about the turn the conversation was taking. 'I'm merely pointing out what a parent has said, and that if there were any truth to it then yes, it would be very serious. Andrea says you kept her behind to do some reading...'

'Yes, I was anxious that she should catch up with the others.'

'Well, fine. But these days, it's never a good idea to be on your own with a child.'

'After this accusation, I can certainly appreciate that! If she's saying I pushed her off a chair, I can just imagine her saying anything. Naughty little girl.' I came away from the meeting unsatisfied, but I was relieved when the rumours about Mrs Best's behaviour stopped. Nevertheless, in this instance, I knew who I believed.

Fortunately, other staff problems during the year seemed relatively minor, although one of the trickiest involved the visiting steel band teacher, Duane. Although I'm keen to promote any kind of music with primary children, I have never really enjoyed steel band music and steel pans aren't instruments I would choose to listen to. Nevertheless, the children were keen, the drums had been given to the school by the ILEA at considerable expense and I certainly didn't want to get rid of them. It was merely a case of dissipating the problems... which seemed legion.

In reorganising the spare classrooms during my first year, I'd stupidly arranged to have the drum set in the room above my office. Although Duane only visited on two days a week, each Tuesday and Thursday the sound would permeate through my ceiling, coupled with the pounding of Duane's feet as he thumped out the rhythms. This made it virtually impossible to do any work in my room and conversations with visitors were very difficult indeed. Other classes near the steel band room were also having problems, and a whole morning of listening to 'Yellow Bird' was proving tiresome. Since you can't turn the volume of a steel band down, the noise had affected Duane's hearing over the years, and having a conversation with him involved shouting at him as loudly as possible.

I'd also been told he had a tendency to disappear into the corner of the room for a smoke while the children were practising the scales he'd given them. Ensuring he didn't smoke in future was done more by sign language than discussion, but this still left the problem of the noise.

Eventually I decided that his work would have to be cut down to one day, and by moving the drums into a small carpeted room at the end of a corridor, at least the disturbance was lessened. And then, at the end of the year, Duane was offered extra work at a local secondary school. It was well paid, and he much preferred teaching older children as they learned the techniques very quickly. Though I tried to find another steel pan teacher for one day a week, it proved impossible and we eventually sold our drums to the secondary school that had employed Duane. The three largest were superfluous to their requirements, so we carried them to the playground, where Fred painted them in bright colours. Then we turned them upside down, filled them with earth, and planted flowers in them. The children who played them didn't miss out because they moved their talents to other instruments I was introducing to the school.

As I neared the end of my second year, I was beginning to realise what an extraordinary job headship was. Barely a day went by without an issue that needed to be resolved, whether it was a child in the infants throwing up in the corridor at a time when Fred was out doing the banking, a radiator in a classroom packing up in mid winter, or a pigeon wandering into a classroom looking for biscuit crumbs early in the morning and not being able to find its way out again.

At times, it would have been easy to think that the school was sinking under the weight of the continual problems that needed to be dealt with, and although I often ended each day tired and spent, I was still optimistic that things would gradually become easier as I became more experienced in the job.

CHAPTER 7
THE NEW INSPECTOR CALLS

*In his news book, Selim wrote 'Mr Kent says I always come in class
with grubby hands, but I am closer to the ground than he is.'*

For over a quarter of a century, my school, like all the other
inner London primaries, had been controlled from County
Hall, a vast building in Lambeth on the south bank of the river
Thames which was the home of the Inner London Education
Authority. The ILEA had succeeded the old Greater London
Council in the mid sixties, and it operated on a sort of Robin
Hood basis, whereby wealthier London boroughs contributed
more funds than the poorer ones, thus ensuring that children in
the most deprived boroughs were given the same opportunities as
those from the richer ones.

For many years it worked well. The fabric of its schools was
well maintained, equipment was readily available, its teachers
were treated professionally, and it set up many worthwhile and
innovational institutions and projects. It had its own film making
and television studios, bought country houses so that teachers
could attend courses in a relaxing atmosphere, distributed its own
weekly internal school newspaper, devised a wealth of curriculum
booklets for use in its schools, set up a massive library of films
and books from which schools could loan material for a term at a
time, and it provided all its children with a wealth of opportunity
in the arts.

Though County Hall was the central hub, each inner London
borough also had its own divisional office, to which schools in
the borough were accountable. The divisional office had its own
local school inspectors, it employed and distributed teachers, and
it financed and arranged buildings maintenance for its schools.
When I began headship, all this was extremely useful to me,
because if a problem occurred there was usually somebody I

could appeal to at the end of a telephone. Alan Green's help, for example, had often been invaluable.

The Achilles heel of the ILEA was its political stance, particularly during its final years. Fiercely left wing, it was often attacked as being profligate with money, unacceptably bureaucratic, and towards the end of its era, hopelessly inefficient. It was also strongly criticised for its support of trendy, informal teaching methods, which, its critics said, taught children precious little.

There was a considerable amount of evidence to support this criticism. During the fifties, primary classrooms contained up to forty children who sat in straight rows, chanted tables and used set text books which gave a basic grounding in factual learning. The teacher stood at the front of the class with a box of chalk, a blackboard, and often a cane, and rote learning was the order of the day. Whether you were able, less able, or distinctly unable, everybody learned the same thing at the same time. If you couldn't keep up, you were often labelled educationally sub-normal.

And then, with the release of the innovational Plowden Report, entitled 'Children And Their Primary Schools', primary education was suddenly set free. Children, it said, should be agents in their own learning, with teachers being friendly learning facilitators rather than mere instructors. The starting point for education should be the children's interests, and the curriculum should grow from topic work related to those interests. Desks should be changed for group tables, classrooms should be joined or opened up into learning areas, and children should work on their own chosen projects. These would incorporate a range of curriculum areas, developing the children's skills as they went along and, most important of all, allowing them to work at their own pace. There would be no more organising children into able and less able classes. Clever children would mix with those who struggled, because this would raise the aspirations of the strugglers, and in many schools age groups were mixed too. Since children were now learning at their own pace, it didn't matter if Charlie was six and Frederick was ten, and anyway, wouldn't this be beneficial socially too?

New schools that were being built were now purposely designed to accommodate the new teaching styles. They contained learning areas rather than classrooms, were carpeted throughout, and had specially designed, colourful storage furniture that children would find easy to use. Children moved from area to area, depending on the activity they were undertaking, and they would meet with a number of teachers as they worked through the day, rather than having their own classroom and one class teacher. A handful of these new schools were promoted as shining examples of the new teaching styles, and they were visited by hundreds of teachers, parents, college lecturers and academics, sometimes to the detriment of the children's learning.

Traditional primary school buildings, built many years ago, were totally unsuited to Plowden influenced teaching. Large amounts of money, particularly in London, were therefore spent in adapting them, removing walls, changing furniture, adding the luxury of classroom carpets, installing audio and visual aids equipment and fitting linking doors between classrooms to permit a free flow of children. Teachers who doggedly persisted in keeping their teaching traditional tended to be frowned upon by the visionaries at the new cutting edge.

Reading schemes were now considered outdated and old fashioned, and 'real books' replaced them, the idea being that if children were offered a wide range of good quality story books, they would intuitively choose something suitable for their level and with the teacher's help gradually learn to read. Phonics teaching was frowned upon.

This immense and sudden change in teaching technique proved a real headache for many teacher training colleges. Lecturers, often elderly and set in their ways, suddenly had to adapt to an entirely new way of learning for young children, and they struggled to cope with it, or even understand what it was all about. Many simply gave up and didn't try. Others gave a half hearted nod in Plowden's direction, and newly qualified teachers often left college confused and concerned, usually spending their first year of teaching finding their feet and trying to juggle lots of activities going on in their classrooms at the same time. If it was done well, children enjoyed learning and it was certainly very impressive to a visitor, particularly someone whose education had been acquired in the old fashioned way.

In the shires of middle England, and in city schools where the learning systems were expertly organised, classrooms influenced by the Plowden report were usually successful. Classes were often small, and children were invariably supported at home by parents who valued education, read to their children, introduced them to the arts, and took them on outings to places of educational interest. Since these children did not come from deprived or disadvantaged homes, they behaved very well and were eager to learn and easy to teach.

But in the poorer boroughs of inner cities, where social problems abounded and buildings were ancient and designed for rote learning, the story was very different. Although in the best adapted buildings the most creative teachers coped well, many struggled, and a lot of children... particularly those with low ability... simply didn't learn anything. With so many activities going on in a classroom at the same time, the atmosphere could resemble a wet playtime, with the teacher desperate to retain control. Children trying to read found it difficult to concentrate if a group in the corner was hammering and sawing bits of wood, and many children would be perfectly happy to paint all day long if allowed to. The most skilful teachers therefore designed a work programme for every child so that each aspect of the curriculum would receive at least some attention during the course of a week. Even so, this was extremely demanding, especially if there were more than twenty five children in the class, and children didn't receive a great deal of personal contact time with the teacher. It simply wasn't feasible.

Nevertheless, the ILEA supported Plowden philosophies wholeheartedly, and its headteachers were expected to embrace them. As older headteachers and inspectors retired, they were replaced by people who trod the prescribed path, and there was little acceptance of any alternative view. If you weren't adhering to what was fashionable, you'd had it as far as promotion was concerned, and your school was likely to be visited by a borough inspector who would apply considerable pressure to make you conform. Which is how I came to meet Harvey Trend.

After a lengthy and very successful career, Alan Green had retired. I'd found it easy to work with him, because although he visited several times a year, he left me alone to organise things in the way that I wanted once he was sure I wasn't going to wreck the school. He was also a pragmatist, and I was running my school in a way he approved of. I was not insensitive to Plowden ideas, and neither was he, but I was acutely aware that my children needed structure and order in their lives and in their classrooms, and I advocated the system I had adopted in my own teaching, whereby some parts of the week were highly structured and others were strictly for embracing the creative arts. This also allowed plenty of time for children to attend groups where they could learn to play instruments, sing in a choir, grow vegetables in the garden, or become involved in a topic that particularly interested them.

But learning to read was paramount. It was a basic skill without which a child would find it very difficult to cope. It was the key to success with everything else in the curriculum, and although I knew I would eventually be criticised for it, I refused to abandon structured reading schemes. I simply ordered the ones I considered to have interesting stories, and for the first hour of every morning, my infant classes were split into ability reading groups. The aim was to make sure no child entered the junior department without being able to read, and the system was working extremely well.

Alan Green's successor, however, wasn't happy, and he was determined to do something about it. He had been a headteacher at two schools in Berkshire, spending a few years in each, before applying to be an inspector in London. In his early forties and a little overweight, he bustled into school for an introductory meeting with me early one morning and I walked him around my school. He looked at the classrooms enthusiastically, shook hands vigorously with everybody, and then sat down heavily in one of my office chairs. Where Mr Green had been a little reserved, quietly spoken and immaculately suited, Mr Trend was the polar opposite, reminding me of a rather jolly, red-cheeked farmer in his casual jacket and effusive manner.

'Well, it's very nice, Mike,' he said, 'but it all seems a bit formal. And what on earth is Gerry doing with those groups upstairs? I thought all that sort of thing died out in the fifties.'

'You have to understand the nature of our children,' I said, resenting his assumption after a mere hour in the school. 'In the mornings, yes, everything is pretty tightly structured, but I've worked out some good systems, the staff are comfortable with them, the children are learning, and the parents are happy. If you stay for the afternoon, you'll be able to see an alternative side to the school.'

'Won't be able to do that, I'm afraid. I've got two other schools to visit today. Tell you what though, I'll come and do a talk at your next staff meeting and show you the way I think things ought to be. I think people will enjoy it.'

Although he exuded a brash confidence and friendliness, I was more than a little edgy. Berkshire wasn't Camberwell, and I felt a little sensitivity and time taken to understand our methods might not have gone amiss. I was several years into my headship and I wanted him to appreciate why we did particular things in the way we did. Nevertheless, the teachers duly assembled in the staff room the following week to hear what their new inspector had to say, and he unpacked the charts, folders, documents and work examples he'd brought with him, rolling them out on the carpet for everybody to see.

'Now look at this,' he said. 'It's a chart made by a child in the school I visited yesterday, just down the road from here. The teacher said the boy was hopeless at maths, and then I got talking to him and found out that his dad was a taxi driver. And you know what? The boy knew the fares to every part of London. He could calculate fares, add up and take away money, and the teacher had said he wasn't very good at maths! All the teacher needed to do was get rid of the text books, and design some practical maths instead to interest the boy.'

My staff stared at him, dumbfounded. It was obvious that he considered our school to be one that needed loosening up, but I imagined how angry the teacher must have been at his insensitive attitude. Practical maths in real situations was a crucial element of the curriculum, but the idea that text books should have been hurled out of the window in favour of talking about taxi fares was just silly. The child would have been interested for half an hour, and then what? But Harvey was just getting into his stride.

'Now, these reading schemes you're using. I'm really not comfortable about those. I want to see the children learning to read from working on their own topics and project work. In my last school...'

'But hang on,' Georgia interrupted, 'Mike and I have carefully set up the system we use. The parents like it because they see progression, and they hear their children read at home. And the schemes we use are good. We read little plays together, we write poems, the stories are interesting...'

'I'm sorry, but no reading schemes are interesting, period.' he interrupted. 'You should be replacing them with real books. Children will learn to read naturally if they are given good books that fire their urge to interpret them.'

'But that would mess up our system? And where would the money come from?'

'I might be able to find you a little extra funding. But I want you to get cracking on changing your reading system as soon as possible.'

I could see how annoyed my infant teachers were becoming, but there was no time for debate because Harvey moved rapidly on to other things he said he was passionate about. The whole school day should be based around each child's interests, they should be left to choose what they wanted to do, children's writing should not be marked because it defaced their work and depressed them, every subject should be taught in a practical manner wherever possible, and work for display should be double mounted and then attached to rolls of coloured corrugated card draped around the classrooms, using dressmaking pins to fix the pieces of work in place.

This was hardly Plowden Lite, and I was certain that much of what he was advocating simply wouldn't work with my children, or with children in similarly challenging schools. Although I was often too busy to go to meetings and meet other headteachers, I knew the ones closest to my school and I telephoned them. It seemed they too were concerned about the pressure being applied to make them conform, and I decided the best way to reach them all would be to write a short article for the ILEA's internal weekly newspaper, outlining my concerns. It proved a popular piece. By the following Friday, I'd filled a display board in the staffroom with letters of support and agreement from teachers across the authority. But it also brought a telephone call that evening with a sinister edge.

I'd gone home early because I had a dreadful head cold, the week had been a difficult one, and I had a huge amount of planning to do. When I discovered I had a temperature, I decided to leave working until the morning and after drinking a stiff whisky and swallowing a handful of tablets I crawled into bed. At ten o'clock I was woken by the telephone ringing. Assuming I was still asleep, my wife answered but didn't tell me about the conversation she'd had until the morning.

The Chief Inspector of the borough had called, and asked for me. My wife told him that I was asleep. The inspector was insistent that he needed to talk to me. My wife refused, explaining that I was unwell and extremely tired.

'Then you need to tell him that he will be called to County Hall next week,' the inspector said.

'For what?' she asked.

'The article he wrote. He has let down his colleagues and criticised the teaching policies advocated by the authority,' he replied. 'We do not expect our headteachers to behave in this way.'

'I've no idea why you're telling me all this,' my wife retorted angrily. 'My husband works extremely hard and for very long hours, and you have absolutely no right to ring our home like this. Ring him at school and speak to him on Monday, because I am now ending this conversation.'

When I heard what was going to happen, I was appalled. I had merely put up a point of view for discussion. What's more, it seemed an awful lot of people agreed with what I had written. But I was also nervous, because I was aware that another local headteacher had been forced from his school for organising it in a highly structured way that the authority didn't agree with, but which the parents strongly supported.

Nevertheless, I was not going to be railroaded into changing the way I'd decided to run my school. Furthermore, I knew Georgia and I had placed the school on a very sound footing. It was extremely popular in the neighbourhood, our roll was rapidly rising, our parents were happy about the progress their children were making, and teachers enjoyed working at the school. For an hour or two, I ruminated about consulting my union and refusing to attend a meeting unless I had a representative with me. After all, I still had memories of the racial tribunal several years ago. Ultimately, I decided to tackle whatever was coming on my own. I also decided to be pro-active. Though I was still unwell, on the Sunday afternoon I wrote a long letter to the inspector, describing the successes of the school, and explaining how changing all our systems would be very disruptive for both staff and children.

Throughout the following week at school, I jumped nervously every time the telephone rang, fully expecting Lucy to come into my room and say that I was wanted at County Hall that afternoon. The week wore on, and so did the following one. By the end of the month I had still heard nothing. I realised that the panic was over, and that I wasn't going to be hauled over the coals, or forced to lose my job. I had no idea what had happened, or why I wasn't called. Perhaps my letter, written with passion, had decided the matter. Perhaps it was realised that I wasn't really that much of a threat. Perhaps, because my school was popular and working well, the powers that be had decided to leave well alone and keep a cautious eye on me.

I was safe for the time being. But only for the time being, because I was soon to be involved in far more serious disagreements with the school inspection process.

CHAPTER 8
A TIDAL WAVE OF CHANGE

'It's very very hot today. Let's have a barkerboo.' Grandson Jake, age
two and three quarters.

Eight years into my headship, Margaret Thatcher's Conservative government made two massive changes to education. One affected what every child in every state school in the country was learning and the other completely altered the status of every inner London school.

It seems extraordinary now, but throughout my classroom career and well into my headship, there was no set curriculum for primary school children. Indeed, the Plowden Report of 1967 had actively discouraged it, although there was general agreement that children still needed to read, write and manipulate numbers. Apart from that, schools could teach what they liked within reason, and children were encouraged to learn through projects and topics of their own choosing, the idea being that the chosen project could be made to absorb most curriculum areas without them being formally taught. Within the ILEA, geography and history were known as social studies, English became creative writing, practical science was actively encouraged, and all the arts were considered to be of great value for primary children, the authority giving strong support to music and the learning of instruments at an early age.

Nevertheless, most primary schools felt it necessary to design a basic curriculum for reading, writing and mathematical skills, with the rest of the week being given over to creative topics that would appeal to the children. This, unfortunately, often led to what became known as 'the dinosaur effect.' Because children love learning about dinosaurs... and our dinosaur exhibition had certainly proved that... dinosaurs, or something equally popular, might be the chosen topic in several consecutive classes.

The curriculum, such as it was, could therefore show a certain paucity, and the children's knowledge and experience in a variety of curricular subjects was often nothing like as broad as it should have been.

Towards the end of the eighties, the enthusiasm for children learning to read with the use of 'real books' rather than reading schemes... always a hotly debated and highly contentious subject for educational theorists... was rapidly waning. The practice worked reasonably well for children in wealthier areas whose parents surrounded them with books and read to them every day, but for inner city working class children, whose parents often didn't have time, children could reach their final primary years without being able to read properly at all.

Similarly, the insistence on practical mathematics, whereby children might be encouraged to learn their tables by playing bingo, or creating graphs by standing in the street counting the passing traffic, was also becoming unacceptable. Children were leaving primary school without being able to add up properly, and secondary school teachers were very unhappy about it, especially as success at secondary school depended on passing tests and exams.

Children at primary school were rarely tested. Indeed, any kind of testing other than a brief calculation of their reading ages was frowned upon by the inspectorate and educational philosophers, so it was difficult for parents to know whether their children were reaching appropriate levels or not. Within a class of eleven year olds, about to transfer to secondary school, there could be enormous differences in achievement, some children being able to write a three page story and others unable to string a few words together or read a simple book. Parents had to rely on the information they received at annual Open Evenings, and if their child's teacher wasn't very experienced, the information they were given could be less than helpful, particularly if the parents weren't academically able themselves. For the schools that adopted it, mixed age teaching also proved a disaster. In a classroom where the teacher was trying to supervise a dozen different activities with a mixture of several different age groups, any canny child with a bit of determination could avoid doing very much at all.

By the late eighties, the government had had enough. It decided that schools and teachers, and certainly teaching methods, must change and become far more accountable. Standards needed to be set, safeguards needed to be put in place to ensure that all children had the opportunity to acquire sensible, basic skills, and teachers needed to be told what to teach, and when. It therefore spent a great deal of money on designing a national curriculum.

The new curriculum would be taught in every state school, and it would define, in considerable detail, what would be taught at every stage in a child's schooling. Infants and juniors were no longer labelled as such. They became Key Stage 1 and Key Stage 2 children. Schools were provided with a set of national curriculum folders, one for each subject, and in a short period of time teachers had to familiarise themselves with everything they were required to teach. There was to be no dissent. All schools had to follow the prescribed path, the aim being that when children left their primary schools, they would all have had access to the same curricular opportunities.

Educational thinkers and theorists were horrified and thought that this level of prescription would be like stepping back to the fifties and disastrous for very young children. So did many headteachers. After all, almost a quarter of a century had been spent giving teachers and children flexibility and freedom. Others weren't so sure, especially those who thought primary children weren't learning very much. Teachers, particularly the less imaginative ones, would now have a strong framework for children's learning to lean on, with proper continuity and progression.

Many parents were delighted; not only would they know exactly what their children would be learning each year, but they could see the levels their offspring were expected to achieve, and they could compare their child's achievement with that of others in the class and an agreed national standard. No longer could a teacher get away with half-hearted explanations of why Cynthia still couldn't read at nine. Now parents could hold the school to account. And if they happened to move house, requiring a change of school, the disruption would be minimal because all schools now taught exactly the same syllabus. In a remarkably short space of time, and with little dissent, the national curriculum was embedded firmly into the nation's educational system. The age of educational freedom and innovation had finally been put out to grass.

Determined not to do anything by halves, the Conservative government had also decided it had had enough of the Inner London Education Authority. It had been a worthy idea and achieved many positive things for London children, but now it was well past its prime, overtly political, and massively expensive. Headteachers were becoming disillusioned with it too, culminating in a wave of anger when the much loved annual Christmas carol concert for schools, held at the Royal Festival Hall, was abandoned because ILEA officers considered carol singing to be unrepresentative of the increasingly diverse religions in its schools. Instead, a huge sum was paid to a popular folk group, and their programme of mediocre songs was piped into the authority's internal television system for schools to watch at their convenience.

Educational thinking was changing fast, and the ILEA, now an unwieldy thorn in the government's side, had to go. It would be far more productive and certainly less costly to the taxpayer, the government insisted, if each London borough was responsible for educating its own children. Smaller would be better, if only for cutting red tape and unacceptable levels of bureaucracy. Almost overnight, the change was made.

It caused enormous upheaval and worry, particularly as every borough now had to appoint a chief education officer and education team at great speed, and it quickly became apparent that wise choices hadn't been made in every London borough. Nevertheless, each borough did its best to cope, inviting headteachers and senior managers to frequent meetings, not only to discuss the changes that were being made, but to ask their advice about how local education should be managed. It was also soon obvious that London schools were not going to be as generously resourced as they had been under the ILEA, although like most headteachers, I had no idea just how much austerity my school was heading for.

I was not particularly concerned about the demise of the ILEA, however. I too had become disillusioned with it, and its ability to work effectively, or to provide the best possible education for the children in my school. I had also experienced its growing waste and inefficiency. While trying to obtain some classroom tables and chairs to replace ancient ones, I'd dealt with five different furniture officers and waited four months for the tables to arrive. The authority's senior inspectors were increasingly remote and unhelpful; the inspector for Literacy, on a very respectable salary, seemed to contribute little more than organising an occasional half-hearted course at one of the authority's country house venues and an annual poetry competition. There were also long delays before any remedial building work was carried out. The electrical wiring in my school was outdated and dangerous, but nothing was done until, in desperation, I sent a parcel of burned wire to the authority.

But at least during the death throes of the ILEA there were opportunities for its schools to obtain additional and badly needed equipment. Once the decision had been made to give education back to the boroughs, the ILEA's massive book and film library was divided up, television and audio-visual equipment was available in abundance, and piles of furniture and office equipment was offered to schools at giveaway prices. It was rumoured that anything not sold was hurled into the River Thames, mainly out of spite for the government's savage action.

During this period, inner London's population was changing rapidly. When I had taken up headship, the majority of my children were from indigenous white working class homes, but within a few years the local ethnic population had increased dramatically. This meant that my school, like most across inner London, was required to accept an increasing influx of children from African and Asian families, many of whom could not speak

English well. Schools struggled to manage, often needing to allocate part of the school budget for setting up special tuition groups for these children.

More money was eventually demanded from central government so that they could cope, and in recognition of the problem the government set up a special programme which became known as 'Section 11' provision. Incredibly, it was felt that African and Asian children who needed language and basic skills support would be best taught by people from similar backgrounds, and schools were required to recruit suitable ethnic teachers. Part-time white teachers already on the staff, who tended to work with a range of children needing additional support, were required to undergo hastily arranged additional training before they were allowed to work with ethnic groups. Understandably, they found this patronising and unnecessary, particularly as many of the hastily recruited trainers didn't seem to have a clue about what training they were supposed to offer.

Most schools soon found that the Asian and African teachers who applied for the jobs were gentle people used to a culture where education and teachers were highly valued. They expected children to sit still, work hard, and be extremely obedient. But inner city children simply weren't like that. The African children, often subjected to severe and sometimes physical chastisement at home, relished the freedom and relaxed discipline they found in the schools they joined, and they frequently took advantage of it. Disillusioned, many of the specially appointed teachers gave up, and Section 11, having created more problems than it solved, was quietly shelved.

Alongside the national curriculum, the method of financing schools was changing too, and much more of the education budget was being released directly to schools under the new 'local management of schools' scheme. This was a new and exciting opportunity for headteachers. They could now buy in specialist educational services as and when they needed them, they could employ tradespeople directly instead of going to the authority first and filling in lots of paperwork, and they had a much greater involvement with staff employment. While most headteachers were delighted with the changes, it was a disaster for borough education offices, which were now required to slim down their staff and tender their services. If schools didn't like the price of these services, they could go elsewhere, and most did.

There was a downside to all this, however. Headteachers at the time were just that; good teachers appointed to be with children and lead an effective teaching staff. It had never been part of their job to worry about the intricacies of appointing staff, find a suitable company to re-wire the school, or deal with burst pipes and groaning boilers in the winter. And they certainly weren't chartered accountants or necessarily good at handling large budgets. Up to now, this had been done by the local authorities. Life's sharks and cowboys quickly realised this, recognising that there was money to be made from schools, and they moved in for the kill. Like many heads, I fell for what seemed a very persuasive deal.

One morning a salesman called at my office and said he could cut the school's fuel bills by 20 percent. All he needed to do, he said, was fit a couple of his firm's special devices to the boilers. I spoke to Fred, who agreed it might be a worthwhile idea, and we paid for a two year contract. The salesman fitted his little boxes and when he returned a month later he played around with a meter and said yes, everything was working well and we'd soon see a reduction in our bills, but it would take a while before things settled down and we reaped full benefit. He visited twice more and then, suddenly, the salesman and his firm became impossible to contact and I was shocked to receive a memo from the borough saying that schools should be wary of salesman offering fuel saving devices, because they could seriously damage the boiler...

But at least I avoided being snared by the worst scams. Photocopier salesman were notorious for the pressure they applied at the time. It was very easy to bamboozle school leaders with misleading calculations and many schools inadvertently tied themselves into very long contracts which would eventually cost many thousands of pounds. Once again the boroughs had to write to all their schools urging them to seek expert advice before they signed anything at all, let alone a photocopier contract, and they refused to bail the reckless schools out.

This period of intense change was challenging for all heads, and London primary schools in particular. Though I welcomed a national curriculum, the government's first version proved unwieldy and almost impossible to implement due to time restrictions within the school week. Even though panels of academic experts had been employed to design the curriculum, it was soon obvious that not enough thought had gone into how many hours could be allotted to each subject area, and before long the first of many revisions appeared.

Keeping up with what should be taught soon became time consuming, and additional money was made available so that staff members could apply to become subject co-ordinators, overseeing one or two curriculum areas and making sure teachers in their schools were kept up to date with the constant changes. I was also anxious to make sure we didn't desert the creative curriculum; art, music and drama are essential for young children and I was determined not to lose them to the now very heavy emphasis on literacy, mathematics and science.

The curriculum wasn't proving a problem for me, but managing the budget was. Despite the government alleging that devolving education to the boroughs would give us more money, the central budget was being pruned severely each year. My priority was to attract and retain first class teachers, but this wasn't easy because salaries had risen and experienced teachers were becoming very expensive. And since schools were now required to work out complex salary and tax calculations for every person working in the school, the beginning of the new financial year and the creation of the new school budget each April was a nightmare. Maths had never been my speciality, none of my school governors had any expertise in this field, and at the start of the financial year each April it meant setting aside many evenings and a full weekend to attempt the number crunching that computers make so simple today.

The enormity of the changes had made many older headteachers decide that now was a good time to retire. They hadn't come into the profession to be dictated to, and they certainly hadn't envisaged accountancy becoming part of their brief. I'd survived it all, though I rarely had an evening free to spend with my family and my workload was constantly increasing. Whenever possible, I took my office work home so that most of my school day could be spent working with the children and enjoying the exciting things that were happening in and around the school.

It was invigorating work, I was fit and healthy, and I felt equal to the challenge. Which was just as well, because events were looming on the horizon which would eventually prove the ultimate test of my leadership.

CHAPTER 9
APPEALS, APPOINTMENTS AND QUESTIONABLE GOVERNANCE

Francis Drake circumsized the world with his very large clipper.
Frankie, Age 11

My twelfth year of headship began with an electricity bill. Under normal circumstances, not an event a headteacher would take much notice of, but this electricity bill was different. It was for fifty seven thousand, five hundred and forty eight pounds. And sixty two pence.

Several years previously, we had suddenly stopped receiving electricity bills and a credit note had arrived. This seemed odd, but the meter had been read and I had assumed we were getting a refund after being overcharged on the previous estimated bill. The credit slip was duly filed for using against the next bill. Three months later, another credit note arrived, but for a different and far higher amount. Rather pleased we didn't have to pay any money, we filed this one too, and put the money we would have used to pay the bill into our interest earning account.

Another three months passed and once again a credit note arrived, even higher than the last two. We'd either overpaid drastically last year, or something simply wasn't right. I suspected the latter and rang the electricity supply company. A nice lady at the other end thanked me for ringing and said she'd get back as soon as possible. She didn't, days passed, and school life being what it is, we forgot all about it.

Until yet another credit arrived. This time, the Premises Officer phoned the company. He was bewildered because people arrived regularly to read the meter, the meter appeared to be working correctly, the numbers on it were heading upwards, and we still hadn't received a bill. Once again, there was a thank you for calling, it would be investigated, and someone would be in touch. Once again, we forgot about it.

By the time the next quarter had passed, almost a year had gone by and still the credits came. This was becoming irritating, although we weren't unduly concerned because we'd put money aside to pay the bill each month, so that when matters were eventually corrected we'd be able to settle the account in our usual good customer fashion. The only person who showed concern was the school's diligent accountant, who visited the school each month to do the difficult financial stuff. 'It's crazy, and it can't be right,' he said. 'You must keep trying to contact them… and make sure you don't spend the money you've put aside.'

Almost before we knew it, several years had slipped by… and we were now used to a credit note arriving regularly in the post. I wrote to the electricity company, received a reply saying the contents of my letter had been noted, and we phoned several times more, although half-heartedly because the interest on the savings was building up nicely. Meantime, whenever the accountant arrived, his first question was always 'Surely they must have realised by now…'

And then suddenly, they did. A fat package arrived in the post, containing estimated bills and the most extraordinary letter from the company's debt collector. Sorry about this, he said, but your meter seems to be a very old type and for years our meter people have been reading five digits when they should have been reading six. This has caused our computer to miscalculate. I'm afraid you owe a great deal of money, but I didn't want to write before the summer break because it might have ruined your holiday. I also appreciate that schools are very reliable at settling their accounts.

But this was one account I certainly wasn't happy about settling, and for another two months letters were sent between the school and the power company. Eventually, I made what I felt to be a very reasonable offer. We were aware that money was owed, but we had tried many times to sort the matter out and the power company has been extremely inefficient, not only in not responding to us, but also in employing people who couldn't read a meter properly. I pointed out that the company was welcome to take me to court, but I certainly had no intention of sending them nearly sixty thousand pounds. Eventually, the company realised it didn't have much of a case, the mechanics of court proceedings would have been troublesome and time consuming, and we agreed to settle at twenty thousand. Since we had saved more than this during the years the bills hadn't been paid, it was something of a result, especially as we'd earned a fair amount of interest from the bank. I was learning that it often pays to dig your heels in.

In fact, by this time I was thoroughly enjoying myself. Originally, I'd intended to stay at the school for five years and then consider moving to a larger one, but I was very happy, there was still much to do and it seemed pointless moving on. I knew many people in the neighbourhood well, our school was continually over-subscribed and its reputation meant that good teachers were easy to attract.

Southwark is an area of London rich with history, and the school was close to a wealth of interesting places and amenities that our children could take advantage of. They were taken to museums, collected historical artefacts from the banks of the Thames, enjoyed outings to London's parks, toured the Houses of Parliament and spent much time in the city's galleries and exhibitions. We linked up with local theatre groups, invited artists, sculptors and entertainers to come and work with our children, and took part in youth productions of Shakespeare at the Globe.

I had always felt music, art and drama should be at the heart of a primary school, and now I promoted them strongly. Visitors to the school were amazed at the variety of art on display in every classroom and corridor. All three halls now held colourful, themed displays of work stretching from floor to ceiling, and the success of our Dinosaur World in the top hall inspired us to create other exhibitions… one on famous artists, another on life-changing inventions, a third on the rain forests. The knowledge the children gained… and in most cases the staff too… was immense. Visiting the school was like walking into a child-centred art gallery, and the children were extremely proud of what they, and their teachers, had created.

Our dramatic productions were becoming well known in the neighbourhood too. I had discovered that Gerry was a talented musician, and it wasn't long before he was composing songs and music for the school plays I wrote in my spare time. Although these were performed at the end of the summer term, I wanted other creative activities during the school year for the whole school to be involved in, and I introduced a Science Week, a Maths Week and a Poetry Week. At lunchtimes and after school there were additional activities for the children... a film appreciation group, and a range of practical clubs, where children could learn to cook, build working models, explore simple chemistry, or grow vegetables and flowers in the section of our playground that we had made into a garden.

All of these activities supplemented the regular curriculum, and gave school life for every child an extra richness. New teachers appointed to the school were asked about their hobbies and interests, and what extra-curricular activities they could offer to our children. Interestingly, it was now very noticeable that incidences of bullying and aggressive behaviour had virtually disappeared, almost certainly, I felt, because the children loved coming to school and there was a wealth of things for them to enjoy. By now, the weaker teachers had retired, moved on, or left because the pace of change and the new demands being made in the primary education curriculum meant they were no longer able to keep up.

The school was now accountable to two very different groups of people, its governing body and the officers at the borough education office, and although their intention was to be supportive, both could be a hindrance as well as a help. Some of the staff at the education office had previously worked for the ILEA and therefore had relevant experience, but there was still a great deal of inefficiency and tiresome bureaucracy. For a time, many of the borough's schools seemed to become islands, solving unique problems on their own with very little support.

This was immensely challenging, and several of my headteacher colleagues either became ill from stress, or felt that the job had changed so much it was no longer something they wanted to do. Almost overnight, I was required to find a firm that could sort out my staff payroll, another firm that could supply me with a set of cleaners, and a catering company that could provide healthy hot meals at a reasonable price. I also needed an accountant with a knowledge of how school budgets worked who could sort the money out, assemble reports for the governing body, and visit regularly to keep our spending in check.

Although it was a difficult year, while both borough and schools struggled to acquire new skills, I inadvertently benefited from the borough's lack of experience; the money allotted to a state primary school at the beginning of a financial year is divided into twelve instalments, with one instalment credited to the school's bank account each month. By mistake, the borough had somehow arranged for a double monthly instalment to be paid to us, and by the time the error was discovered the account had earned nearly four thousand pounds in interest... a very useful sum indeed.

For some reason, my borough also thought it would be a good idea to appoint a school inspector for every area of the curriculum, plus a few to oversee multiculturalism and racial awareness. During the ILEA's tenure, each borough had been allocated just two primary inspectors, one for the north of the area and one for the south. Until now, I had dealt with only Alan Green and Harvey Trend, and seen them infrequently. When they visited, they simply chose a few curriculum areas to look at in depth. Now, my school was suddenly inundated with visits from a large group of newly appointed inspectors, all of whom had to be introduced to staff and given a tour of the school. Many of them also seemed to have acquired rather nice cars that needed accommodating in my tiny car park. Each new inspector asked the same questions, and when I was eventually visited by inspector number twelve within the space of a month or two, I questioned why the authority hadn't considered a bit of information sharing, since I'd now given the same school tour and said exactly the same things twelve times. Apparently it hadn't occurred to anybody.

Each of these subject inspectors had been allotted a small group of schools to oversee as a general inspector, and mine was a slight, quietly spoken gentleman whose speciality was secondary school information technology. He had never taught in an inner city primary school, had little knowledge of what went on in one, and seemed very hesitant to talk to any children when he visited. Although he knew a great deal about computers, his knowledge applied almost universally to the secondary sector, and had little relevance to what was happening in my own school. It wasn't long before the borough realised that schools were becoming fed up with constant visits from inspectors, and since it had also discovered that it couldn't really justify such an ambitious level of inspectorate anyway, some hasty pruning was undertaken with generous redundancy payouts.

At this time, there was much information gathering by the borough too, and although I appreciated that it needed to know a lot about its schools in a short period of time, it seemed to be constantly starting afresh rather than looking at the information it had inherited from the ILEA. Every day, my postbag contained forms to be filled in, often duplicating requests that had been made on a previous occasion by a different department. This soon became increasingly tiresome. I found the best solution was to ignore anything that wasn't essential, and if there was a telephone call, pretend that I'd already sent the form. Usually, I heard nothing further.

Some of the requests made no sense. On one occasion I was asked to give an extraordinary level of detail about every person working in my building, including whether they were male, female or 'of an unknown gender'. I was also required to state the make, colour, and registration number of their cars. When I questioned the need for this information, I was told that the survey had come from the government, and the borough had merely forwarded it. There was little they could do about it, and every school was required to comply.

When I phoned the government's Department for Education, I was told it had indeed sent a questionnaire, but the requests for unnecessary personal information such as the colour of teacher's cars must have been added by the local education authority. Incredulous, I contacted the borough again, who denied this, saying they would never request the colour of a teacher's car. Determined to get to the bottom of this mystery, I phoned the Department of Education yet again, and was told the school itself most have added the car questions. I flatly refused to look at the questionnaire again, let alone complete it, although I imagine many poor, harassed school secretaries dutifully complied.

But now that it was no longer mandatory to go via the education office to find a teacher, making effective appointments became far easier. I had set up good links with two local universities who specialised in training future teachers and twice a year we took groups of their students on teaching practice. First class primary teachers tend to be born rather than made and invariably, at least one of the students would prove to be particularly talented. If I had a vacancy, I was very quick to offer a job. This meant the school had a useful mix of teachers; Some, like Georgia, Gerry and Wanda were extremely experienced, others had five or six years of solid teaching behind them, and the newest recruits from college, though inexperienced, were eager, enthusiastic and brimming with ideas.

Due to the popularity of the school, it wasn't long before the infant classes were full. Most parents know instinctively what they want from primary education, and they soon discover which schools within travelling distance are worth investigating. A parent new to an area will usually chat to her neighbours, assemble a shortlist, and then, since the government constantly assures them they have the right to send their offspring to any school they fancy, off they'll go to the one they've chosen. Usually it will be full, simply because it is a good school and many parents want to send their children there. This was the situation we were now constantly facing.

After a parent had looked at me blankly because I'd said there wasn't even room on the reserve list, I would explain the admission criteria laid down by the local authority, but the more

I tried to explain it, the less the parent seemed to understand it. Mrs Jones was typical, and determined that her children should join us.

'But I only live two streets away,' Mrs Jones says. 'I must be entitled to a place.'

'That's true,' I reply, 'but everybody we've admitted into that year group lives nearer.'

'Well, how has Mrs Smith got her children in here? She lives further away than me.'

'That's also true, but Mrs Smith's children are in a different year group, and there were spaces for that age.'

Mrs Jones becomes a little irritated. 'Well, what about Mrs Brown, then? Her kids come from East Dulwich and that's miles away.'

I sigh because I've been over this ground so often. 'Mrs Brown originally lived just across the road,' I explain. 'She's been rehoused in East Dulwich but her children are still entitled to come here.'

'Then how did Mrs Green get her Jimmy in here? She lives in the same flats as me.'

'I know. But Jimmy lives one floor lower than you.'

'So what?'

'It makes Jimmy ten yards nearer. And we have to measure it all out on a large-scale map. Look, I'll show you. You can measure it yourself if you like...'

I could understand and appreciate the parental frustration. One of the admission rules was particularly irritating for a parent who had more than one child, since it stated that other children in the family could be admitted to the school if one of them was already attending. The problem was that you needed to get one child on roll in the first place, which brought everything back to distance from front door to school again. It can all be very confusing for parents, but they do have one potent weapon: the admission appeal.

Provided they can make a good enough case to the appeal panel for getting a child into the school they've chosen, the school will be legally obliged to take the child, whether or not the year group is full. If there are lots of appeals, and half a dozen are successful, the school can suddenly find itself with a serious overcrowding problem. This was happening to us, and I was finding that parents were becoming increasingly wily in the methods they used to gain entry.

At that time, appeals for the schools in my cachement area were heard by three independent panel members. They were often governors of other schools, or local councillors. The parent and school would put their cases, the committee would ask questions, and then, after the parent and headteacher had left, a decision would be made. For a while, I seemed to be at the mercy of two regular panel members who believed everything a parent said, and very little that I said. The numbers in my two Reception classes were expanding alarmingly, and it seemed that appeals were being heard virtually every fortnight. I began to take photographs to the appeals, to show how crowded my classrooms were becoming, but it made little difference. I needed to find a solution quickly, and I talked to Georgia about it after one particularly gruelling appeal.

'We need to prove that we just can't cram any more in,' she said. 'Look, I've got an idea...'

Her plan was bold, but I thought it had a good chance of working. I wrote to both panel members, inviting them into my school to see what effect the overcrowding was having. When they arrived I opened the door to one of the Reception classrooms and they were horrified; children were crammed into every nook and cranny, while the harassed teacher rushed around trying to accommodate everybody's needs. We moved through all the infant classrooms and they saw an identical scene in each. Both visitors left the site subdued and concerned. Once they'd gone the thirteen extra children we'd been shipping from classroom to classroom just ahead of the visitors were returned to their normal classes. It seemed to do the trick. In subsequent appeals, the two panel members made decisions a little more cautiously.

Working with school governors could also be time consuming and difficult. I'm still not sure what makes anyone want to be a school governor. A taste of power? Spare time to kill? Or a passion for education, and a real desire to see a school do the best it can for its pupils? There are, I suppose, many reasons, but attracting lay people who have the right kind of knowledge can be a difficult task, especially in deprived inner city areas, where people often feel, wrongly, that they need to be academically inclined to make a worthwhile contribution.

These days, school governors have awesome responsibilities over the curriculum, health and safety, the budget and teacher's salaries, and they have to attend many meetings and training sessions. Furthermore, all this has to be done on a voluntary basis, because no governor ever receives any money for the work. School governors are elected for four years, they need real commitment to stay the whole course, and only the most dedicated do.

It wasn't always so. Years ago, governors had a minimal workload. They were simply required to turn up for one evening meeting a term. Visiting the school wasn't a requirement, so many didn't bother. Some were helpful, others were not. Some gained full marks for eccentricity and used meetings to air their own prejudices and dubious advice at considerable length. For a headteacher who'd already had a long and hard day at school, this could be very frustrating.

In my early years of headship, I'd arrive at meetings laden with documents and find myself listening to earnest but pointless discussions. Invariably, a resolution was made for the headteacher to present more documentation and I'd work for the next few evenings producing it. Then a more experienced colleague let me in on the secret.

'Show what a co-operative chap you are by smiling and agreeing to absolutely everything, and then only do what's important,' he advised. 'And the only important things are those which directly affect the children.'

It was good advice. At the next meeting, an elderly governor demanded to know why our school was no longer allowing visits from home beat police officers. I was astonished. We'd done nothing of the sort and I said so. He merely repeated the accusation, thumping his fist on the table until a hearing aid shot out of his ear and I realised he had a hearing defect. He was also on three other local governing bodies and often got us hopelessly mixed up. While he hunted under the seat for his hearing aid, the chairman moved the meeting rapidly on.

Back then, most governing bodies had elderly members like Miss Johnson and Mr Eldridge, whose hearts were in the right place but whose minds meandered alarmingly. Although petite, Miss Johnson had a ravenous appetite, marking her place at the table with sandwiches cut to a thickness that suggested they only came three to a loaf. She'd wait for what she considered a tedious agenda item, and then tuck in. Assorted fruit and veg would fall softly to the table. Once, she forgot her sandwiches altogether. She'd been for a day at the seaside and came to the meeting armed with a collection of shells she thought the children might find interesting. Becoming bored halfway through the meeting, she took a magnifying glass from her bag and spent the next agenda item closely studying a family of periwinkles.

Mr Eldridge did his bit for the community by coaching the local youth in football skills, although his enthusiasm far outweighed his ability. He had a tendency to slip on the ball, and often appeared at meetings with appendages covered in sticking plaster or a bandage. Around the third agenda item, he'd often place finger and thumb on a furrowed brow and dip his head with intense concentration. It took me several meetings to realise he'd fallen asleep.

Like juries, school governing bodies have always contained a fair cross section of society. This throws up anomalies from time to time. When we co-opted a retired headteacher from a small, respected academy for young ladies, she was never able to reach a real understanding of life at a tough London primary. Offering to do a regular slot on Tuesday afternoons reading to a class of infant children, she said plummily: 'I've decided on Beatrix Pottah. All the younger children at my school adored Beatrix Pottah.'

She stuck it out for a full half-hour, only losing her patience when a child sitting at her feet scrawled, in felt-tipped pen, on one of her suede shoes. 'What on earth are you doing?' she snapped. 'Drawing Peter Rabbit,' said the child. For the next few months she spent her volunteer time digging the school garden instead.

Times change, though, and governors with them. To cope with the massive workload, a prospective governor today needs an enthusiasm bordering on insanity. Nevertheless, new governors do often have this sort of enthusiasm. The morning after appointing two new parent governors, I found one pounding the playground beat, handing out questionnaires on school dinners, while making sure no parents parked on the zig-zags or dared to light a cigarette under the playground shed, and generally letting parents know that if there was a complaint about the school, she'd be very happy to take the matter up with the headteacher.

But enthusiasm could sometimes be followed by a rude awakening. On the morning she'd volunteered to man the security camera overlooking the front gate, she was astonished to see a parent slipping a just delivered two litre bottle of staffroom milk under her coat and disappearing rapidly down the street.

Like all headteachers, I had great respect for the governors who were committed to my school and who genuinely had something to offer, but the timewasters irritated me, and none more so than Anthony. In the year that he joined our governing body, Lucy, our hard working school secretary, retired. Secretaries, or School Administration Officers as they are now called, are crucial to the success of a school. Appoint a bad one and they can cock everything up with alarming speed.

Fortunately, we had the ideal replacement to hand. Sandra was one of our teaching support assistants, adept with any age group. She had the right qualifications, excellent relationships with everyone and she was efficient with parents and paperwork. She also had a delightful sense of humour and was very keen to do the job. At the next governors' meeting, I suggested that we should appoint her. Everybody agreed except Anthony, who rarely came to meetings, and when he did, he was always late. Since he was on the small appointing committee of the governors, he said it was important that we followed the rules by advertising and interviewing. Other governors nodded, so we discussed dates for the personnel committee to meet. Unfortunately, Anthony couldn't make any of them, but he said it was fine for us to go ahead without him.

We spent an evening drawing up an eye-catching advertisement, and I phoned the local paper to see how much a couple of insertions would cost. Horrified at the price, I reduced it to one, which was fortunate, because the phone rang constantly for two weeks after it appeared. I asked Anthony if he'd like to help me draw up a job description, but unfortunately he was busy that day.

By the end of the week I'd printed, packaged, posted or e-mailed 73 application forms and detailed job descriptions. It took a great deal of time to go through the applications and give them the attention they deserved. I'd asked Anthony to help, but unfortunately he was too busy, so I divided them between the remaining three of us on the personnel committee.

Ten applicants were invited to look around the school. It's always fascinating to compare reality with what's written on an application form. I hadn't bargained for Caroline turning up in what looked suspiciously like a pair of carpet slippers, and Deirdre may have been nervous, but after half an hour of being unable to get a word in edgeways I felt I'd been verbally ravaged. After another long evening with the personnel committee, minus Anthony, we eventually managed to whittle the number of applicants down to five people. Plus Sandra.

I'd hoped Anthony would at least be available for the interviewing panel, but unfortunately he was very busy that week. On a rainy evening, all the candidates turned up in their Sunday best, ready to convince us that salary was the last thing on their minds, because they all knew how cash-strapped schools were. All six smiled a great deal and said how wonderful they thought children were. Particularly Sandra.

By 10.30 that night, it was all over, and we'd appointed the best candidate. Her name was Sandra. I didn't even bother telling Anthony...

Although the year had gone well, it was to end on a note of appalling sadness. Classroom assistants sometimes don't seem to have much going for them. They're paid too little, they supervise playgrounds for long periods in bitter winter weather, they don't do the most exciting work in the classroom, and yet they'll be the ones who sit in hospital accident and emergency departments with sick children for hours while the school attempts to contact a parent on a mobile that's usually switched off.

Certainly the job has changed over the years and it is far more interesting now, a far cry from the days when they dispensed small bottles of milk for the children to drink, washed paintpots, brewed tea for teachers on playground duty, or tried to control classes during rainy playtimes while teachers went off for a quick break. Because they needed no qualifications, it took a long time to realise that untrained people could actually be very capable and of real value in the classroom. Nowadays, they are indispensable cogs in the educational wheel and properly used in a primary school they can enjoy as much work variety as the average teacher. And some, if given the freedom, can display the most amazing talent, adding fruitfully to the school's human resources. Elaine was such a person.

Elaine was the kind of teaching assistant headteachers would like them all to be. She'd come into school early in my headship, looking for a place for her son. Unfortunately that year group was full and although he seemed an exceptionally pleasant boy, I had no option but to turn them away. Then, before they'd left the building, a member of staff mentioned that she'd just passed a woman in the bottom corridor who was saying to her son how attractive the school seemed, and what a shame it was that there were no places. I sent a child downstairs to find them, and Simon had a place the next day. Soon, his mum had joined us too, working full time as a teaching assistant.

From the start, her talents were remarkable. Her warm personality and delightful humour ensured she related well to everyone. Children, especially those with special needs, made rapid progress with her, and she'd spend hours at home preparing interesting things for them to do. Perhaps because she'd been through a disastrous relationship herself, she had great empathy with children who were enduring family crises that affected them deeply. Fights and arguments in the playground dwindled; she had the knack of dissipating tension with gentle humour and the talents of a skilled judge and jury.

She was artistic, too, and a meticulous model-maker, demonstrating to fascinated children in assembly how she created Victorian doll's houses. The quality and detail was exceptional, and they could have sold in the finest toy shops. Her talents extended in every direction. If anybody needed a complex costume for a class play or children's work fashioned into a beautiful wall display, they knew what to do. Ask Elaine.

We thought the world of her. And then, shortly after her thirty eighth birthday, we found out that she had been diagnosed with cancer, although she'd said nothing to us. I knew that she'd had stomach trouble for some time, and been prescribed various pills and potions, but she didn't want anybody to fuss. Ultimately, a scan revealed the worst. Determined to overcome this latest obstacle in her life… after all, she'd overcome the others… she tackled the awful rigours of chemotherapy with a grim determination and, apart from the hospital sessions she needed to attend, she was seldom away from the job she loved.

Support from colleagues was abundant. She struggled on, walking around school with a small concealed bottle that injected doses of painkiller into her, determined that her friends, colleagues and children at the school should never know how ill she really was. One afternoon, I came down a flight of stairs and found her in tears at the bottom. She'd just returned from the hospital and it was the worst possible news. I stopped on the stairs, took hold of her, and hugged her tightly. Tears streamed down my face and I felt totally helpless.

A month later she was dead. This gentle, kind and unbelievably brave woman had given years of dedicated service to my school and been much loved for it. The funeral was some distance away, and I took the unprecedented step of closing the school so that all of us could attend. Just two parents objected… one saying it would be extremely inconvenient to keep her child at home that day and the fact that somebody had died really wasn't her problem.

People's capacity for extraordinary kindness or devastating indifference has never ceased to amaze me.

CHAPTER 10
ALL CHILDREN GREAT AND SMALL

Soft water is good for washing close. Hard water isn't. It's called ice.
Simon age 9

In the poignant last scene of that classic film about teaching, 'Goodbye Mr Chips', Mr Chips is about to join that great classroom in the sky. 'Shame he never had any children of his own,' another master says softly. 'No children?' overhears Chips, 'I'm a teacher... I've had hundreds of children...'. This is the fascinating thing about being a headteacher. All those children. All different, all so interesting.

Like Robert. When he joined us, his mother didn't mention that he was autistic, but all those years ago autism went almost unrecognised in schools. She did say that he seemed to have a remarkable ability for retaining information and that she called him her little Mr Memory, and I soon discovered why. Talking about dinosaurs in the first assembly Robert attended, I mispronounced 'diplodocus'. Up piped a surprisingly loud voice. 'It's not docus, as in crocus. It's od, as in plod. The diplodocus is one of the longest dinosaurs from the late Jurassic period. It was a herbivore and it ate plant material. The reptile attained lengths up to eighty feet and had a long neck, body and flexible tail...' I hadn't known about Robert's passion for dinosaurs and he continued for a full two minutes. The other children watched, mouths agog....

Becoming a headteacher is rather like gaining an instant and very large family. All its members have to be looked after carefully, especially in a socially deprived and challenging inner city area, although I have never ceased to be amazed at how resilient children are. Throughout my years as a headteacher there were constant instances of intense pleasure at seeing just what a young child can achieve, such as six year old Kwai-Ann earning a grade in her violin examination normally only reached by a very talented sixteen year old, and the occasional times of appalling sadness, epitomised by Cheryl, also aged six, who developed eye cancer. She was very attached to a scruffy old teddy bear in the play corner of her classroom, and before she went into hospital for the final time we presented her in assembly with the biggest and fluffiest teddy bear we could buy. She loved school and was desperate to be back, but it wasn't to be. The cancer had been diagnosed too late and her brief life was over far too soon.

Between those extremes were the characters who, for one reason or another, stood out from the crowd. Children who could be intriguing, exasperating, challenging, wildly amusing, or surprising in a way that none of us expected.

When Andrew joined our nursery class, he announced his presence by making the loudest wailing noise I had ever heard. It was astonishing that such a noise could emanate from such a very small boy. It was so loud, classes everywhere could hear Andrew being escorted through the building towards my room in the days that followed.

On his first day, Andrew had bounded enthusiastically into the nursery. The nursery teacher had previously visited Andrew's home, and had noticed within seconds that mum had no control over Andrew whatsoever. Now, overwhelmed by the array of equipment in the nursery to play with, he began to throw it around. When he'd finished hurling building bricks, he went to the book corner and tried to throw the books instead. Wherever he went, there was a trail of devastation, and when anyone tried to call a halt to his activities, he gave them a punch on the leg, or a head butt, or a kick. Other children looked at him in astonishment, and then quickly learned to avoid him in case a missile or a fist came flying their way. A handful of children are always difficult to settle when they start, usually because it will be the first time they have been parted from their parents, but this period is normally over quickly. Andrew, though, was something else.

The time-out chair, complete with sandtimer to indicate when he could get off, was soon brought into play. There was only one problem. He absolutely refused to sit on it. He wriggled, squirmed and shuffled until he could slip out of the adult's grasp and create further havoc. Ultimately he was a danger to other children and the teacher decided there was only one thing for it. He'd have to be brought to the boss.

When he arrived, I thanked my lucky stars that he was so small, and I lifted him bodily into the corner of my room by the desk. He wasn't having any of that. Whoooooing loudly… and it was quite obvious by now that it was only for effect… he jumped up, ran round the room and began twanging my guitars. I lifted him again, put him gently back in the corner, and fifteen minutes passed before he realised I intended to keep doing this until he sat still. While I worked at my computer, his eyes flickered from the screen to my face as he assessed whether it was worth heading for the guitars again. Eventually, the nursery teacher came at the end of the morning, smiled at him hopefully, and led him quietly back downstairs to go home.

Like groundhog day, the next three weeks passed in similar fashion until, at last, he began to change and visit me less frequently. As his behaviour improved, the teacher put colourful stickers on his chart, and he was told that ten stickers would mean a trip to me for a very special badge. On the day he'd earned his tenth sticker, I was in the library chairing a meeting with teachers and a social worker. Suddenly, the door flew upon, and there was Andrew wailing as loudly as he had on his first day. The social worker's eyebrows shot up questioningly. What on earth could the school be doing to this little child?

Unfortunately, Andrew still associated coming up to me with being made to sit still on my carpet. Then, as I fixed a large badge on his jumper and everybody in the meeting smiled and gave him a huge cheer, he suddenly realised what was happening and the most delightful grin lit up his face. I whooped for joy too, which made him giggle loudly. We were succeeding with him at last.

Oliver was a top infant and he couldn't settle in his class either. It was worrying his teacher because he was an intelligent and able child, but his parents had spent little time with him since birth and left him to amuse himself. While surrounded by a choice of equipment in the early years classes, he'd been manageable, but now that he was getting older his day needed to be more structured and he wasn't having any of it. Unable to contain him, his teacher frequently brought him to me, and it was all I could do to manage him either. Wherever I sat him in my room he found something to mess about with, and one afternoon I placed him in the middle of the carpet where there was nothing he could touch or interfere with.

Glancing up from my work after a while, I thought he'd fallen asleep. In fact, he was busily pulling tiny pieces of wool from the carpet, rolling them into balls, and teasing out eight strands from each of them. Jumping up, he dropped his miniature creations onto my desk. 'They're for you,' he said, 'it's a family of tarantulas.' Since he was sent up to me every afternoon for the next couple of weeks, I took to providing him with a range of junk material and allowed him to make me a different model each day, provided he worked hard in the classroom each morning. Fortunately, he eventually began to realise that reading and writing were also worthwhile, and that he could be quite good at those activities too.

Throughout my headship, I placed a lot of emphasis on settling children at an early age, even though it took up a great deal of my time. I reasoned that it would always be much harder to sort out behaviour problems when children were older, and I quickly found that things could be particularly challenging if we admitted a child who'd already been behaving badly in another school and nothing had been done about it.

Leon was such a child. Six, and knee high to a grasshopper, he and his angelic smile had come into school accompanied by his mother, who asked if we had a vacancy. It was my policy never to refuse anyone if we had a place, but we always telephoned the previous school for some background information on a new child before the personal file arrived. On this occasion, the secretary at the other end of the phone hesitated for a few seconds, and then said 'Hang on a moment. I'll pass you to our teacher who oversees children with special needs....'

The teacher couldn't believe her good fortune. 'He's coming to you? What a relief! He's a thoroughly objectionable little boy. His behaviour is appalling, he does no work, he hurts children, and he hides under tables and spits at staff. I wish you luck. You'll need it.'

When Leon's file arrived, things looked even more depressing. Police often arrived to turn his home over, his older brothers and sisters had all been in trouble, one had been permanently excluded, and there had been serious involvement with social services. I worried about our chances with this one, but at least he was going into Amanda's class... and Amanda was the sort of teacher who'd continually tell me how delightful her class was, unaware that it was due to her brilliance as a teacher. Things went fairly well on day one. Leon was allocated a friend to help him through his first day, and apart from watching the other children cautiously, wandering around the classroom whenever he felt like it, and calling out during lessons occasionally, he seemed like most children we'd taken on. He also seemed genuinely surprised at how well the class behaved. He obviously wasn't used to it.

The problems started on the second day. Leon was very late and looked as if he'd just crawled out of bed. His mother had sent him to the DVD rental shop before going to school. He'd had breakfast.. a small bar of chocolate as a reward for going to the shop. We gave him fruit and a hot drink, but he was clearly very angry. Later on we discovered he'd had very little sleep... the police had found his little sister wandering in the street late at night.

At the end of playtime, he refused to line up with his class, and ran off to climb onto the Playtown. A child was sent to fetch me. I wasn't sure how I was going to handle the situation, and as I walked up to the Playtown he scuttled into the tiny shelter on the top level. 'Well, I'm not dragging you inside,' I said. 'If you want to run home, you can. If you want to stay out here, it's up to you, but it's going to rain. And your class is cooking cakes this morning.' I crossed my fingers and went back inside. Ten minutes later, I found him under a table outside his classroom. 'Do you want to go back in?' I asked. He nodded and I slipped him back into the room.

By the end of the week, he'd discovered school was a place where you could do lots of interesting things instead of spending the time being told off. He was bright, alert, talented at art, and desperately keen to learn how to read.. something that seemed to have been ignored at his previous school. He quickly formed a strong relationship with Amanda. He knew she liked him and he was anxious to please her, even arriving one morning at eight o' clock to see if she needed any help.

In those first weeks, I often popped into Amanda's classroom, but he was fine. Apart from habitual lateness, which wasn't his fault, he settled quickly and well, but I wondered how two schools could perceive a small child so differently. We couldn't cure his home situation, but I often chatted to Leon, or listened to him as he discovered the excitement of learning to read, and when I returned to school after a few days with flu, he ran up and hugged me. 'I missed you', he said quietly. I was reminded of just how awesome my responsibility as a headteacher was.

But it was a greater struggle if we accepted an older child who saw little point in school and was determined to be as disruptive as possible. Eddie had attended four other schools, and it seemed that his parents moved house, and school, when the neighbours couldn't stand the family's behaviour and noise any more and his headteacher was on the point of permanently excluding him. He was deceptively quiet and attentive when he stood beside his mother as Secretary Sandra took down the family's details, his piercing blue eyes watching me carefully, as if assessing how long I'd tolerate him. On his first day, I smiled at him in the corridor as he went to his class.

'I'm sorry you haven't enjoyed your other schools, Eddie,' I said. 'But I hope you'll like it here.'

'So long as nobody tells me what to do,' he said. 'I don't like being told what to do.'

That became very apparent within his first hour. I'd allocated him to a charismatic young teacher who already had several difficult children and she'd had great success with them all. Eddie, however, didn't even feel the need to sit down. He wandered around talking loudly, disrupting the work of other children and giving them the occasional shove when he felt like it. Earlier, I'd telephoned the other schools he'd attended, and it appeared that all of them would have been happy to insert a nuclear device in his bottom.

By late morning, Eddie's teacher felt it would be a good idea if I had a word in his ear and she managed to entice him out of the classroom on the pretext that she needed to show him something. At that moment, I was rehearsing the choir in the hall that also doubled as a gymnasium, and as soon as Eddie realised I was going to tell him off, he climbed to the top of the wallbars and sat there gesticulating obscenely. The children in the choir were fascinated, particularly as they wondered what I was going to do about it. I started by asking Eddie if he'd mind getting down, because his behaviour was messing up my time with the choir.

'You can't make me,' he said.

'Oh, I'm well aware of that, Ed,' I said. 'I just don't want you to fall off. You know, health and safety and all that. If you break your legs, I might lose my job.'

'Couldn't care less,' he said. 'I'll sit here till I feel like coming down.'

'Okay,' I said. 'You can enjoy our singing from up there.'

The children in the choir smiled, and I turned back to the lesson, ignoring Eddie's increasingly ardent attempts to make himself noticed. At playtime, as I dismissed the choir, I suddenly realised he'd climbed down from the wallbars and taken himself off to the playground as if nothing had happened. When the teacher on duty had attempted to chat to him, recognising that he was a new boy, he'd informed her that no teacher could control him. His previous school had apparently let him do what he liked all day.

'That won't happen here,' she said.

'We'll see,' he replied.

By the end of the morning, his class teacher was really suffering, and because he wouldn't leave the room, I was sent for. Fortunately he wasn't a very big boy and I picked him up bodily and carried him to the chairs outside my room, where he sat thumbing through some reading books on a table. One of the borough's school advisers was waiting to talk to me, and as she watched me plonk Eddie on a chair she looked at him sympathetically.

'Hello young man,' she said,' Aren't you very well?'

'Nah,' Eddie replied. 'I've just bin assaulted by the 'edteacher.'

It was obvious Eddie was going to be a tough nut to crack, but then, we were pretty resilient too, and bit by bit we began to understand his anger and resentment. His older brother had been permanently expelled, his mother had little time for him, and his father felt that giving him a good whack every evening was the best way to keep him in line. But we soon discovered that Eddie was a very intelligent boy with an excellent command of language, a real passion for science, and a love of animals. He was also devoted to his little sister, and loved reading to her. As we'd found with Leon, once Eddie discovered that his class teacher was an interesting, caring person with a great sense of fun and an ability to create highly enjoyable lessons, his behaviour began to change rapidly. On the occasions when she found him just too wearing, she'd send him to the nursery or a Reception class, where he loved to help teach our very youngest children.

Eddie's father was astonished. A school refuser himself, he had undoubtedly influenced Eddie with his views, and now he began to influence his son positively. 'This is a great school,' Dad said to me one morning. 'I keep telling him he's got to make the most of his two years here.' And ultimately, Eddie did. Although I wasn't convinced he'd make it through secondary school and there was always a strong possibility that he could end up like his brother once he'd left the security and family atmosphere of our primary school, at least I knew we'd given him a chance.

Sometimes, a child could present the school with a serious problem, but not through poor behaviour. Rahmid had extreme special needs. Born prematurely with a large section of gut missing, he wasn't expected to survive, but surgeons effected a partial solution by connecting his stomach to a colostomy tube and feeding him using a special machine. The first three years of his life were precarious, but he progressed, and was eventually able to attend a small local nursery for a year. At this point mum decided he should come to us, because his older brother had done well since he had transferred to our school.

My special needs co-ordinator and I visited his nursery, so that we could get to know him a little before he joined us. He was constantly supervised by adults and, perhaps unsurprisingly, extremely indulged. His language when he couldn't do as he wanted could best be described as ripe, and his medical needs were extreme, causing him to be followed round the room by his two helpers to make sure he didn't trip over or bump into anything.

We had a dilemma. We felt unable to admit a child who needed such close medical attention. Compared with the space at his nursery, our Reception classrooms were tiny and we'd need an extremely capable support assistant. Although we'd been told Rahmid's incontinence was gradually being overcome, we weren't convinced. And we were unhappy about the electric feeding machine supplied by the hospital, which the class teacher and support assistant would have to attach to his stomach and operate every day. What if it went wrong?

I decided to make a stand. I refused to take him without adequate support from the borough, which annoyed the nursery he was attending because the staff were unwilling to keep him there any longer. In a bid to hurry matters forward, the local education department offered a little additional money, but not full time support. Once again I refused. A week later I was visited by a social worker and the borough inclusion officer, who sat stiffly on my chairs and looked vaguely threatening.

'I'm afraid you can't refuse to take this child, Mr Kent,' said the inclusion officer. 'Inclusion of children with special needs into mainstream schools is now a legal requirement, his mother wants him at this school, and I shall have to ask you to make the necessary arrangements immediately.'

'I don't have a problem with the legal requirement, provided it comes with the proper backing.' I said. 'This little boy's needs are extreme. He is seriously incontinent, he will need somewhere to bathe, he requires feeding from a machine and I cannot expect my staff to cope. They are not medically trained to handle this.'

'But you will be given extra resources. Once he is on your roll there will be extra money for you to employ additional help, and the whole situation will be monitored by the school nurse.'

'I'm sorry,' I said, 'but I seriously doubt that. We hardly ever see a school nurse and I suspect that once I take this child any extra resources will be a long time coming.'

'That's rather a negative view, Mr Kent,' said the social worker.

'It may be. But I've been in this situation before.'

'Unfortunately, I'm afraid you don't have any choice,' said the inclusion officer. 'I shall expect you to take the child immediately.'

'I'll be happy to,' I said. 'Just as soon as I get the facilities and support the child is entitled to. Until then, I'm afraid I flatly refuse.'

The two left my room, and I sat down heavily. Once again I was in for a battle. But Rahmid deserved every chance. He'd had quite enough to put up with in his short life to date. While I was fired with emotion, I wrote a letter to the authority, with a copy to Rahmid's mother. I had a suggestion for the authority to consider.

We had a small shower room in one of the mezzanine rooms, and although it hadn't been used for some time and needed a little refurbishment, it would help us cope with the incontinence problem. If the education authority would agree to fund the work, and pay for full time support, we would be able to guarantee Rahmid the schooling he deserved. Since Mum refused to consider any other school, and I was determined not to budge, the authority reluctantly agreed. Rahmid joined us at the end of the summer term, to acclimatise before September.

We had a hell of a time. The incontinence was worse than expected, creating difficulties until the shower room was finished. It also took some time to find a suitable support worker, and the feeding machine often broke down. Nevertheless, the patience of his class teacher and the determination of our special needs co-ordinator meant we soon began to see changes in Rahmid. As he moved through his infant years and his medical needs declined, he matured into a happy little boy, warm, caring and enthusiastic about learning, and his mother told me he often woke her early in the morning asking if it was time for school. Sometimes, I thought, it really pays to dig your heels in.

Frankie was very different. He wasn't a challenging child, he had no medical problems and he was never absent from school, but he did have an all-enveloping passion for buses. He'd also joined us from another school, and it was a fortnight before I met him properly. I was in the playground, chatting to his teacher while she supervised playtime, when he wandered up to us.

'Shall I do a bus, Miss?' he asked. Seeing my baffled expression, his teacher smiled. 'Frankie's my very own bus service,' she said. 'Shut your eyes and listen'. He launched into an impression of a bus in motion, with gear changes, stops and starts, and hissing air brakes. It sounded just like the real thing. 'What bus was that?' he asked, expecting us to know.

'I reckon it's a 53,' said his teacher. 'Of course not!' he replied indignantly. 'It's a Bendy bus. This is a 53...' He embarked on a second impression, which sounded very different.

By half term, we'd adapted to his quirkiness. Each day, as I stood on the staircase and chatted to the children as they passed me after playtime, Frankie would hurry past me making motoring noises. One day he decided to play bus conductor, announcing the stop we had reached.

'This is East Dulwich. Along that corridor is Peckham Rye. If we go up another flight of stairs we'll be in Forest Hill.'

'Your bus route knowledge is very impressive,' I said.

'Yes, it is,' he agreed. 'Ask Miss if you can look at my maps.'

I discovered that Frankie had drawn elaborate maps of the school, re-creating the building as a large chunk of south-east London. Bus routes were marked with coloured lines, and stops were marked at intervals. To catch the P13 to Streatham, also known as the school dinner hall, you had to wait outside Class 9, where buses should appear at ten minute intervals if they were on schedule.

Frankie could give any school activity a transport slant. On an outing, while other boys sat comparing the contents of their packed lunch boxes, Frankie unfolded a huge bus map, laid it out on an empty seat, and carefully studied the route they were taking. I was relieved he wasn't sitting directly behind the coach driver, outlining alternatives. His South African class teacher was initially unfamiliar with London, but after teaching Frankie for a year she felt that she could travel anywhere in London by bus. Frankie simply loved them. He studied them incessantly and even at that early age, we knew he'd eventually find a career with them.

Soon after he'd left us for secondary school, I met him with his mother in a shop, miles from where he lived. 'You're a long way from home,' I said. 'How did you get here?'

'Dear God, please don't ask him that,' his mother said. 'We'll be here all morning!'

It's always rewarding when a potentially difficult child eventually settles down and finds that school can be a pleasurable experience. It's even more rewarding when children come back to visit and tell you proudly that they're training, or studying at college. Jeffery was such a child. He was in his final two years when I joined the school as headteacher, and I learned that he'd been very difficult in Year 5. I was warned that I'd probably have to exclude him in his final year.

He could certainly turn on the charm. He was the first child I encountered when I arrived at Comber Grove, since he was usually the first to arrive in the playground each morning. He offered to carry my bags upstairs, and when we reached my office his eyes darted quickly around the room.

'Wow, you've changed this room around a lot, haven't you Sir?' he said. I had the impression, even then, that half an hour later he could have drawn me an accurate map of everything it contained. Within days, I discovered that nothing was safe when he was in the vicinity unless it was firmly fastened down, but catching him taking something was impossible. I also found that he could irritate his classmates with consummate skill, causing arguments that degenerated into fights, and sometimes utter chaos.. at which point, like MacCavity, Jeffery wasn't there.

By the time he reached Year 6, he was becoming impossible to handle. In my determination to get him through his final year as successfully as possible, I offered him a leading part in the school play I was producing. This occupied him for several hours a week, to his teacher's delight, but gave me undeniable grief instead. Jeffery constantly re-wrote his part, demanding that other cast members keep up with his changes and giving them a tongue lashing if they didn't. He'd take himself off to the stockroom and use copious amounts of expensive card to create intricate props he'd designed. He'd persuade teaching assistants that I'd said he could stay in at lunchtime to practise... and chocolate bars would suddenly disappear from lunchboxes. Ultimately, the cast rebelled and said they wouldn't be in the play until I'd sorted Jeffery out.

On one occasion he was sent to the library to work. A group of children was also in the room, reading with a part-time support teacher. At lunch time, the teacher popped out to the shop.. and realised that her little wallet of credit cards was missing from her bag. Frantically, she rushed back to the library but found nothing. I sent for Jeffery and told him I'd have to search him, but he raised no objection, merely expressing his sympathy for the teacher's loss and offering to help look. The empty wallet was found on a ledge in the boy's toilet that afternoon, and it had obviously been removed from the teacher's handbag with the skill of a magician while the group was concentrating on reading.

Somehow, we reached the end of the year and Jeffery moved on. Then, seven years later, a smart young man appeared in the corridor. It was Jeffery, and he wanted me to know how well he was doing. He'd almost finished his business studies course and was going into partnership with a friend. Pleased to know that things were going well, I invited him to say hello to the teachers he knew. Four years later, he appeared again, in a tailored suit and carrying a very expensive briefcase. His business was successful, he was marrying soon, and he hoped he could put his children into our school as it had given him such a good start in life. I smiled inwardly, but once again expressed pleasure at how well things had turned out.

Until, reading an evening paper a year later, my eyes stopped at a photograph of a young man who was wanted for a string of daring robberies in one of London's smartest districts. Always immaculately dressed, said the headline, and carrying an expensive briefcase......

Babamide, one of our West Indian boys, was another child who could be disarmingly polite and charming. He came from a family of five children, all of whom were spread across the school. Dad was rarely at home, and Mum had more or less given up trying to keep her offspring in line. Though she cared very much for her children, she worked long hours and by the time she'd fed and watered them, all she could do was collapse into a chair while they more or less did what they liked. If her older children caused her too much stress, she beat them, often telling us that we had her full permission to do the same if they were a nuisance in class. In fact, Babamide rarely got into serious trouble at school, but almost unwittingly, he could drive a teacher insane. I'd usually find him working (I use the term very loosely) outside my room at least twice a week. I'd sigh, and the usual bizarre conversation would ensue.

'Hello, Babamide.'

'Hello Sir. I....'

'No, don't tell me, you've come to see me because you've been working especially hard.'

'No, my teacher sent me down here.'

'Really? For a sticker because you've done some good work?'

'No, because Nancy fell over on the stairs.'

'Don't tell me. You pushed her?'

'No, I was jus' walkin' like a chicken and she got in the way...'

'That was unfortunate. You are aware that walking like a chicken is not our recommended method of travelling up the staircase?'

'Pardon?'

As usual, it is pointless pursuing the matter unless I want to be there until lunchtime, so I leave him, tongue enthusiastically emerging from the side of his mouth, struggling to draw the legs on a Roman soldier. The next day, I'm listening to one of the violin groups, and I notice that Annisola, Babamide's sister, isn't using her own violin. Tentatively, I ask her where the violin is. I already know the answer.

'Me brother broke the string again. He keeps trying to play it.'

'Then why don't you hide it from him?'

'Me mum did. She put it on top of the wardrobe.'

'And he found it? How?'

'He sleeps on top of the wardrobe sometimes...'

But like all children, Babamide had many good points. He was an able reader and he loved taking books home, although this quickly proved problematic because he kept losing them. Eventually, I had to tell him that he couldn't take any more home until his father had at least made a contribution towards the ones he'd lost. Worried about a walloping, he took matters into his own hands and a day later his teacher intercepted a letter to his dad, purportedly from her, that he'd written himself. 'Dear Babamides Dad,' it said, 'I am pleesed to say Babamide as found his books so you won't hav to pay no munny.'

But invariably, by the end of the Summer term, his class teacher had developed a great affection for him. 'He can be such a drain on my patience,' said one. 'And he takes up far too much of my time. Funny thing is though, I shall miss him next year.'

I reminded her that she wouldn't have long to wait. There was always another member of the family on the way up...

CHAPTER 11
NO PARENTS PAST THIS POINT

The Greeks were very good at sport. In the Olympic Games they did things like throwing the javlins and hurling the bisciuts.
Danny, age 8

Parents are a school's customers. If parents, children and teachers are in harmony there is no limit on what can be achieved, and the majority of parents are keen to co-operate and work alongside the school. But, like any institution that deals with the general public, a school will also encounter people who can be very difficult to deal with, and just a few who make you want to put up a notice in the playground saying 'No Parents Past This Point.'

I can remember the first time I was approached by an aggressive parent. I was teaching a class of seven year olds in my first school, in Islington, in the sixties. At that time it was a tough, uncompromising working class area and I had been sent there after finishing my training because I had wanted to work in a deprived part of London. I loved my first class, but I had been warned about Juliette's mum, who had a reputation for throwing open the classroom door and shouting at the teacher. Juliette had been described to me as pretty, petulant, and rather devious. In fact, I rather liked her. At first she often sulked, but when I imitated her facial expressions I found it was easy to make her laugh, and we soon got on very well indeed. She was also an able child with a real talent for writing, unlike her mother who was unable to read or write very well at all.

At the Autumn Open Evening, I was disappointed not to see Mrs Barnes. I wanted to tell her how well her daughter was doing, and I had sent a report home with Juliette the day before, asking her to read it to her mum. As I was going through the dinner register, another teacher put her head round my door.

'I think I should tell you that I've just seen Mrs Barnes storming up the stairs,' she said. 'Do you want me to stick around?'

'No, it's okay,' I said. 'I've got to meet her sometime.' I turned back to my register. Within seconds the door handle was rattled furiously, the door flew open, and Mrs Barnes strode into the room. She was enormous, and her huge, shapeless form filled every hollow in the threadbare winter coat she was wearing.

'I want a word with you,' she demanded. I noticed with fascination that she only had one tooth.

'Certainly,' I smiled. 'Let's go into the corridor. Children, carry on with what you're doing and don't make a noise.' They didn't. They were too eager to hear how I would handle the situation. As soon as we were outside, I made myself as tall as I could and looked Mrs Barnes firmly in the eye.

'Now firstly,' I said, 'I'm always happy to see you, but next time make an appointment. Don't ever come into my room like that and don't wag your finger at me. It's extremely rude. And don't shout at me. I wouldn't let your daughter do it and I'm certainly not having you do it. Now, how can I help you?'

I smiled warmly and she hesitated. She wasn't used to this. Usually people backed away. She took the crumpled report out of her coat pocket. 'What do you mean by saying my daughter is careless and can't concentrate really well and she ain't made much progress and she's really late for school?

'I think you need to read the report more carefully. I've written that your daughter has charisma… Juliette loves big words and I asked her to explain that to you. And if you look closely you'll see it says Juliette can concentrate really well and made much progress. It also says she's rarely late for school.'

Mrs Barnes looked at me suspiciously for a few moments and then stuffed the report back in her pocket.

'Hmm. All right then. I must say she seems to like yer. I said to her if she's got any issues I'll come up and sort it out, but she won't have a word said against yer.' This was as near to an apology as I was going to get, and she hurried off down the corridor. It was the only time I ever spoke with her, and since her daughter seemed to have formed a positive relationship with me it seemed she had no wish to become involved any further with her daughter's education that year.

I learned something that day. Children instinctively know when you like and care for them, and they have a strong sense of fairness. Provided they feel you're doing the best you can for them, they will communicate this to their parents and in many cases even the most difficult parent can be brought onside. This is very important for a school, because a child can only make the best progress if teacher, parent and child are all working in harmony.

Nevertheless, any professional dealing with the general public will always experience problems, and teachers are sometimes seen as an easy target if parents want to unload their anger, frustration or dissatisfaction with whatever is going on in their own lives. If primary aged children are disruptive in a classroom, there is almost always a good reason for it, and as a teacher becomes more skilful and experienced, it becomes easier to discover and deal with the underlying causes.

For headteachers, however, it is harder. If there are inadequate teachers on the staff, parents have an entitlement to be unhappy and the head has to address both sides of the situation. Carefully considered advice and practical help has to be given to the teacher, and usually this soon makes a difference. Sometimes, however much help is given, improvement doesn't happen. Things can become very fraught indeed when a teacher seems unaware that the children are bored rigid or becoming difficult to control, and then thinks the best way to deal with an unhappy parent is to argue back.

Headteachers meet parents on a daily basis and very early in my headship I made it known that if a parent had a concern, I would always try to resolve it the same day. I made myself accessible, often appearing in the playground to meet parents, always being available at the beginning or end of the day to talk to them, and making sure I quickly followed up any complaint that was made. However unreasonable the complaint might have seemed, I soon realised how important it was never to become angry, although as I'd found with Mrs Barnes, it was often necessary to be firm and decisive. On very rare occasions it wasn't possible to resolve a dispute and the parent would decide to take the complaint to the governors, where a panel of three would hear what both parties had to say and then make a reasoned judgement. This involved much evidence gathering and letter writing on my part, and could take up many evenings. Fortunately, most problems were resolved quickly, although the sheer variety was astonishing, ranging from aggressive, unhappy young mums who seemed intent on being as difficult as possible, to people who just wanted advice on dealing with their offspring or reassurance that they were doing the right things with them.

Too often, there was a tendency for parents with time on their hands to become involved in their offspring's petty squabbles. One Monday morning, Jasmine's mother followed the class into the corridor and pushed Andrea's mum forcibly, saying that Andrea had stolen Jasmine's coloured pencils and she wanted them back, right now. Andrea's mum, no stranger to confrontation, snorted angrily in denial. Fortunately, the teacher had got her class safely inside the classroom, distracting them by reading a story very loudly. In the corridor, the voices of the two parents became increasingly loud, and then they began shoving each other. Minutes later they were tussling on the corridor floor, at which point the Cook strode out of the kitchen and threatened to pour cold water over them. By the time I got there, both parents were leaning sheepishly against the wall, breathing very heavily and apologising profusely to each other.

Serious arguments between parents are rare, but if they're going to happen it'll often be in the playground, usually when the weather is very hot and tempers are short. One early September afternoon, just before hometime, a woman strode into the playground and accused a much smaller mother of shouting at her daughter. A row broke out, and what the smaller mother lacked in stature she certainly made up for in strength, ripping the large woman's blouse open and revealing her ample bosom just as a

Year 6 group of boys were coming out of school. Before long, the women were surrounded by hordes of intrigued children and a dozen mothers who were trying desperately to calm things down.

We had just appointed Danny, our new Premises Officer after Fred had retired in July, and he moved hesitantly towards the group, not daring to get in between them but aware that they needed to be moved swiftly off the premises. Fortunately, the larger woman's boyfriend suddenly drove up in a battered van and she ran off to join him. The relief on Danny's face was palpable. Incidents like these were flashpoints that could occur without warning and at any point in the day, but they also had the benefit of being over very quickly, unlike the occasions when an irrational parent is convinced her child is without blame and determined to prove it at any cost.

Rather than giving her son the affection he needed because she was always too busy, Mrs Ahmoud bought him the latest toys instead, and the toy of the moment was a miniature spinning top called a Beyblade. For about six months, every young boy wanted one. You wound a strap round it, pulled hard as you flicked your wrist, and let it spin across the playground at great speed. You could have competitions with your mates, and they were even more fun at lunchtimes than having fights. Until, of course, somebody stole one, which is what happened to Samuel.

I'd set out the Beyblade ground rules clearly in assembly. As long as I saw them only in the playground, and nobody played with them after the whistle had blown, I'd be a happy man. For a while, the children stuck to the rules, and then the toys began appearing inside, mainly because they spun wonderfully on the large stone slabs connecting the school's staircases. Samuel had already been told several times not to play with his toy in the classroom, and in desperation his teacher took it from him, put it on her desk, and then forgot about it. When Samuel asked for it back, she realised it had disappeared. She spent time trying to track the toy down, but it didn't reappear and the theft was discussed with Samuel's mother the following morning. The teacher explained that even though she didn't condone the theft, the children had been told very clearly that they mustn't play with Beyblades inside the building. She also explained that she'd carried out an exhaustive search, it hadn't re-appeared, and given the circumstances the school couldn't take any responsibility for the toy. And that, the teacher assumed, was the end of the matter.

The next day, Secretary Sandra received a phone call from Samuel's mother. After further consideration, she wasn't satisfied. Didn't the teacher look after the things on her desk properly? What else went missing in her classroom? And what did the headteacher intend to do about the missing Beyblade? When Sandra told me about the phone call, I got the feeling that I was expected to go out immediately and buy the boy a new one. The following morning, Samuel's mother appeared at my door. Two teachers were off sick, a class was waiting for me, and the whistle was about to blow. Nevertheless, I agreed to discuss the matter very briefly.

She asked me why the Beyblade hadn't been locked away safely in a drawer. I was astonished. The fact that Samuel shouldn't have been playing with the toy hadn't seemed to occur to her. She folded her arms and settled in for a long argument. I pointed out that the discussion had finished and I had a class to teach, whereupon she strode off down the corridor, pausing only to ask Sandra how to make a formal complaint.

An hour later, the Chair of Governors was on the phone. Mrs Ahmoud had been to the education office, he said, and the person who handled complaints had passed the matter on to him. The parent was demanding an explanation, an apology, and a replacement, and although he hadn't time to deal with the matter now, he'd decided to make the complaint an agenda item at the governors' meeting the following day. With so many important matters to attend to, I couldn't believe we would shortly have a group of adults sitting around a table discussing Beyblades. Fortunately, when all the facts were known, common sense prevailed and the governors instructed Alan Warren to write a short, curt note to the parent and sadly for the children who used them sensibly, I decided to ban Beyblades the same day.

Parents can sometimes be intimidating, and occasionally aggressive, but the incidences of school staff being struck by a parent are still relatively rare, although sadly they are increasing. The pace of life today, the difficulties parents face in bringing up their children, the lack of deference for any kind of authority, the increasing levels of violence and unpleasant language in television dramas and the ease of being abusive using social networking devices are all contributory factors. Sometimes, headteachers feel that a school is the last bastion of reasonable and responsible behaviour.

Some of the most difficult situations I dealt with occurred when the affection that two parents must have originally felt for each other turned into extreme loathing and the child was caught in the middle. Children are incredibly resilient, even when awful things are happening at home, but occasionally all headteachers experience situations that tear them apart inside.

Stephanie had always been a challenging child, but we were successful with her and she achieved well. Years later, she brought her daughter Angela to us, asking if we could enrol her. There'd been an aggressive dispute with a neighbour and Stephanie and daughter were living temporarily with Stephanie's mother. I accepted willingly. I had a soft spot for Stephanie and I'd been pleased at what she'd achieved with us, but I soon learned things hadn't gone well for her. Out of work, she'd split with Angela's father and he'd made threatening phone calls, upsetting Angela. But Angela wasn't the easiest of daughters; she had her mother's quick temper and despite everything, she really missed her dad.

Nevertheless, after a difficult first month, Angela settled into our school routines and made several close friends. Before long, I barely noticed her, apart from the smiles we shared as we passed in the corridor. Then, when I gave her a part in our Summer musical, she seemed withdrawn, and unable to learn her lines. I didn't know that relations between mother and daughter had deteriorated to the point where Stephanie told her she intended to get sterilised, because she didn't want any more annoying children like Angela. And Angela wasn't getting on with mum's new boyfriend either.

One afternoon, her father came into school asking to see me. He'd been drinking heavily... Dutch courage before talking to me, since school had never been his favourite place. Angela, it seemed, was going to live with him now because Stephanie was refusing to tolerate her any more. I called Angela to my room and she sat beside her dad. No, she didn't mind living with him, but hoped she'd be able to see mum occasionally. Dad explained that his new girlfriend was expecting a baby and Angela managed a smile, telling him she was pleased. I explained to dad that we wanted to support Angela, and that if there was anything we could do he should call us. We never saw him again.

Weeks passed, and Angela's appearance deteriorated. She was having difficulty forming a relationship with dad's girlfriend and often came into school tearfully. She was allowed to speak to her mother on the telephone, but dad would stand behind her, making aggressive comments about his ex-partner. Angela's class teacher patiently explained that adults sometimes had relationship problems, reassuring her that mum and dad still loved her, even though they no longer loved each other.

Suddenly, dad decided he didn't want her any more and told Stephanie she'd have to take her back. He packed her things into a small case, and sent her to school. But Stephanie now lived outside London, and it meant Angela would have to leave her friends and the school she loved. Mum arrived at lunchtime, telling her she'd have to behave, because she wasn't putting up with any nonsense. I gave Angela a hug, and said how much I'd miss her. I had never seen a child so distraught. That weekend, she went into her mother's bedroom, put a black plastic bag over her head and fastened it with sellotape. She was eleven years old.

Fortunately, mum found her in time. Police and social workers became involved, and while lengthy investigations were made, Angela went back to live with her grandmother. She returned to us and we eased her through the final few weeks of her primary years, until eventually her mother was rehoused outside London and took Angela to live with her again. I never knew what happened to her after she left us, but barely a month went by when I didn't wonder.

Just occasionally, a situation could escalate to a frightening level, usually when the parent was suffering from severe stress bordering on mental instability. Mrs Pearson's son David was a withdrawn child who found it difficult to make friends, often coming to school looking as if he'd just fallen out of bed. Although generally well behaved, he could be roused by other children into bouts of intense and extreme anger. He'd clench his fists, his body would shake violently, he'd lash out, and then he'd avoid speaking for long periods.

But his general knowledge was good and his teachers worked hard to keep his interest. As we got to know his mother, she seemed literate and well educated and asked for lots of homework because she 'wanted him to go to university', but the homework was never completed. One morning, when David's teacher asked her why, she said she didn't need a lecture because she'd been a teacher herself. And a performer, writer, social worker, and psychologist. At that point, we began to worry. During the following weeks, David gradually became more unkempt and we learned that his father had walked out. David bitterly resented this. He began rebelling against his mother, arriving very late at school. When I met with mum, she defended her son unconditionally. 'I've examined the relevant statistics,' she said, 'and it's a proven fact that children who are late for school always do better in later life.'

Things didn't improve and we met with her repeatedly as David's behaviour continued to deteriorate. I was concerned that he'd told us he was allowed to do whatever he liked and tiredness indicated he'd been on his computer into the early hours. I felt Mum might need help too... a view reinforced when she withdrew him from school lunches on the contention that he was being bullied in the playground... and then to his utter embarrassment sat with him on a tiny patch of grass opposite the school, feeding him kebab and chips.

Then the school began receiving bizarre daily e-mails, always preceded by a telephone call telling us to check our e-mail box for an important missive that was about to arrive. The letters were threatening, accusatory and offensive. The following week,

Mrs Pearson managed to bypass our security system, slipping into school while a stock delivery was taking place. She strode into assembly, attempting to give every member of staff a letter stating that she'd spoken with people at a very high level, and had arranged with the governors to have me removed from the school immediately. I led her gently, but very firmly, to the school gate.

The e-mails resumed and I passed the matter to the local beat officer, who visited the house to give her an official warning. The next day an e-mail told me that she didn't take kindly to a visitation from a bumbling Mr Plod, and that she had employed a top barrister to mount a case against my evil regime at the school. I contacted the welfare services who gave her what they referred to as a 'telephone assessment' and then told me that she didn't appear to have any signs of mental breakdown. I feared even more for David and refused to let the matter lie. Mrs Pearson promptly removed her son from our school, only to put him in what she described as 'a delightful school with a proper headmaster.' Unfortunately, it had just been inspected and deemed a failing school. It was just what he didn't need.

Possibly the most spectacular parental incident of my headship occurred during an after-school meeting with social services and a family who were constantly re-housed because neighbours couldn't stand the chaos they created. The mother was Jamaican, and she had seven children, only two of whom had been fathered by the same man. We'd enrolled the youngest child. The mother dressed in violently coloured inappropriate outfits, she wore a wig and alarmingly long false pink fingernails, and she had a temper to match her appearance. Nevertheless, because her son had settled well and seemed very happy she gave us little trouble. On one occasion after dropping her child at the classroom door she offered to read my dreams. She was, she said, a specialist in that field.

Social workers were her mortal enemies. Understandably, they were required to check up on the well-being of her children, especially as the father was known to the police and had occasionally dealt drugs from the family home. Five minutes into the first meeting we'd arranged at school, mum decided she'd had enough of being dictated to by two white middle-aged women and began arguing about their right to question her. Shoving her chair backwards, she stormed into the corridor and kicked over a filing cabinet, making me relieved that I'd arranged the meeting for after school when no children were around.

At this point, father arrived, furious that he'd only just heard about the meeting and hadn't been officially invited. His eyes revealed that he'd been taken drugs before arriving, and the mother screamed at him to get out of the building. A teacher, putting up a work display at the other end of the corridor, saw what was happening and quickly phoned the police, while the mother took one of the metal music stands that were in the room and chased her partner along the corridor. He hurried down the stairs, while I tried to calm the mother down. Meanwhile, the two social workers hovered in a corner of the room looking ashen and frightened. I felt as if every serious parental incident in my career had been mere preparation for this one. The law eventually arrived at school an hour later, in the form of a very young bespectacled constable, but by that time everybody had gone.

I'm glad he didn't meet the mother. She'd have eaten him alive.

CHAPTER 12
THE COMPUTER REVOLUTION

'How do you spell bok, Miss?' asked Ahmed, age 10, deeply engaged in writing his story. 'There's no such word,' said his teacher. 'Do you mean back, or book, or block?' 'No Miss,' said Ahmed, 'I want the sound a chicken makes.... bok bok bok...

During the last forty years, technology has completely changed our world and never was a phrase so apt as 'the global village'. We own a bewildering variety of increasingly clever electronic devices and the pace of change is staggering. When I was small, if you wanted to make a telephone call you needed to find a big red callbox in the high street and push some pennies in a slot. Nowadays, we can keep in constant touch with anybody, anywhere in the world, using tiny mobile phones that can also take photographs, capture videos of family and friends, guide us to a travel destination, give us games to play, allow us to store thousands of our favourite tunes, stream a film, TV show or radio programme, find a good local restaurant, put us on the internet and give us access to a wealth of information which at the current rate of growth doubles every couple of years. From a very early age, children now experience everyday electronic items with buttons to push, touchscreens to swipe, toys which just need the insertion of a battery to do an amazing variety of things, or paperback sized tablets which offer a curriculum-wide range of activities.

When the first micro computers for home use arrived in the early eighties, there was enormous interest in them. Although they only had tiny memories... 16K was the standard to aim for and 32K was regarded as massive... they sold like hot cakes to everybody except the older generation, who saw no need for them and had no interest in trying to understand them. Education authorities looked very cautiously at this emerging new technology, and for a while saw no real need to put it into their primary schools. It was expensive, fragile and prone to failure, and the technology was not considered cost effective or useful enough to include in the curriculum. On a personal level, however, I found the whole idea of computers in the classroom fascinating, probably because I was interested in amateur film making, and the construction of a computer programme seemed to have much in common with making a home movie. Nevertheless, at that point I had no idea how to bring computers into my school, and anyway, our lean budget wouldn't allow it.

I had, however, purchased one device which was midway between a calculator and a computer, advertised as the latest thing in electronic wizardry for primary children. Called a Digitor, it was the size and shape of a dinner plate and had a number keypad with four selection buttons. Push the addition button, choose a difficulty level, and the child was presented with ten adding up sums. If the correct answers were typed, the device showed a beaming face. Get one wrong, and the face grimaced. The children thought it was wonderful.

Then, one evening, our Chair of Governors telephoned me. He'd bought a Sinclair Spectrum Z80, one of the first and cheapest home computers, and he'd practised a little programming using the standard computer language known as BASIC. He'd written a short counting programme that he thought might be fun for infants to use, and he wanted to demonstrate it to the staff. I agreed immediately, the teachers were interested to experience this new phenomenon, and in due course he brought along his computer, a portable black and white television to plug it into, a multitude of leads, and a cassette recorder.

In those days, computing really was an enthusiast's hobby, and the staff didn't find the talk very interesting, especially as our chairman wasn't very good at explaining what home computing was all about. Certainly, the whole process was primitive and crude. You bought a specialist magazine, found a programme you wanted to try, and then typed a couple of hundred lines of BASIC code into your computer, in numbered lines of text. The computer then read these lines of code at great speed, producing chunky animated pictures, characters and shapes that could be viewed on a television screen. Writing even the simplest programme was enormously time consuming, and if you made the slightest error, the programme wouldn't run. Once you'd spent many late nights debugging your programme, you could save it onto cassette tape. This was a risky procedure, because if it didn't record properly you'd had it, and it wouldn't load back into the computer, meaning all the code had to be typed in again. The simple addition and subtraction programme Alan Warren had written didn't impress the staff, even though he'd spent hours on it, and most of them thought a pencil, paper and text book, or indeed a Digitor, would be far more useful.

But it wasn't long before the BBC Microcomputer was introduced, and although far more expensive than the Spectrum, it had been specifically developed as part of the BBC's computer literacy project and was strongly targeted at schools. Here was a machine that had a proper keyboard, a large memory, a good sound system, an excellent and easy to use version of BASIC for programming, and the opportunity to store programmes on floppy discs, which were much faster and far more reliable than cassette tapes. Furthermore, programmers were quickly developing a superb range of software for primary schools, both on cassette and discs, and many education authorities flocked to buy these machines so that each of their schools could have at least one.

The ILEA, however, thought that the BBC Micro wasn't robust enough to withstand a hammering from lots of small fingers, and it opted to go with a different manufacturer, who produced a machine with the aesthetics and durability of a Sherman tank. Every London primary school was provided with one, together with a trolley for trundling it from class to class, a dedicated viewing monitor which was at least better than a television, a rugged cassette recorder for programme loading and a handful of simple educational software that had been designed by programmers employed in the authority's own newly formed computing department.

It was an expensive disaster. Most London primaries had at least three floors (one close to mine had thirteen) and hauling the computer up and down steep flights of stairs was a major task. At best it took ages, at worst it was dangerous. The programmes, designed by computer boffins rather than teachers, were primitive and dull. They were also prone to failure and some took fifteen minutes to load... useless if you wanted to incorporate them in a lesson.... and one computer for two hundred children was a non-starter. I decided there had to be a better way for my school.

In contrast the Spectrums were relatively cheap and the range of educational programs available to buy on cassette was rapidly increasing. After a couple of intensive staff meetings, we decided to arrange three fund raising days, with the intention of raising enough money to buy a Spectrum, screen, cassette recorder and tiny thermal printer for every class. Since I only had seven classes at the time, this didn't seem an impossible task. Fortunately, the parents were very enthusiastic about this emerging technology and gave great support to our fund raising. Within three months we'd achieved our aim. I built special wooden tray units for containing the equipment and its wiring, so that the computers could be easily transported to a store room for locking away at the end of the school day.

At first the scheme was very successful. Every child now had the opportunity of operating a computer several times a week, and although it wasn't seen as a serious educational tool, the computers gave the children a lot of pleasure as they played simple learning games and watched short animated stories that helped them with word identification and number rules. Even watching a computer ask for your name and seeing the screen greet you in person seemed a minor miracle at the time. And the local press was very impressed... here was a primary school with a computer in every classroom, and even children in the Nursery were using one at the age of four. Whatever next!

In fact, we'd known all along that the BBC Micro was a much better machine, and this was the way we needed to go. The graphics were more advanced, the sound possibilities vastly superior, and the new dot matrix printers were far more capable than the thermal type. Word processing, simple data handling, and desktop publishing were quickly becoming essentials for the IT curriculum, and the software for the BBC Micro was far more sophisticated. Also, instead of continually loading a word processor or data handling programme into a computer, the BBC Micro could be opened up and a dedicated chip directly inserted, giving permanent and instant access to these facilities. I telephoned the authority and asked if I could trade the clunky black machine they'd supplied for a little extra funding to purchase a couple of BBC Micros, but my request was refused. They'd be broken within a couple of days, they said, and they certainly wouldn't consider servicing them if we went ahead and bought some.

Back to the fund raising, and the diversion of some of our school budget. Within a year, we'd managed to buy six. Since we had an old stockroom that was no longer used, I decided to convert it into a special computing area for our new machines, and after Premises Officer Danny had obligingly spent a weekend repainting it, I persuaded one of our parents, an electrician, to wire it with multiple sockets. Now we had a small but impressive technology room for the older children to use. Since I had taught myself to programme in BASIC I felt confident enough to teach groups of children how to programme too, and they thoroughly enjoyed the experience. I felt we were really moving forward; many schools across the country still had only one machine, whereas at my school, every classroom still had Digitors, at least one Spectrum, and we now had a useful number of BBC Micros as well, plus the machine the ILEA had originally provided us with, although this was now rarely used.

My only concern was the refusal of the ILEA to repair anything the authority hadn't provided, and a peculiar problem began to emerge with our BBC Micros. Although disc drives were available at the time, they were expensive and relatively rare, so our programmes still had to be loaded into the computers from cassette tapes. Our computers were on for much of the school day, and they had proved eminently reliable, but now they seemed prone to refusing the tape signal, rendering the machine useless.

Although one of our teachers lived near a shop which repaired computers, it charged £25 pounds… a great deal of money at the time… just to open the case and have a look. Since there weren't many skilled repair technicians around, we had no option but to pay up, but as the machines started to fail regularly, this began to be an expensive worry.

Nowadays, virtually any problem with any piece of machinery can be investigated and resolved by spending half an hour on the internet, but that wasn't possible in those web-free days. I scoured every computer magazine I could lay my hands on… and found that one parts supplier was advertising replacement tape control chips. That seemed to be what I might need and I ordered one. To my great relief it was, and it came with a printed note saying that the original chips were prone to overheating. The greatest bonus, however, was that the new chip cost just 19p, so I ordered a box of them. The manager of the shop who charged £25 to look inside a computer now seemed a highly successful opportunist. Unfortunately, schools are always very vulnerable to these people.

And then, one morning, our school computing took a massive step forward. Georgia said that her brother, who lectured at a London college, had phoned the previous evening. The college was updating its computers and there were thirty BBC Micros with dedicated monitors that were longer needed. They were ours, provided we could collect them. I jumped at the chance. Fortunately Gerry owned a large battered old van, so Georgia, Gerry and I headed into central London the next day, parked tentatively on a yellow line, and staggered down two flights of stairs with the equipment. The monitors were massive… basically large televisions adapted to work as screens for the computers. Our small computer room at school was far too small to hold them all, so I decided to convert one of the unused classrooms on the top floor into a dedicated computing centre. Danny was proving to be an accomplished handyman, and I paid him to resurface the old tables with modern, stylish worktops.

By the time we'd finished, it all looked extremely impressive, until I switched everything on and discovered an annoying problem with the computers. They'd been adapted to work in tandem, fed with software from a central server, and it wouldn't be possible to use them as standalone machines. This was really worrying... I couldn't face heaving all the monitors downstairs and if we couldn't make the gear work, we'd need to hire a skip to get rid of it all.

In desperation, I phoned the company who'd provided the cassette control chips. It shouldn't be a problem, they said. You just need our conversion kit that will make your BBC Micros work independently again with disc drives. He could barely contain his delight when I said we'd be needing thirty of the kits. Some of the components and wires inside the machines had to be disconnected and the new boards carefully soldered in... a delicate process that took me a fortnight to complete. Fortunately, everything worked well and the staff were delighted. Now an entire class could be taken into the computer room and given a technology lesson, with all the children having a computer to themselves. We seemed to have reached the ideal situation at last.

But technology never stands still and already the BBC Micro was gradually becoming obsolete. Microsoft was capturing the computing market with its early Windows software, the design of the home and office computer was changing rapidly, and ICT was assuming a much greater role in the primary school curriculum. During our first Ofsted inspection we were left in no doubt that we needed to upgrade to Windows computers as soon as possible to comply with modern requirements, and since one of the inspectors worked for the authority, he promised to investigate some funding. We were eventually given enough money to buy five of these new, completely different machines.

But having had the luxury of a computer for each child, five wouldn't do, and I postponed ditching our older machines until I could afford some more new ones. Then, one afternoon, I was phoned by a company who specialised in fitting computer systems into primary schools. Would I be interested in receiving a quote? When the salesman visited, not only was the quote extremely reasonable, but if I paid up front and added another couple of thousand, their technicians would redesign our computer room and give us an additional three machines at half price. This meant that I would have twelve computers. Not as good as thirty, certainly, but it would mean a class could still comfortably have a useful computing lesson, with no more than two children to a machine. It was an offer I couldn't refuse, and I duly signed the cheque. During the Easter holiday, our computer room was rearranged and updated, and when we returned to school the children were highly impressed with our new, gleaming, state of the art ICT suite.

Everything worked well for seven months and then the problems began. A monitor overheated, made a loud pop, and smoke poured from the back. Three days later, another followed. Then components in the computers began to fail, several of the disc drives wouldn't load anything, and the screen colours faded or became inconsistent. At first, a technician from the company arrived promptly to put things right, but it became more and more difficult to contact anybody, until eventually we couldn't get in touch with the company at all. My only compensation was that other schools, equally short of adequate ICT funding, had got themselves into a similar predicament when the sharks had moved in. It was a bitter blow, and only through careful second hand buying, and yet more fund raising, were we eventually able to recover our position and buy equipment from reputable companies. I had been extremely naïve, and it was a trap I determined never to fall into again, although shortly afterwards I was tempted by an offer that would apparently give us more computers, but cost the school nothing at all.

A computer salesman called, and said that the government had put money aside, in the form of a bursary, for teachers to own a desktop machine. I checked his story out, and discovered that it was true. The government was very anxious for teachers to get up to speed with computing, and the funding could be applied for. The salesman said that as his company could produce computers in bulk, all we had to do was sign his form. He would then deliver our computers within six weeks and claim the bursary.

The computers didn't arrive. I phoned the company's managing director, who said he was extremely sorry, but lots of schools had taken up his offer and production was therefore taking longer than he'd hoped. And then, as I'd experienced with the previous firm, he became impossible to contact. I wasn't unduly concerned, as I could buy elsewhere and each teacher could claim their individual bursaries. Or so it seemed. Then I discovered that, incredibly, the government had already paid the company without confirming that the computers had been supplied. It was infuriating, and once again the taxpayer was footing a bill caused by incompetence.

But we had to keep moving forward. I was sure that computing skills were going to be increasingly important for primary aged children, and because I was fascinated by the changing technology anyway, I kept abreast of each new development. But this wasn't true of primary teachers in general. Many had found learning to use computers an unacceptably steep learning curve and they simply weren't interested. Others felt that technology had no place in the primary school and that skills of this sort could wait until children were in their teens.

Nowadays, it is accepted that all primary school teachers must have first rate technology skills, and ICT is a required feature of almost every subject in the classroom. The equipment is infinitely more reliable than it was in the past, but software can still crash, and since schools rely totally on computers for office administration, data handling and progress monitoring, it can be infuriating when things don't work properly. It is essential, therefore, to invest in repair technicians who can come to the school at a moment's notice and get things up and running again very quickly. Often these people are technophobes whose weekends are spent pulling computers to bits in the garage or making them do things they were never designed to do in the first place.

During my headship I encountered several talented repair technicians, none more so than Marcus Browne who arrived on the scene when school computers were in their infancy. Marcus was a hard-wired computer anorak, employed by the authority. Nervous, shy and very quietly spoken, he disliked contact with human beings, much preferring to solve intricate computer problems. At that, he was little short of miraculous. The local authority had quickly appreciated that computers would be a real asset to headteachers and their secretaries for financial accounting purposes and the fact that the available software was remarkably primitive didn't deter them from providing each school with an office computer, which came with an enormous steel storage safe, since computers were a highly desirable target for thieves. No longer would office staff have to struggle with calculators and reams of paper. Now everything could be done using a tailored accountancy package.

Unfortunately, the authority's finance people hadn't been happy with the package chosen by the IT department, and they arranged for a second company to integrate a reporting package into the accounting software. Very little field testing was done and almost as soon as the package was rolled out to schools, problems arose as the two pieces of software rapidly set about corrupting each other. Fortunately, Marcus was at the top of his game and was able to sort out anything. When he visited me, I'd show him into the stock room, where I had a computer set up for him, and he'd open his packet of sandwiches... invariably cheese and pickle plus a small pork pie... before starting work, because he knew he would probably have to re-install all the software. At the time, all software was stored on low memory floppy discs and he would persevere diligently for several hours before emerging triumphant from the stockroom. On one occasion in his excitement he leaned on a can of paint I'd been using to decorate a Nursery tricycle, and inadvertently sprayed the crutch of his trousers Prussian blue. On another occasion, a cleaner had inadvertently locked him in the room and it was an hour before he noticed.

But my personal favourite was Italian Angelo, who'd started work for a small computer firm in 2006 and then branched out on his own to service the schools he'd got to know, including mine. Angelo could dissect a computer like a fishmonger filleting a kipper and never had I needed him more than on the January morning Secretary Sandra came into my room with a very worried look on her face.

'Something's wrong with my computer,' she said. I sensed an edge in her voice. All our important pupil data was held on her machine, and she'd just updated everything for the annual census. 'Don't worry,' I said. 'I'm sure we can sort it.'

Like a naughty child refusing to move, her screen sat defiantly displaying a message that said a system file was corrupted and nothing could be loaded. I wasn't too worried. I'd backed everything up on a portable drive, and we had a recovery disc to sort the corruption out without disturbing the data files. I loaded the disc and left it churning away while I did something else. When I returned, it said that everything had been successful and I could now re-boot the machine. I did. And up came exactly the same message as before.

Now I began to worry too. Meantime, the rich pageantry of primary school life carried on around us. Ahmed from the Reception class had been sent up with diarrhoea, Charlie had lost his coat, Ben was soaking because Aaron had sprayed him with drinking fountain water. There was only one thing for it. Stop worrying and send for the cavalry.

Angelo sensed the urgency in my voice and arrived within the hour. 'Ah,' he cried, 'Issa seemple problim. I just replace-a the bad file.' Using diagnostics discs from his crumpled holdall, he transferred some files and booted up again. The same message returned and now Angelo looked concerned. 'Interesting...' he said, in the way that computer geeks do when they're baffled. 'It seem issa not a seemple problim after all...'

He explained that he'd need to disembowel the machine, remove the hard drive and try to recover the school data in his workshop. If it was still on there, of course. Sandra blanched visibly. I wanted to cry. What if we had to type everything in again? It would take forever.

And then I remembered the portable back-up drive. We plugged it into the computer in my room and checked the data was all there. It was. But the program running it wouldn't work. Angelo tapped away, but nothing. 'Donna worry,' he said. 'I come back sometime maybe next week. Then we feex.' I held his hand gently, and explained that if he couldn't feex it by tomorrow, I would be committing hara-kiri. A teacher popped her head round the door to ask something, but withdrew when she saw my face.

Although my computer skills didn't equal Angelo's, I took the portable drive home and sat up half the night trying to interpret messages saying that file lib.dib.exe.diddly/doo needed moving to C:/exe.lollipop.beta.bin. Eventually, success as things began to piece together. In the morning, elated, I plugged the portable drive into a notebook computer to re-assure Sandra we hadn't lost anything. Before my eyes, the notebook died, emitting a burning smell. Then, just as I'd decided that now was an ideal time to run screaming into the hills, Angelo re-appeared, smiling. He'd retrieved the data, and installed it on a newer computer he'd found in his workshop, which Sandra could have for a pittance if she wanted. I'm rarely over-emotional, but frankly, I was extremely tempted to give him a kiss.

By the time I retired from headship, technology in the primary classroom had gone through yet another evolution. Dedicated computer rooms had all but disappeared, along with the ungainly monitors and desktop computers that had seemed so sleek and desirable at the turn of the century. The electronic whiteboard… a large and highly versatile screen that could connect to the internet, show digital movies, allow a child to manipulate and move screen images, play music, tell stories and make every aspect of the curriculum more entertaining… ruled the roost for five years, but as miniaturisation became ever more desirable and inexpensive, the individual tablet took its place. It could do everything the class whiteboard could do, but on a personal level, and access a mountain of information at the touch of a button.

And all the time teachers have to keep abreast of what is happening in the world of technology, incorporating each new development into their lessons. But there's no going back, and in twenty years time the classroom of today could well be unrecognisable.

CHAPTER 13
CHALLENGING OFSTED

Miss, where are the elephants you're going to bathe?' asked Sophie, aged 6. 'No Sophie, said her teacher, 'I said I'm going out into the rain to brave the elements...'

In Victorian times, teachers dreaded a visit from the school inspector. If the knowledge and academic performance of the children wasn't up to scratch on the day the inspector visited, or the children were nervous and performed badly, the teacher's wages suffered and she was in danger of losing her job. It was hardly a fair system, but all the evidence indicates that today's school inspection system is just as unsatisfactory.

State schools have always been inspected, and it is right that they should be. After all, how else will taxpayers be satisfied that the education of their children is of a good enough standard? Few people would disagree that the possibility of a visit from an inspector is a surefire way of keeping a school on its toes, but the manner in which schools should be inspected has long been a matter for intense debate, which is why we are still far from getting it right.

When I began my headship at the start of the eighties, local authorities across the country appointed their own school inspectors. In inner London, The ILEA appointed inspectors centrally and allocated them to the boroughs. They'd often been successful headteachers who would have an intimate knowledge of the borough they were appointed to, and this was important. The needs of a school like mine, in an area of enormous social deprivation, were vastly different from those in a comfortable tree-lined suburb.

Because inspectors knew the requirements of their schools well, they always attended headship appointments. Indeed, they invariably knew far more about education, and the school, than the school governors themselves. Then, once a headteacher had been appointed, the inspector popped into the school regularly, until it was certain things were running smoothly. The inspector's role was to be supportive, helpful, and to occasionally find a little extra funding for projects that a new head wanted to initiate, especially if the outgoing head had let things slide a bit. Certainly, this had been my experience, and I was grateful for the support I'd received.

Occasionally, I was visited by an inspector from Her Majesty's Inspectorate. HMIs were highly trained and exceptionally astute inspectors who travelled the country and usually only stayed in a school for a day. Nevertheless, in that short time they were able to sum up what was going on with consummate skill. At the end of one in-depth visit several years into my headship, an HMI settled comfortably into one of my chairs after school and said 'Mike, your school is extremely impressive. It's no wonder the children are so happy and involved. But your room is a tip. It's the first port of call for visitors and it really doesn't create a very good impression.' I hadn't even considered it, but he was absolutely right. My room was filled with equipment needing repair, musical instruments we had nowhere to store, sets of books being sorted for classrooms, and even a pile of lost property. I attended to it immediately.

In those days inspectors were usually far more of a help than a hindrance. The school only saw them a couple of times a year, and even a local inspector with an inflated view of his own importance was little more than a minor irritant who'd be gone by the end of the day. And anyway, I welcomed inspectors. My school was running extremely well and I was proud of it. I enjoyed showing off what we were achieving, the staff were happy and relaxed, and the children loved chatting to visitors about their work. And then, in the early nineties, the method of inspecting schools changed dramatically.

Following the introduction of the national curriculum, designed to ensure that every state school in the country followed a prescribed curriculum in each subject, the Conservative government decided it would also be a good idea if all state schools were inspected in exactly the same way. This, it said, would be the fairest way of doing things. Parents already knew exactly what their children were learning, so now, with the new radically revised inspection format, they would also know how their child's school compared with any other across the borough or, indeed, country wide. Increasingly sophisticated computers in schools also meant the gathering of pupil achievement data was beginning to assume much greater importance, and the government could easily gather, analyse and disseminate it. Each school was already receiving an 'Autumn Analysis Package' detailing exactly how its achievement compared with other schools.

There were, however, serious flaws in the government's reasoning. Schools vary enormously in ability intake, local environment, social conditions and staffing levels. Some schools are highly selective in their intake, while others achieve exceptional results because the children are extremely able even if their teachers aren't necessarily of the highest quality. Some schools, working extremely hard with a low ability intake, can appear to be achieving poorly even when they are doing the very best they can for their pupils, and actually achieving many good things. Equally, data and statistics can be notoriously unreliable, sometimes giving a very distorted view of a school…. and they can be manipulated.

Nevertheless, the great inspection initiative went ahead, and the Office For Standards In Education, shortened to Ofsted, was born. It was decided that schools would be inspected every four years. At first, school inspections lasted a week and a team of at least six inspectors, plus a 'lay' inspector from the general public, would descend on a school and investigate every aspect of it. Since many schools were now being inspected at the same time, contracting companies had to be set up and a virtual army of inspectors recruited, and although some inspectors were very capable the abilities of many were questionable. Because so many were needed, it wasn't hard to be selected, and more than a few disillusioned teachers, deputies and heads saw it as an easy escape route out of the classroom or school office. Schools could therefore be put under the microscope by briefly trained people who had little knowledge of local conditions and often didn't have enough relevant experience to make valid or worthwhile judgements.

To add to schools' concerns, a chief inspector with very little teaching experience had been appointed, and he attacked teachers as never before, saying that 15% of them were ineffective and that Ofsted would play a strong role in rooting them out. The number seemed to have been conjured from highly questionable evidence, and it was virtually a mandate to bully. The only upside was that schools would be given more than a term's notice of an impending inspection, at least giving them ample time to prepare for the ordeal.

My first experience of an Ofsted inspection was not unpleasant. The lead inspector was keen to make this new, in-depth investigation as painless as possible, and although only one of the six had any experience of teaching in a primary school... something I would be far more concerned about today... the children and staff were keen to show what they could do. It seemed, also, that the team valued what my staff and I considered to be the essentials of primary education; creativity, healthy exercise, individual expression, art, drama and music. Since we were also achieving good standards in the basic skills of reading, writing and mathematics, the report we eventually received was highly pleasing. Our parents, children and governors were delighted, and we seemed to have been given a recommendation to carry on doing what we were doing. Perhaps this lulled us into a sense of false security, because four years later when we were given notice of our second Ofsted inspection, I had no idea that I would be experiencing the most worrying and frightening week of my entire career.

Two weeks before the inspection began, the team leader visited us for the day to gather the necessary paperwork, clarify arrangements for the inspection, and introduce herself to the staff and children. The day went well and she was made welcome by everyone in the school. She was impressed on her tour of the building and commented positively on the colourful displays in the classrooms and around the school, stating that we obviously had much to celebrate. We showed her our latest exciting project, an environmental park area being built at the far end of the junior playground.

As she left the school she was asked how she had enjoyed her day and she said that our children seemed exceptionally well behaved and hard working. Then, after the mandatory evening meeting with the parents, she telephoned to say that they were supportive of the school's work and that last year's Year 6 national test results, which had been a little disappointing for us, shouldn't be an issue. It all sounded as promising as our first Ofsted, but one thing nagged at me. When we'd first met, I'd asked the inspector why she'd left headship to join Ofsted, and she'd replied that she'd become bored with being a headteacher. This seemed very odd to me. I didn't understand how anybody could find the job less than fascinating… and I couldn't help wondering what her staff had thought of her. I was also concerned that the lay inspector was a farmer's wife. I hoped her knowledge of the workings of a tough London primary was greater than my knowledge of milking a cow.

On the first day of the inspection the sky was formidably dark and the rain torrential. We were obviously going to suffer wet playtimes and a wet lunchtime, meaning a greater likelihood of the children being fractious. One of the inspectors arrived fifty minutes late, saying that she'd been unwell all weekend and had travelled for hours in the rain and traffic to get to the school. There wasn't a great deal of sympathy; my teachers had all been in school since the crack of dawn, despite the appalling weather.

The manner of the lead inspector seemed to have changed too. There was a stiff formality, apparent in our first assembly. Since every child in the juniors played at least one musical instrument, we had prepared a short concert and the children were excited about showing how well they played and sang. The inspector, however, seemed unmoved. Some of the children, she felt, were 'overblowing' their recorders. How, I wondered, could anybody not be impressed by such a large group of small children playing the Chorus of the Hebrew Slaves, a difficult piece, with so much passion? After assembly the teachers hurried the children back to their classrooms. I'd forgotten how quiet the school is during an inspection. For the teachers it is the culmination of many weeks of preparation and the children catch the air of urgency and anxiety. I walked nervously around the corridors, but everything seemed fine. Then, during lunch, the lead inspector walked into the hall and said she'd like to talk to me in my office. I left my lunch untouched and hurried upstairs. 'I'm afraid we've seen a great deal of unsatisfactory teaching this morning,' she said. 'We're being generous, but from tomorrow we shall be very rigorous indeed.'

I was stunned. I knew my teachers well, and there had been hardly any staff changes since the last inspection. Then she talked about the dangers of the loose bricks on the building site in the playground, and it took me a moment to realise that she was referring to our environmental park area. I explained that the bricks would be built into plant beds within a few days, but she considered this unacceptable, saying that until they were cemented into position it would be possible for the children to throw them around. I said that my children weren't prone to throwing bricks around, but I would ask the premises officer to organise extra barriers during the afternoon. I hurriedly left my room to finish my lunch, passing several teachers on the way who seemed irritated and unhappy and who asked to talk to me as soon as possible.

After school the lead inspector visited me again, saying that more unsatisfactory lessons had been seen and I might want to tell my staff to be very diligent with their lessons from Tuesday onwards. I pressed the issue, asking her to explain which lessons had been unsatisfactory, and why. She quoted three, all taught by experienced teachers, running the lessons down in a casually destructive manner. She expressed doubts about one teacher's ability to be the literacy co-ordinator for the school... and yet that teacher's work had been chosen as a model by the local authority.

The inspectors left for the day and staff flocked to my office. They complained that inspectors had often only seen parts of lessons because they'd arrived late, or early, or not at all when they'd promised they would. One inspector had arrived fifteen minutes into a lesson and then left shortly afterwards, missing the beginning and end completely. On entering the room labelled The Nursery Class, an inspector had asked how old the children were. Although clear documentation had been given about the layout of the building, a Year 1 class had been confused with a Reception class, Year 2 work was mistaken for Year 1, and a Year 4 class was thought to be Year 5. Teachers also felt the inspectors deliberately sat in unnecessarily conspicuous positions and in one case actually at the teacher's desk, shuffling through everything on it, even though a chair had been placed discreetly at the back of the classroom. Feedback had been promised and not given, and only one inspector had spoken to any children. The day ended moodily with many teachers disgruntled, one in tears, and the weather forecast promising heavy rain for the rest of the week.

We managed to grind through Tuesday, the teachers looking more ashen by the hour, and then on Wednesday the lead inspector informed me that something would have to be done about the 'building site'. The additional barriers wouldn't keep the children away, she said, and one of the inspectors had seen a child throw a brick during the lunch period. I was astonished. The children were extremely enthusiastic about the park area and although the bricks had been there for a month, nobody had touched one. Her tone suggested the inspection might stop if the matter wasn't addressed and I spoke quickly to Danny, who immediately hired skips to remove all the bricks from the site. He was upset and angry, since we'd need to buy another consignment before the builders arrived or we'd have no plant beds.

The situation quickly deteriorated further. Wanda had been with me for many years and had proved herself an outstanding teacher, much respected by younger staff and parents. Now she looked drawn, tired and extremely upset. Her history lesson had been savaged the previous day, although only a small part of it had actually been seen. Then her gymnastics lesson had been grudgingly labelled satisfactory, the inspector saying that Wanda hadn't given any words of encouragement to the children, an accusation she strongly denied. I could appreciate the way she felt; tact wasn't emerging as a speciality of this team. Anxious and distressed, she asked if I would be a witness in any future observed lessons.

By mid afternoon there were more rumblings of discontent and I called an emergency staff meeting after school. Complaints tumbled out. Children's work had been sent to the inspectors on Monday and most of it still hadn't been returned. Some inspectors didn't appear to know whether they were supposed to offer feedback to the teachers. Inspectors had yawned through parts of lessons. Much school documentation either hadn't been read properly, or had been misinterpreted. The inspector covering religious education had stated that the school didn't celebrate all the children's religions, although she was forced to retract the comment when the teacher responsible for our RE curriculum gave her a list of the readily visible displays in the classrooms.

Following the meeting, Wanda spent an hour crying in her room. Two other teachers were in tears, and for the first time in my career, I had no sleep at all that night, worrying about my staff. I was extremely tempted to halt the inspection, call in the contractor, and refuse to co-operate further. However, had I done so, the school would have been forced to start the inspection again, and there was no guarantee that a replacement team would be any better than this one.

Interviews with subject leaders and governors caused additional problems. Several inspectors turned up late for the interviews, or had to be hunted down, or hadn't known who they were supposed to be interviewing, or for what. Questions were often aggressively suspicious, and many teachers felt that the inspection was all about trying to catch them out rather than assess them constructively. Towards the end of the week the staff had raised so many issues I called the lead inspector into my room and told her I intended to lodge a formal complaint about the aggressive and haphazard conduct of her team, and that from now on I would not speak to any of the inspectors without a witness present. It was bitterly disappointing, as just a week earlier we'd been so optimistic.

And then our disappointing test results the previous year became an area to be probed. Fifteen children had moved away from the area between Year 2 and Year 6, and they had been replaced by fifteen others, most of whom weren't so able, and I was now required to prove it. Small wonder that my special needs co-ordinator, in the middle of an interview with the lead inspector, asked her why she was so suspicious about everything.

Four school days had never passed so slowly, and on the Thursday evening, after the staff had gone home tired and anxious, I sat dejectedly in the staffroom with Georgia, waiting for the verdict. When it finally came, at 7.45, it wasn't as bad as we'd feared. But then a comment, almost an aside, immediately heightened the tension again. Under the current regulations, we were told, the inspectors had to decide whether we fell into a category known as 'coasting', because their interpretation of the data showed that our test results had been slipping slightly for the past four years. We were astounded. It wasn't true, and after the meeting I hastily scoured my filing cabinets for information to prove it. Right until the last moments of this inspection, we felt we had been fighting an unfair battle just to prove our worth. I went home miserable and depressed.

Schools rarely complain about their Ofsted inspections, however unfair they are, and for understandable reasons. It is far easier to accept the verdict, try to bring the school back to normal as quickly as possible, and leave the bad memories behind, rather than challenge a huge piece of government machinery. I began to understand why the Chief Inspector had proudly stated that schools were more than happy with the current form of inspection because only three per cent had ever complained. But neither I, nor the staff, were willing to leave things as they were. What we had experienced was unfair, and if nothing was done about it the same team could move on to other schools and cause the same distress. I decided that we had to complain, and see it through to the bitter end, however long it took.

Fortunately, the Easter holiday followed our inspection, and it was a much needed break for everybody, although I had little chance to rest. I spent most of it assembling a lengthy document, collating all the grievances that staff and governors had raised and showing how I felt the Ofsted guidelines for the conduct of inspectors had been clearly breached. I also decided to ask for the names of the last three schools inspected by senior members of the team, as it occurred to me that a precedent might be established.

A meeting of the governing body had been arranged at the start of the new term, to discuss the inspection, and I knew it was going to be important to have the governors onside. Those who had been in school during the inspection knew very well what we had experienced and they were keen that we should take action, especially as I'd sent every governor a photocopy of my document. Anthony, who always had a great deal to say but rarely followed it with any action, was less so.

'There is no precedent for a complaint like this,' he said. 'I can't give my support unless I know in detail what went on.'

'You were invited in during the inspection,' I replied. 'But you said you were having a very busy week. And you have all the documentation in front of you. That has all the detail you need.'

'Well, perhaps so, but I haven't had time to read it yet. We need a working party to examine all the relevant issues.'

One of the parent governors sighed audibly. 'I don't agree. Mr Kent and the teachers are obviously angry and unhappy, we all know this is a strong and successful school, and I think we should help.'

There was a murmur of agreement and Alan Warren turned in my direction. 'I think we're broadly supportive of what you want to do, Mike, but you need to be aware of what you'll be up against. From what I've read, you'll need to deal with the inspection contractor first, and then Ofsted if you get no satisfaction. If that doesn't work you'll need to go to the independent adjudicator, and then if you still receive no satisfaction, to an ombudsman. Frankly, I don't think there'll be much chance of success.'

'I know,' I said. 'But I can't let this go without trying.'

'Then do it. But keep us closely informed.'

The following morning I posted my document to the inspection contractor, expecting to wait a long time for a reply. To my surprise, I received a reply within days. There was concern that we'd been upset by our inspection and my document would also need to be passed to the lead inspector for her comments. The contractor's own principal inspector would then make a considered judgement. And sorry, but it wasn't within their brief to tell me which other schools had been inspected by this team.

Three months passed, and I jogged the contractor's memory. I was told that a reply was on its way, but the lead inspector was very busy on another school inspection and a complaint document as detailed as mine had never been received before. I pointed out that I was very busy too, probably even busier than the lead inspector, but I'd managed to put my document together quickly and I saw no reason why a reply should take so long. It arrived soon afterwards and I handed copies to my staff. The response simply increased their anger. It was clear the inspectors' versions of events were completely different from our own and in some cases we couldn't even recognise the scenarios they were describing. We were heading into very stormy weather.

Then, after a random but not very optimistic search on the internet, I couldn't believe my luck when I discovered a school that had also been inspected recently by members of our team, but I hesitated before calling the headteacher. Would she tell me the conduct of the inspectors had been fine? Had her school received glowing praise? Was I wrong in my assessment of our own school? I needn't have worried. The school had gone through a very similar experience to us and the written reports were almost interchangeable. The staff, like mine, were thoroughly demoralised afterwards. 'My teachers work their backs off, and so do I,' the headteacher told me when I phoned. 'I'm working all hours trying to keep up with everything. This was never an easy school, but we've turned it around in the last three years and I simply couldn't do more. Then this happens.' Two months later, I learned that the headteacher was taking early retirement, still angry and upset over what had happened. Her teachers were distraught, and it made me even more determined.

We were now responding to responses. I wrote, again in detail, quoting sections from the inspector's reply to my complaint document and pointing out the many inaccuracies. We'd also been sent our Ofsted report to read through before it was published. After a cursory look, I found spelling and grammatical errors, paragraphs that didn't make sense, sentences that contradicted each other, and serious factual errors. I sent it straight back, insisting it was altered and retyped before I would look at it again.

Then, out of the blue, I received a letter from an Ofsted official. Serious complaints had been received from the inspectors about the 'hostility and intimidation' they had been subjected to by me and my teachers. In a vaguely threatening manner, he stated that he would be sending a copy of his letter to the Chief Inspector. I replied immediately, saying that the manner in which the inspection had been carried out was completely unacceptable, and that I was astonished the inspectors were accusing us of intimidation. I trusted he would send my letter to the Chief Inspector too. He wrote again, saying he didn't intend to respond further, referring me back to his previous letter. I wrote and referred him back to mine.

Towards the end of the school year, we received a letter from the contractor's senior administration officer. Our views had been carefully examined, together with the responses from the inspectors, and he had made a brave attempt at sifting the wealth of detail on all the issues raised. He explained that he was replying in place of their principal inspector, who was on long term sick leave. Since Wanda, the teacher worst affected by our inspection, was also now on long term sick leave, it seemed a bizarre case of tit for tat. I couldn't help thinking what a dreadful waste of money and human resources the whole Ofsted business was, but at least the administration officer was sensitive to the fact that the inspection had been such an unpleasant experience for us, and he offered to visit to talk things over. He came a fortnight later and we warmed to him immediately. He'd been a policeman in South London, a lay inspector, and a chair of governors, and he had a passionate interest in primary education.

After a fruitful hour, some interesting facts emerged. As we'd suspected, it was becoming difficult to recruit inspectors as there was gold in other non-teaching educational hills, all well paid and less arduous. Nevertheless, at the end of the meeting, we had to inform him that we were still dissatisfied with the contractor's responses, and now intended to pursue our complaint through Ofsted itself. Our dossier, now over an inch and a half thick, was posted to the Ofsted complaints department the next day.

I heard nothing for weeks. When I eventually phoned out of frustration, an official apologised and said they had no knowledge of the dossier, although the name of the school did 'ring a bell'. He would look into it and phone back. Half an hour later a different person phoned and said that although it had arrived, it had unfortunately been accepted by a temporary staff member and left underneath a pile of documents. Nevertheless, it would be attended to as soon as possible, although due to their heavy workload this could take up to three months. I pointed out that it was already more than nine months since we'd been inspected.

Another five months passed, and Ofsted's tactics were becoming clear. Each time I phoned, I could never obtain the person I had previously spoken to, and there were lengthy delays before any letters were replied to. Also, the contractor's administration officer was now denying what he'd said to us, and I suspected he'd been instructed not to comment further. Tired of this seemingly deliberate prevarication I wrote and then telephoned again, demanding that the dossier was passed to the independent adjudicator without further delay. An official wrote back, apologising for the delay, but assuring me that our complaint was receiving Ofsted's full attention and that the dossier had now indeed been passed on. By now, my staff had put the inspection firmly behind them and the school had returned to normal, although there was still a palpable residue of anger.

Then, a full fourteen months after our inspection, the final response arrived. On many of the issues, sympathy was expressed but the adjudicator had been unable to make a judgement because the versions given by both sides were so different. Nevertheless, just over half of our complaints had been upheld and this, she said, would be brought to the registered inspector's attention. The team would be allowed to continue inspecting, but there would be careful monitoring by an experienced HMI to ensure it was undertaken correctly. We had made our point, and it was a victory of sorts, when Ofsted was in its relative infancy. In common with teachers across the country, our hope was that Ofsted would change, adapt and improve its practice through meaningful professional discussion.

Unfortunately it has done nothing of the sort. The inspection system has now been in existence for almost a quarter of a century, the public has been conditioned to judge a school by its current Ofsted report, and each year with governmental backing Ofsted has tightened its stranglehold on education... regularly altering its inspection criteria so that teachers are constantly wondering whether they are up to date with current requirements. An Ofsted inspection is now the thing most feared by schools, to the extent that the whole of a school's agenda is geared towards pleasing Ofsted inspectors. Their obsession with levels, data and targets makes a nonsense of everything that primary education is supposed to be about.

There are very sound reasons for teachers' fears. There is still too little control over the quality and ability of Ofsted inspectors. Indeed, when challenged, one Ofsted contractor had no idea what qualifications its inspectors had, or even whether they had qualified teacher status. Too many inspectors are intimidating, overbearing and on occasions bullying, with an enhanced view of their own importance. They have the power to destroy a career. In extreme cases, headteachers and senior leaders have been placed under such tension and stress they have taken their own lives. One senior leader, seriously ill, shouldn't have got out of bed, but she was so worried about letting her colleagues down during inspection week that she crawled into school and died in the school hall. Another took her own life because she was desperately worried her school wouldn't be labelled outstanding... as it had been in the two inspections under the previous head.

Because schools now have highly sophisticated computers and software, they are required to provide vast quantities of data on children's progress. An Ofsted team examines this before coming into a school, and then looks for evidence that corroborates what the data seems to be saying. This is an absurd way of judging a school. Data can be manipulated, it is often highly unreliable, and children are not... however much the government would like them to be... merely 'outcome units' on a sales curve. One headteacher, whose school was enormously popular and very successful, suffered a difficult inspection because her Year 6 cohort had many special needs children in it, and one child had died in a traffic accident during the final term, causing the other children considerable distress. The inspection team, led by a lawyer with no teaching experience who thumped her fist on the desk while asking questions, had little sympathy and gave the school a poor and eminently unfair report. The much loved headteacher was so distressed she hid behind a clothes rail while shopping in Marks and Spencer, to avoid being recognised when she spotted some colleagues from a neighbouring school.

Stories of bizarre comments and actions from inspectors are legion. The inspector who told a languages specialist that primary school children should spend lots of time writing Spanish down, not speaking it; the inspector who instructed a headteacher to conduct the pre-inspection briefing by mobile phone... because she needed to walk her dog; the school that almost failed its inspection because the team was offered coffee before being asked for identification; the inspector who told the head of a country school that the small scattering of autumn leaves in the playground was a serious health and safety hazard; the inspector who yawned her way through every lesson she saw, and then, when her rudeness was pointed out, said she had a medical problem which caused her to take occasional gulps of air...

Today, schools are given only one day's notice of an impending inspection... a far cry from the two terms they originally had. The short notice should, in theory, give a much more accurate vision of a school. In practice it doesn't, because the inspectors are in the school for just two days… barely enough time to make a worthwhile or accurate assessment. Though greater importance is now rightly attached to high quality teaching and learning, Ofsted has been unable to resist creating its own format for what a good lesson should look like, and how marking should be done, seriously stunting a teacher's creativity and freedom. When a school close to mine was inspected, eight of its teachers were graded good or outstanding and one was told she was merely 'satisfactory'. Four years later, in the subsequent inspection, the satisfactory teacher was told she was good, and six of the others were given a 'notice to improve', simply because the ground rules for a good lesson had changed. One teacher demanded to be reassessed, and by carefully following the tick-box guidelines for a successful lesson, he was suddenly outstanding. Another teacher was told her lesson was superb, but she couldn't be given an outstanding because the class was too well behaved and the inspector was unable to see how she dealt with difficult children… one of the tick box requirements.

There is no sense in this, just as there is no sense in trying to prescribe a format for a perfect lesson. Looking back to my youth, many lessons stand out in my mind. I remember Mr Johnson, who told us how Louis Pasteur stayed up night after night struggling to develop a vaccine for curing a nine year old who'd been mauled by a rabid dog. Mr Johnson's lesson didn't have a beginning, a development or a plenary. It was just Mr Johnson talking, from start to finish… but I still remember everything he told us. And we didn't write anything down in Miss Davis's music lessons either, but her enthusiasm fired my lifelong love of classical music. I've never forgotten the lesson in which she made us plug our ears tightly, told us to try composing some simple tunes with our classroom instruments… and then played what Beethoven had achieved when he was stone deaf.

As a headteacher, I gave my staff great freedom with lesson organisation, and I remember some corkers. The teacher who rushed her class off to see a whale that had become stranded in the river Thames… initiating a whole topic on nature and the environment; the lesson where the children were taught to do magic tricks with dice, and at the same time learning an enormous amount about number; the Year 4 children who were blindfolded for an intense serious disability experience… and the children's subsequent fount of inventive ideas for helping people with sight problems. Sadly, none of this would be acceptable today in our Stepford designed, Ofsted-aimed primary school lessons. Mr Johnson with his lesson about Louis Pasteur would be out on his ear.

The written report a school receives following an Ofsted inspection is intended to help it move forward. In fact, because the reports use a vocabulary of stock phrases designed by civil servants, they are of very little use at all. Often, two schools which are remarkably different can have reports which are almost interchangeable, and sometimes the comments made in the reports are merely risible. 'Where lessons were good,' stated one, 'the children were on task and interested.' Another report, commenting on teaching, said that the teachers should make sure 'each lesson is closely matched to every child's individual needs…' Noble words, but impossible in practice. Every child in a class will have differing needs and no teacher could possibly cater for all of them. Nor could an inspector. But then, it's far easier to criticise than actually do the job.

Near my home, a local primary school hired a huge advertising hoarding in the main road to promote its Ofsted rating of 'outstanding'. This in itself seems an extraordinary waste of money, but the comment the school had chosen to highlight stated that 'every child makes exceptional progress.' Since an Ofsted team is now in school for just a couple of days, it seems pertinent to question how the inspectors found time to discover that four hundred children were all making exceptional progress. Furthermore, it raises the question of how an 'outstanding' school should be defined. Another local school was recently rated outstanding, but in three years nineteen teachers have left, due to the stressful conditions and bullying attitude of the senior leadership team. In their final year, the children have no lessons in the arts at all. Instead, they are subjected to a constant diet of practice tests to ensure the data, which Ofsted cares so much about, reads exceptionally well. Frankly, this smacks of the dreadful 11-plus years and it's not a school I would want a child of mine to attend.

Recently, I was listening to a current affairs debate which included some questions about education. When asked whether performance pay for teachers was a good thing, a young publicly educated MP said he felt it was essential. 'It is absolutely right,' he stressed, 'that hard working teachers whose children constantly achieve high exam results should be properly rewarded.' A member of the audience then tentatively raised her hand. 'I'm a special needs teacher with challenging children,' she said. 'I work exceptionally hard, but I call it a success if I can actually get some of them to school. How, exactly, are you going to measure my performance?'

The old systems of inspecting schools were not perfect by any means, but we seem to have come full circle and reached a stage where, just as in Victorian times, good teachers and leaders fear for their jobs because the children's test scores are the arbiter of success. Pleasing inspectors seems, once again, to be the purpose of education.

CHAPTER 14
THE BUREAUCRATIC NIGHTMARE

Joan of Ark was put to death by fire after a bishop tied her to a steak.
Alex Age 9

Ask anybody what a primary school headteacher's job is all about, and they'll probably say 'Making sure all the children are happy, productive, experiencing a wide and interesting curriculum, and making good progress year by year.' To do this, a headteacher has to create a family atmosphere, where everybody from premises officer to deputy head is considered crucial to the success of the school and is genuinely cared for. Teachers who are trusted, encouraged to be creative, and given the freedom to experience real pleasure from their work will seldom be absent from school. They will also give enormous amounts of goodwill time outside school hours. The knock-on effect is that the children can't fail to thrive; they'll be immensely proud of their school and want to do their best for it.

As the years passed and I became more experienced at my job, I realised how lucky I'd been in my early years of headship. I'd had the freedom to shape the school as I wanted, with hardly any interference from the local authority and certainly no incessant demands for paperwork. I'd even had a great deal of time to teach, and if a member of staff happened to be ill, I interpreted the title 'headteacher' literally and taught the class myself.

But gradually the role of the headteacher changed, and now it is very different indeed. Headteachers still have the ultimate responsibility for ensuring children in their schools make good progress, but they have a management team to assist them. They rarely, if ever, teach. Neither does the deputy head or assistant head. The role of these senior leaders is to monitor teaching quality, assess and comment on a teacher's lesson plans, deal with poor behaviour, devise school documents and policies, and liaise with parents, school governors and outside agencies. And as society has become increasingly litigious, demanding, media driven and health and safety conscious, the pressure on schools and on a headteacher's time has increased enormously.

In order to comply with health and safety regulations, finance and employment laws, human resources requirements, fire safety and building standards, a school must store a raft of policy documents, and because they are usually regularly revised, they must be kept up to date. This isn't difficult, but it is enormously time consuming, and making sure you have the current version of a policy requires checking regularly on the internet, or on the local education authority's website. Small wonder that tiny but enterprising firms have made a fortune from offering schools definitive sets of policies that can be downloaded and printed out with the school's name pasted in.

In order to make sure schools are keeping abreast of requirements, they are subjected to an annual audit by officers from the various departments. These audits can take up most of a day, or in the case of a financial audit, up to three days, and they are extremely gruelling. What's more, the inspecting officer from one department, who will be a specialist in his or her particular field, hasn't the slightest interest in the fact that you have a school to run. As the years have gone by, the quantity of information demanded has increased dramatically, to the point where common sense has long since departed. This was amply demonstrated each time the human resources officer, the fire safety officer, or the health and safety officer visited me for the annual check, and each year I found them increasingly irritating.

A human resources officer would always settle back into one of my comfortable chairs, scatter the contents of his briefcase on the carpet, take out his checksheet, and expect me to give him my full attention for the next two hours. Because HR officers work in an office, they seem to have little appreciation that a primary school is full of young children, and whenever one knocked at my door to show me some work or ask a question, the officer would appear irritated, as if expecting me to shoo the child away. All the human resources officers I met seemed devoid of humour, but for graveyard dedication to the task, Mr Hardgrind, who visited me on three occasions, was certainly aptly named.

True to form, he starts by asking to see my grievance policy, a blow by blow procedure for anybody in the building who thinks I've been unfair to them and wishes to take the matter further. Two days previously, Secretary Sandra has updated it with the latest electronic version, and I proudly bring it up on the screen, but apparently that won't do, because the rules have changed. It needs to be on paper, and filed on a shelf with the other hundreds of policies I'm supposed to have. I ask why. My visitor says that it is now recommended procedure. But that's just silly, I say, and what about our carbon footprint? He doesn't like being called silly, and he hurrumphs, moving to the next item on his list. Could he see my Code of Standards and Behaviour for staff? I tell him that, unfortunately, I have no idea what he is talking about. Irritably, he says he needs to see a document that tells him what I expect from my teachers. It's a new requirement. Had I not kept up with the announcements on the authority's website?

I invite him into the corridor, asking him to look and listen. Art is everywhere. A class of infant children who have just finished a games lesson file past quietly. The children are smiling and happy. A nearby Year 6 class is investigating friction, absorbed and interested. Down the corridor, top infants are playing maths games. Every child is on task. The corridor is a model of purposeful, enjoyable primary education. See if you can work out for yourself what I expect, I tell my visitor. But that isn't good enough, and he puts a cross in a box on his tick chart.

Back in my office, I'm asked if the staff are familiar with the new restraint policy. The restraint of what, I ask. Children, he says. Actually, I say, we don't do restraint. Our school's too interesting for children to need restraining, and it's never been an issue. Well, he says, suppose I'm a supply teacher in a class where a child has gone berserk. I'd need to view the restraint policy before dealing with the child. I say that by the time he'd read it, the child would have beaten his mates up and broken the furniture. He harrumphs again and tells me I'm open to litigation if I don't restrain an unruly child in the approved manner.

I point to my computer, and the vast compendium of mandatory policies that sit on it. Does he realise, I say, that reading every detail in them all would probably take six months? I mention a frightening story from the previous day's newspaper about two part time police officers who wouldn't risk jumping into a lake when they saw a child out of his depth struggling frantically. Their superior officer regretted the fact that the child had drowned, but said that 'proper procedures' had been followed. What kind of bureaucratic state have we reached, I ask my visitor, when dreadful news like this merits only a couple of paragraphs in a newspaper? Mr Hardgrind raises his eyebrows, furrows his brow and looks at me steadily for a moment. Then he returns to his checklist. He doesn't consider commenting on the story to be part of his brief.

By the time another hour has passed, I have a thumping headache, I'm annoyed and frustrated, and we are still only halfway through the policies check. He examines each one carefully to make sure it is the current version and then purses his lips and shakes his head when he finds I have a copy that went slightly out of date last week. Fortunately, at that moment the silence is broken by Secretary Sandra knocking at the door. 'I'll be busy for a while', she says. 'Darren's messed himself again.'

'Choices', I say to the visitor I have mentally dubbed Mr Jobsworth. 'Sandra has several; Darren's mum's away. Gran won't come out. Sandra can walk him home, clean him up and risk mum suing the school because his trousers have been removed, or she can leave him covered in shit. What would you do?' Unsurprisingly, he doesn't seem to have a policy for that.

The visit from the Health and Safety officer is a similar drain on my time. Nobody would deny that health and safety is important, and we've certainly come a long way since Victorian times when young children were dying from the lead in the toys they played with, the arsenic in wallpaper dyes, or the poison from the bacteria in their feeding bottles. Unfortunately, though, we seem to have reached a state of overkill, causing some schools to stop children playing conkers, sliding in the playground in case of an accident when there is snow on the ground, or making leaf prints in case they get street dirt on their hands.

Taking a class to a place of educational interest... or simply on an outing for a day... now involves a host of risk assessment form filling and usually an initial visit by a teacher to assess the hazard level of the environment. And some things simply can't be predicted; a school sent a class on a nature trip to a safe countryside location, and while the children were waiting for the coach to take them home, a boy at the back of the line threw an uneaten bread roll at a child near the front. The roll missed its target and flew into a bush, disturbing a small hornet's nest, and a girl was stung. The parents sued, claiming the teachers in charge didn't have proper control of the group. Fortunately for the school, the parents lost, the judge stating that although the bread roll shouldn't have been thrown, the teachers couldn't possibly have known that there were hornets in the hedge.

I always knew, each time the health and safety lady visited, that we'd start off politely and then I'd quickly become frustrated by her demands. On this occasion, I'm not looking forward to the visit because she is a new, aggressive broom recently employed by the local authority. She had given my staff a talk two months previously and told them that their risk assessments for taking classes swimming weren't comprehensive enough because they didn't include provision for terrorist attack. Since the swimming bath was only one street away I didn't think we were at red light danger level and nor did the staff, who gazed at her in astonishment and sheer disbelief.

The lady begins by reminding me that we live in a litigious society. Yes, I say, I know. A society where attractive flower baskets are removed from lampposts in case they drop on people's heads, children's playground equipment is removed from parks in case somebody falls off a see-saw, and the parents' races at sports days are abandoned because at one school a parent tripped over in a field, broke her ankle, and successfully sued. It seemed the judge thought the headteacher should have examined the running area very closely for furrows before letting the race go ahead.

As the meeting shifts into gear, absurdities soon rise to the surface. Have I any pregnant teachers and if so, have I done risk assessments on them? They could be struck in the stomach by violent children, or fall over a trip hazard, or collapse from weariness if their teaching schedule isn't shortened. I explain that I do indeed have a pregnant teacher. I also explain that I have an excellent relationship with her, and that she'd tell me immediately if there was a problem, thus eliminating a lengthy risk assessment. And no, I don't tolerate violence from children in my school, so the likelihood of the teacher being hit in the stomach is virtually zero. Ah, but that's just the problem, she says. Virtually zero doesn't mean it would be impossible for the teacher to be struck. And verbal agreements are unacceptable, because however well I happened to get on with her, the teacher could suddenly change her disposition and deny that there had been any verbal agreement at all. I feel my shoulders sagging with the weight of it all.

We move on to portable appliance testing. Years ago, teachers could bring their own electrical items into the classroom. They often came with dodgy wiring or a plug that had been badly fitted, and looked at with hindsight this obviously wasn't a very good idea. Hence the emergence of mandatory appliance testing, where local electricians make a killing by inspecting pieces of equipment, their plugs, and the wires going into them, and then charge four pounds per item to put a little sticker on them that says they are safe to use. Affordable in the days when a school might have one magic lantern and a portable gramophone, but now? I ask the lady to count the electrical items around us and there are twenty in my office alone. Surely, I say, there isn't much need for portable appliance testing these days? Even an electric toothbrush comes with a moulded plug. Ah, she says, the wires could be frayed... and don't forget we live in a litigious society. Adding up the cost of a three day appliance testing inspection, I point out that it will cause a severe dent in the school budget, not to mention the upheaval getting all the equipment into one place to be tested. Well, it needs to be done, she insists, and our main electrical system needs to be checked too. I point out that the building was rewired a few years ago, but she tells me the current requirement is to have it checked annually. Just in case somebody decides to sue....

We're not even safe when we turn the staffroom tap on. Have I had the water tested, because there's always a remote risk of Legionnaire's Disease? I explain that I wouldn't let a diseased legionnaire within a mile of my school, but the lady has no sense of humour and her cold eyes simply stare at me for a few seconds. I explain that the loft tanks have recently been replaced at considerable expense, that we don't have air conditioning, and that water doesn't have a chance to stagnate... the three conditions that just might, if we're really unlucky, promote this disease. Nevertheless, I'm told it would still be a good idea to have it checked. Just in case. Better safe than sorry. Because we live in a litigious age. And no, the check isn't cheap because it's quite a complex test. By the end of the session, I'm wondering whether I should insist that our infants come to school in hard hats and combat boots before I allow them to climb on the playground equipment.

Two months later the fire safety officer arrives for a full inspection of the building, and this year he is more officious than usual because there has been a serious fire in a public building in the neighbourhood and the council has been severely criticised for not giving it a proper annual inspection. Schools are particularly vulnerable and every school in the borough is being given an intensive survey, he says. In the past we have not encountered problems with the fire safety inspection, mainly because Danny, and Fred before him, walked around the building every fortnight, checking that the alarms worked, the extinguishers were properly in place and functional, all the doors shut tightly, and any chemicals and combustibles were locked away. They also made sure the fire gates were easily accessible for a fire engine, particularly important when a fire safety officer suddenly arrives. Since I insisted the premises officer's records were always kept up to date, the fire safety officer was normally impressed, making a quicker inspection than he might otherwise have done.

But not on this occasion. This gentleman is grim-faced, disagreeable and determined to find as much wrong as he possibly can. I'm the first to admit that fire safety in school is essential and I point this out to him, but I also say that my school was built in the reign of Queen Victoria, when a bucket of wet sand was the cutting edge technology for dousing any flames. The corridors are narrow, the conditions are cramped and like many schools built last century, it's a stone fortress with incredibly thick walls. I tell him that I am not aware of any school like mine being burned to the ground and I ask him if he knows of any that have. Immaterial, he says. I mention that the only fire I recall in one of these stone learning emporiums during the last fifty years was a minor one and caused by arson… and then only because the school had foolishly decided it didn't need an on-site Premises Officer with a big dog.

He isn't interested and strides off down the corridor ahead of me. It is soon apparent that these gentlemen have a lexicon all of their own. Our walls are covered with 'hazardous substances' which need to be removed immediately. For a moment I wonder what he is talking about, and then I realise he is referring to the colourful children's paintings, sculptures and models that adorn every wall. Display has always been a strong feature of our school. Visitors, governors and inspectors constantly comment positively on it and the staff and children are exceptionally proud of what they have achieved. The fire officer, however, is not interested. He is concerned that if a fire occurred, the paper on the walls would rapidly burn.

I ask him what he recommends. It appears that the only solution is to remove all the art work and mount some fire resistant display cases in each corridor to hold a few pictures. I point out that this would strip our school of its unique character, and buying the number of cases we needed would be prohibitively expensive. That, he says, isn't really his problem.

As we move along an upstairs corridor, he points to the ground. A 'trip hazard', otherwise known as 'a child's coat that has fallen off its peg and dropped to the floor'. Ah, says the fire officer, but the coat shouldn't be on a peg in the corridor anyway. It should be in a locked cloakroom. I remind him that school cloakrooms were converted into mandatory inside toilets during the seventies, so the only place coats can be stored is on the corridor coat rails screwed to the wall. The officer licks his pencil, puts a cross on his tick chart and writes a few sentences, saying that it is his job to point out the dangers, not suggest what should be done with the coats.

Then he examines the classrooms and halls. Hopeless, he says. Breaking every rule in the book. The school should be equipped with smoke alarms and water sprinklers that turn on automatically if a fire is detected. The small panes of frosted and wired glass set into the corridor partitions could explode if heated and they need to be changed for fireproof glass. The kitchen should be double lined and the serving hatch bricked up to avoid fire escaping from the kitchen. Each hall and the end of each corridor should have automatic doors which glide shut if the temperature rises. And those cabin hooks on the doors to keep them open as the children come in and out of assembly? Dear oh dear. Fetch a screwdriver and get them off immediately, never mind the fact that the knob on a swinging door could take a child's teeth out. And although our fire alarm has been deemed fine in the last inspection, I am now told it needs updating. At the end of the morning I calculate that we would need to find at least £200,000 pounds if we are going to implement everything he has recommended. And we simply haven't got that kind of money.

Within days, his report arrives in school, with a covering letter stating that the building will be re-inspected in six months, by which time it is expected that the most serious deficiencies will have been attended to. If they haven't, the fire department has the option of shutting the school down until we are fully compliant with their requirements. Two days after that, a letter arrives from the local education authority, saying that a copy of the fire report has been passed to them, and if required they can arrange three quotes from approved building firms, including one from their own in-house team. Any of these building firms would, they say, plan, oversee and undertake the required works if my school governors and I want to take that option.

I immediately wrote back and said that we couldn't afford any of it, particularly as we'd already had to pay for a massive water leak from a pipe under the playground earlier that year, and that I'd be extremely grateful if they could shoulder most of the cost. Sorry, they said, we can't afford it either, but if the work was carried out by their own team, the money could be paid back in monthly instalments from the school budget over the next four years.

This was extremely worrying. Although I still felt that the likelihood of a fire was virtually nil, we were in a precarious position, and failure to stay within the law could leave us seriously vulnerable. I talked through the problem with my school governors at their next meeting and it was agreed that we would need to stall the work. Our budget was already extremely tight, and even if we shaved a little money from other intended expenditure, we could still only afford to spend a few thousand on the fire safety work.

And then an astute parent governor, who'd run a local pub and experienced problems with officious fire safety officials himself, suggested we scrutinise the fire officer's report with extreme care, investigate which recommendations were legally mandatory, and then pay for a second opinion from a private fire safety expert. Meantime, representatives from three firms visited the school, drew up comprehensive estimates for the work and submitted them for our approval and a decision. It was no surprise to us that although all three estimates seemed extortionate, the authority's estimate was slightly cheaper than the others.

But there was even better news to come. The report from our expert second opinion seriously questioned some of the fire officer's recommendations. We did not need automatic water sprinklers, the existing extinguishers were up to date and adequate and so was the alarm system, the glazed glass did not need to be replaced, the kitchen equipment was satisfactory and safe, and filling in the serving hatch was unnecessary. It would, however, be important to site fire sensors near all the classrooms, extend the wiring so that the alarm could be clearly heard in every corner of the building, and fit proper self closing fire doors on every corridor, all of which would bring us inside the law. What's more, he could recommend firms that could do the work quickly and at a reasonable price, probably no more than £30,000.

'What about the 'hazardous wall substances?' I asked. 'I really don't fancy stripping all the children's work from the building.'

'Just argue the toss,' he said. 'Every primary school worth its salt has children's work all over the classroom walls and corridors. It's what every parent expects to see when they walk into a school. You just happen to have a lot more than most, and it looks terrific. I wouldn't mind betting that if you offer to keep it six feet away from any door or hall entrance, they really won't worry too much.'

And fortunately, they didn't. I also discovered some contingency money that hadn't been spent, and within four months the essential work had been completed and passed by a different inspector. Another crisis averted, but it certainly brought home to me how much time all these issues took away from the one thing that really mattered... spending time with the children in my school.

CHAPTER 15
POLYTHENE, PIGEONS AND
ECCENTRIC ELECTRICS

'Is there anything your class teacher could provide that would make you happier at school?' the Ofsted inspector asked naughty Simon, aged 10, dumped unceremoniously on the threadbare matting outside his classroom. 'Yeah,' said Simon, 'Thicker carpets.'

Much of a primary headteacher's time is taken up with minor inconveniences caused, either innocently or deliberately, by the little human beings in your school. A day would seem to be going well, and then you'd be informed that a sink in the cloakroom had been blocked with tissue paper, causing water to overflow, cover the floor, and seep into the stockroom beneath, wrecking piles of exercise books. Since we had no CCTV, and putting it in a cloakroom would be frowned upon anyway, it was usually almost impossible to catch the culprits unless somebody had seen them and decided to 'grass'.

Toilets seem to hold a fascination for children, and my school seemed to have more than its fair share of young plumbers who would enthusiastically rearrange the piping so that a sitter would suddenly be showered with water, or a seat would slide from its moorings, or a bowl would be blocked with an entire roll of toilet paper. Even when we spent a great deal of money refurbishing the toilets on each floor, instructing the plumbers to bolt everything down as tightly as they could, the children still had a great deal of fun with the taps. Originally we'd had screw turn taps and these could easily be left running to flood the floor, so during the refurbishment we opted for the push button type, which cut the water off when the button was released. We were certain this would stop little hands leaving the taps running, but of course it didn't, because after a while the push buttons stopped working and despite liberal doses of easing fluid the taps either ran continuously, or they didn't run at all.

During most weeks, I would be called to an incident. A parent might be using abusive language in the playground, a dubious stranger might have wandered into the school, a problem with stolen money or belongings might need to be addressed, a piece of technology might be refusing to work meaning a teacher couldn't start a lesson, a visitor might have parked across the fire gates, or a child might be misbehaving in a classroom and need removing to the quieter confines of my office. But these were all part and parcel of school life and things I expected, and since I tended to do most of my administrative work in the evenings at home, I usually had plenty of time for troubleshooting, and moving quickly from corridor to corridor helped to keep me fit and agile.

However, in every headteacher's life there will also be bigger problems to deal with, and I certainly had my fair share. Some seemed to be perennial... a boiler would behave erratically as soon as the ground was thick with snow, and spare parts were always difficult to locate; there would be a problem with the electricity, suddenly plunging us into darkness in the middle of winter; a pipe in the kitchen would become blocked in the middle of serving lunches to everybody or the freezer would pack up. But often, the biggest headaches were caused by upgrades to the building, such as the fitting of a new roof or the refurbishment of the windows.

The windows at my school had needed attention since the day I arrived. Although they were Victorian and rather attractive, most of the sashes had broken and many windows wouldn't open, or they'd stick halfway, usually when it was pouring with rain outside, because the wooden frames had become distorted over the years. Some were so weather-beaten Danny had nailed them shut in case they fell out of their frames. And then, after a particularly hot Summer when children had been sweltering because their classroom windows wouldn't open properly, I was delighted to receive a letter from the local authority saying that they'd taken notice of the letters my governing body had written, and they were sending one of their buildings officers along to inspect the windows, with a view to renovating or possibly replacing them.

The buildings officer was a very pleasant chap, and he agreed that something certainly needed to be done before a window fell out and injured somebody. Perhaps naively, I'd assumed the local authority would arrange for a firm to do what I'd done to my house: remove all the old windows and replace them with tough white polycarbonate ones closely modelled on the originals. Then, unlike the wooden variety, they'd probably last until the building fell down.

Unfortunately, the officer explained, it wasn't as simple as that. Firstly, there was the question of expense. The authority didn't have the money to replace the windows, but it could make them as good as new with a skilful but less expensive refurbishment.

Then the officer explained that even this route wasn't straightforward. At the time, issues with improvement or renovations in London schools were complicated. The responsibility for decorating the inside of the building, including the window interiors, lay with the school, while the local authority looked after anything to do with the outside. And since some of the windows in the sheltered sections of the building weren't disintegrating, only the worst ones in danger of falling out would be replaced. The rest would just be sanded and repainted. Nevertheless, it was agreed that something needed to be done quickly, and the officer said that he'd arrange for estimates from three approved firms. After further meetings with the buildings officer, the school governors, the finance officer and the head of the building firm appointed to undertake the work, a contract was signed. It was all rather bewildering; the outsides of the windows were to be refurbished and the insides untouched, unless the insides were damaged while the painters were refurbishing the outsides, in which case they'd touch up the insides…

After an extended half-term holiday during which the school was covered in scaffolding, the work began. The authority had decided to kill two birds with one stone; the brickwork would be steam-cleaned while the scaffolding was up and to prevent muck flying everywhere the building was shrouded in thick sheets of polythene. From the inside, the building resembled the Palm House in Kew Gardens, but it was impossible to see out of any window to know whether the sun was shining or the rain was pelting down. Since we were experiencing April showers, runners had to be organised every few minutes before a playtime to check if the children could go out. When the wind blew, the polythene often broke from its moorings and flapped about like the wings of the mythical Roc, making the teachers' voices difficult to be heard in the classrooms.

But far worse than this was the brick cleaning machine, which made a fizzing, high-pitched squawking noise. Teachers complained that if it was directly outside their rooms, teaching became impossible. You could guarantee that if you moved out of your class for the morning, the next bit of wall to be done would invariably be just outside the room you'd escaped to. Several times I'd just started assembly in the main hall when the machine fired up, drowning my voice. It certainly amused the children, who began to think that the workmen were doing it deliberately. After a while, so did I.

Nothing seemed to have been co-ordinated. When we stopped for playtime, the workmen stopped, too. When a class moved to a different venue while the scraping and painting was done, it always seemed to be half-finished when it was time for the class to return. A teacher could be in the middle of a lesson, with the children's attention finely tuned, when two workmen would wander along the planks outside the window, discussing in colourful language how many pints they'd downed the previous night. Another workman removed the nursery door one morning to replace the glass panel in it, thereby offering an escape route for thirty very small children. Even worse, he'd left his Black and Decker plugged in on the bench by the door. It only takes one inquisitive little finger.

Danny watched the proceedings like a hawk, determined that the work wouldn't go on a day longer than necessary,. His good nature meant that it was hard to upset him, but he refused to budge when a workman drove into the car park with a bald tyre and no tax disc. And I felt sorry for the painter who reached through a window and accidentally knocked a guitar off its hook in the Music Room, damaging the tuning pegs; Danny pursed his lips, shook his head gravely, and told him it was the headteacher's personal instrument and had cost £600.

And then, two months later, just when the work had been finished and we thought the ordeal was over, the muck from washing the brickwork clogged a drain in the playground. Since the painters had a high pressure hose with them, one of the workmen had a bright idea and said it would only take a moment to shift the blockage. Unfortunately, the playground drain was linked to the one in the infant toilet, and a barrage of filthy sludge suddenly shot around the toilet walls and into the corridor. Danny nearly had a heart attack, and had to hire outside help at the weekend to make the place habitable again. At least there were no children in the toilet at the time. I've no idea what I would have told the parents...

Fire alarms can be another source of misery. At least once in a school year, our alarm would be set off, a small hand having whacked one of the little glass-covered red boxes screwed to each corridor wall. This had been an impossibility when the boxes had been fitted well above the reach of a child, but under new health and safety regulations it had been decided that our school should receive a brand new alarm system and a set of the latest alarm boxes that would be discretely positioned at various access points on every corridor.

I listened in awe as the electrician proudly explained the high-tech console that controlled the red boxes positioned around the school. It worried me that the boxes were well within the children's reach, and one was perilously close to the juniors' playground exit, but the electrician explained that the authority's current thinking was that children were sensible, mature little beings whose fingers wouldn't possibly go near a fire alarm unless they had actually spotted something burning. I felt I knew young children rather better than the pundits who had such faith in their innocence, and during the first fortnight after the fitting of the alarm my fears were repeatedly proven.

On Tuesday, the alarm suddenly goes off. It's an incredibly piercing sound… far louder than the previous alarm and worse than Year 3's first descant recorder lesson. I come out of my room to find teachers in the corridor, their bodies vibrating. Then the noise stops as suddenly as it started. I hurry to the control console, where Danny, who has heard the alarm from his house, has switched it off. Meanwhile, two teachers have discovered eight year old Mary, a child with special needs, standing sheepishly near a little red box with its glass broken. Her brother George is beside her. George is into high-tech. He looks at me carefully. 'Me sister dunnit,' he explains.

The next day, while I'm supervising lunchtime film club with a room full of infants, the fire alarm goes off. Teachers emerge from the staffroom, puzzled. A fire drill? Should they go outside? Should they fetch their registers? Aaron is discovered, his mates having grassed him up. Aaron is no saint but he swears he didn't mean to do it; he just happened to be waving his arms about when he hit the funny little red box. The following morning in assembly I explain the importance of treating the new alarm with respect. I tell the story of the boy who cried wolf, and the children listen intently; the message seems to have struck home. At 3.30pm, the alarm goes off again. By now, the staff have almost come to expect it, and I have a sinking feeling in the pit of my stomach.

The bell rings interminably. Dammit, Danny is at a premises officers' meeting, so I open the control box myself. I stare at the flashing console, but it might just as well be the flight deck of the Starship Enterprise. I try to remember what Danny had said. Turn the key twice, pull the lever across, push a button. After five permutations, the noise stops. Meanwhile, a parent governor has cornered Andrew by the playground gate. Andrew left us last year. He swears he leant against the button by accident, with the innocent expression he'll no doubt be using to tell the judge he was only borrowing the motor to do some shopping for his gran.

The following week, I call the electrician. Could he remove this particular box? It is so close to the playground and a child can easily break the glass at hometime and scoot out of school. There is a sharp intake of breath. Difficult, with this new high-tech system. It would mean some wiring adjustments and he'd need permission for that. And there's the expense, of course. Could it, then, just be put out of the children's reach? Another intake of breath. It could, but you've got the same wiring problem, and what if a child discovered a fire? The alarm goes off again the next afternoon. I rush downstairs to find a quivering delivery man in the corridor. He tells me he was just unloading some boxes of netball equipment and he smashed the glass accidentally and Jesus doesn't it make a racket…

Since the corridors were filled with children's art work, I was extremely tempted to cover the little red boxes with pictures, but decided this would get me into a lot of trouble with the fire safety officer and was merely tempting fate. Fortunately, as time passed and my warnings in assembly seemed to be having some effect, the children began to realise that breaking the glass in the boxes was not really a good idea, and their little fingers moved on to other misadventures that didn't involve turning out the entire school into the playground.

An old building, architecturally attractive though it may be, can give rise to many annoying problems, and since most London primary schools were built around the turn of the century, heating and electrical systems could be particularly troublesome and expensive to sort out. During one Winter, after a particularly heavy snow fall which made me wonder how my teachers were going to get home, our struggling electrical system simply gave up and broke down.

The building was prone to draughts at the best of times, and the temperature quickly plummeted. Although I sent a message around the classes saying that children should put their coats on, this wasn't easy because many of the classrooms, and two corridors, had been plunged into darkness. Before long, Danny appeared to tell me that he'd traced the source of the problem. A fuse had blown. I breathed a sigh of relief. I was certain he would have a spare, and things would be back to normal within minutes.

I should have realised that things are never that simple. In this case it was a massive 160 amp cartridge fuse, encased in metal and as big as a child's fist. There was also an acrid whiff of smoke coming from the main electrical cupboard in the hall. I assumed that the fuse had been there for many years... one of those things that nobody ever checks or worries about until it goes wrong. While classroom assistants searched the toilets, retrieving terrified infants who'd stumbled for the door in the semi-darkness, Danny quickly checked the contact breakers. Several teachers poked their heads around doors demanding to know which twerp from Year 6 had run around the school switching the lights off.

The problem quickly escalated. The cook hurried upstairs to tell me that her freezers were down and it wouldn't be that long before the food supplies started thawing out. I had to make a quick decision. I didn't want to close the school, but if we couldn't feed the children, keep them warm or teach them effectively we didn't really have much option. After a hasty consultation, the cook decided she could just about manage sandwiches and salad, and the teachers said they could probably get through the rest of the day with just the meagre amount of emergency lighting on. I breathed a sigh of relief... until Danny told me that the boilers had gone down too. There'd be no heating or hot water. Now there was no alternative; we would have to close.

There was one other option. If we could get the fuse repaired before the end of the day, it would save me sending out a letter to the parents about the closure. Many of them worked and I knew how inconvenient it would be if they had to find somebody to look after their offspring for a day or two. Secretary Sandra quickly rang the local authority for the name of a reliable electrician, they put her in touch with one, he arrived quickly, and probed the fuse cupboard with a torch and a test meter. 'That's definitely your problem!' he said triumphantly, pointing to the massive fuse.

'So you can change it?' I asked.

There was a sharp intake of breath. 'It's a very old one. Must have been there since the place was built. I reckon it'll take a good couple of days to find one of these. That's if we can find one, of course. Frankly, I doubt it. Might have to completely rewire this lot, but I'll see what I can do. I'll be back on Friday morning.'

I informed the staff that we'd have to close until then, and I hurriedly photocopied letters to the parents, explaining what had happened and apologising for the inconvenience. Next morning, I stood at the school gate with Danny. Many parents had come along to see whether, by some miracle, we were opening. Most, as usual, were very understanding when we said they would have to take their children back home. Mr Smith, as usual, wasn't.

'So, what's all this about, then?'

'Sorry, we've no lighting, heating, hot water, or cooked meals.'

'Don't you lot have any contingency plans for emergencies?'

'Not for this, I'm afraid. It's a unique situation. We've never had this one before.'

'Well, it's fucking inconvenient. God only knows how we managed to win two world wars.'

He stalked off down the road, his wife trailing behind him and looking embarrassed. Neither of them worked for a living, but the idea of simply looking after his three lively children for an extra day instead of handing them over to the school must have been a bridge too far.

I couldn't believe my luck when the electrician drove into the car park early in the afternoon. He'd managed to locate a fuse, the building was soon light and warm again, and we put a large notice outside the school gates saying the children could return in the morning. On Friday, I received a call from a parent governor.

'Is school open again, then?' she asked. 'Nobody wrote and told us.' It was one of those moments when I felt that whatever I did, there'd be somebody wanting to complain about it.

Closing my school was something I tried to avoid at all costs, and throughout my years at the school there were very few occasions when I had to do so. Most problems, even major ones, could be dealt with while the children and teachers carried on working, often unaware that I was wrestling with a problem caused by a warning from an official that if a particular repair wasn't carried out, the human beings in the building could be in danger. And there was no finer example of that than the day I suddenly realised we had a problem with pigeons.

There's nothing pleasanter than hearing wood pigeons cooing in the countryside on a warm, fresh Spring morning. But town pigeons, well, they're a different kettle of feathers altogether. They'd always been something of a nuisance to us. They would fly down from the roofs of the flats surrounding the school and stroll into the playground, heads bobbing, hunting for food scraps. Before we became an accredited healthy school, we had sold breaktime biscuits and the pigeons scrabbled for crumbs in the playground, calling their mates to join in the feast. Pigeons might not be very bright, but they soon become bold. Once the playground scraps had been swallowed, a few wandered into the building searching for more, and then couldn't find their way out again. When children discovered a pigeon in school, some, unsurprisingly, were frightened. Others wanted to stroke them. A few chased them up the corridor, causing the birds to make rapid bowel evacuations on the floor. Or even worse, in mid-air.

Then the days of increased school security arrived, and doors were no longer left open. But teachers sometimes inadvertently left classroom windows open at hometime, and pigeons began flying through those instead. There's nothing more disconcerting for a teacher than sitting the children down while the register is called, and then finding a pigeon cooing from its perch on a high window ledge. Fortunately Danny had been working away at the problem. He'd bought a telescopic metal pole, and screwed what looked like a fisherman's net to one end of it, and a brush to the other. The brush end soon proved useful when a cleaner was sweeping the stairs after school and was startled by a flapping noise coming from behind a staircase radiator. A pigeon had perched on it for warmth, fallen behind it and then sat there flapping its wings in fright… until Danny managed to give it a releasing shove with his brush and trap it with his net. Armed with a couple of these home-made tools, we felt equipped to tackle any avian intruder.

And then the pigeon problem suddenly became very serious indeed.

Sweeping the playground one morning, Danny noticed three pigeons flying into the loft area of the building. Danny rarely went into the loft. Provided the water tanks aren't leaking it's not a place you spend time in, but he thought it best to climb up and have a peep. His eyes opened wide with horror. Grilles at both ends of the loft had broken away, the whole area was thickly covered in white bird droppings, adult birds were careering to and fro around the roof beams, eggs were nestling in the rafters, and recently hatched youngsters blinked at him in the sunlight. Hurrying back down the ladder, Danny immediately sent for the cavalry.

When the pest control specialists arrived they were extremely concerned. Because the pigeons had been using the loft space for a long time, the rafters had begun to rot, and it seemed it would only have been a matter of time before some of the timbers collapsed and plunged through a classroom ceiling. Covering themselves with special protective clothing, the workman spent a week in the loft removing the eggs, scraping out the worst of the mess, sealing the skylights with metal mesh and fixing pigeon resistant spikes to the roof and window sills. A sigh of relief and two thousand pounds later, we thought the problem had been solved. Until Monday morning, when a teacher on the top floor discovered four pigeons in her classroom and mess all over the place. They'd probably been hovering all weekend, annoyed that they couldn't get into the loft as usual. Presumably they couldn't believe their luck when they found an open window nobody had noticed. From then on, all teachers had strict instructions to close every window at the end of the day.

A headteacher always has to be ready for the unexpected. The staff and children need to have confidence that you're ready and able to deal with any difficulty that arises, whether it's bullying in the playground, a broken water pipe or a major disturbance. One warm and sunny May morning, my goodwill towards the world was suddenly shattered when a teaching assistant hurried up to me as I munched my meat and two veg at lunchtime. The neighbourhood surrounding my school had never been known for its tranquillity, and there'd been a gangland shooting in the main road at the weekend. There was a murmur of gossip about it as the children filed into school on Monday morning, and then it seemed to be gradually forgotten. Until Wednesday lunchtime, 'A bloke has just rushed into the corridor,' said the teaching assistant breathlessly. 'He says he's being chased. Can you have a word with him?' Several children had overheard the assistant and were peering outside as I approached the man. He was leaning against a cupboard, panting.

'I need help, mate,' he said. 'I'm a reporter and I went to interview the family of the bloke who was shot. I'm being chased by a gang of youths.'

I'd heard this kind of thing before. Some years ago, a woman had walked into the office, said she wanted to register her fifteen children and then proceeded to remove her clothes. The same year, a gentleman who told the children he was a school inspector quietly removed three handbags from the staffroom and legged it over the wall. People aren't always what they seem. I asked if he had any identification and he produced a laminated card with a faded photo and a title saying 'Press'. I wasn't convinced, although he seemed genuine enough. By this time, little faces were staring through the hall doors with interest, and I suggested that we walk towards the gate, away from the children. He blanched.

'I'm not going out there in the road, mate. They'll kill me. I need police protection.'

I said that Danny, our premises officer, happened to be working in the playground, and he always had his mobile phone with him, so we'd get him to phone the police immediately. More children gathered as we came outside, and Danny summed up the situation in a flash. Within minutes, a police car and a police van roared up the road, sirens blasting. By now, children were scrabbling up the walls, hanging over the fences, or lying flat on the playground trying to get a view under the solid metal gates. I opened one of the gates, led the 'reporter' quickly outside, explained the situation to the boys in blue, and left them to deal with it. There didn't seem to be any threatening youths loitering in the street, and I never did find out whether the worried intruder really was a newsman.

However, persuading the children that nothing much had happened was a far bigger task. Rumours shot around the playground and Daniel, never our best attender, ran up and asked if school would be closed tomorrow because of the gangsters. It occurred to me that I should write and reassure the parents, but I quickly dismissed the idea. After all, it was over very quickly, and nobody had been in danger.

The phone calls began at eight o'clock the following morning. Was it safe to come to school, asked Mrs Gray; Samantha had said three gunmen were holed up in the school yesterday and there were rumours one was still in the building. Is it true the school will be closed for three days, asked Mrs Williams, only Daniel said some of the teachers had been trapped in the corridor and one had been attacked. Why weren't we alerted about all this, demanded Annie's mum, who cries bully if somebody so much as brushes against her daughter. Are you all right, asked a friendlier parent, only I heard you'd been attacked by a huge man who rushed into the corridor yesterday...

Within a day normal service had been resumed, and the incident had been all but forgotten until the local minister, one of our parents, came in to take an assembly at the end of the week. 'I hear you're a hero,' he said. 'I'm told you were chased around the playground by a man with a samurai sword, and that you grappled him to the ground in seconds.' It was the most extreme example of Chinese whispers I'd ever heard. I was very relieved that the story hadn't reached the local newspaper.

When the media does takes an interest in something that is happening at school, a headteacher has to be very wary, which is why I was in two minds when Harriet Harman, our local MP, asked if Gordon Brown could visit and chat to the parents, hopefully fired by election fever, outside the school gate. Harriet had visited my school on a number of occasions, always taking the trouble to enquire about Thumper, our school rabbit. This was interesting, because we'd never had a school rabbit, a fact that I pointed out to her each time she came. Nevertheless, she was always very pleasant, showed great interest in what was going on, and was exceptionally helpful on two occasions when I needed help with housing for two of my parents, both of whom had large families and were at their wit's end. But it seemed that nothing much could go wrong, especially as Gordon wouldn't actually be coming into the building, and since we'd been talking to the children about elections and how they work, I said I'd be happy to help.

Harriet had also asked if I'd mention the Chancellor's visit to parents, and since I was finishing a newsletter, I suggested I put it in that. 'Good idea,' she said. Within three minutes she was back on the phone, saying that actually, it wasn't such a good idea after all. Her advisors had pointed out that half the neighbourhood might descend on the school, and then there would be all kinds of security problems. Within the next hour, a call came from Labour's Central Office, asking if I could send an email with a full description of the school and its work so that Gordon could be properly briefed before arriving. I hurriedly typed some notes, saying what an utterly wonderful school we were, and that we wouldn't mind a little monetary donation to help us finish the school garden we were creating.

By eight o'clock in the morning photographers and journalists had commandeered the road outside the gates. Labour party aides arrived soon afterwards, several asking if they could pop into the school and use the powder room. I agreed, warning them that our powder room might not meet the health and safety standards they were accustomed to at party headquarters, and to watch out in case one of our amateur plumbers had removed a pipe or a lavatory seat. Then, as school time approached and parents and children began to wander inquisitively towards the school gates, boxes of leaflets and stickers were unpacked in the playground, and bright red balloons distributed. My little group of 'challenging' mothers, always ready to grumble about anything to do with school as they whiled away their day between dropping and collecting their offspring, perched themselves on the low wall opposite the school, inspecting the scene suspiciously. 'If you want all them balloons blown up,' advised one of their husbands, nodding towards the group, 'pass 'em over there. That lot have got enough hot air between 'em to fill a gasometer.'

Children were now arriving in droves, asking what was going on and whether the Queen was coming. I told them about our visitor, and how he held the purse strings to the country's finances. 'He'll talk to your mums and dads,' I said, 'and he might even talk to you. So tell him about the school garden...'

One of them soon spotted the stickers and the other children, astute as ever, quickly realised the aides weren't sure who'd been given one and who hadn't. By hiding stickers under their coats they could keep going back with innocent faces, saying they hadn't had one. Ten minutes later, many of the children looked like walking sticker banks.

Meanwhile, our distinguished visitor had arrived with his group of minders in a huge chauffeured car, and was already shaking hands with a growing crowd of people. I hung back, interested to see how he would work the crowd, but Harriet insisted on introducing me and he gripped my hand warmly. 'It's a nice little school you have here Mike,' he said. I started to reply, but he obviously felt he'd done his duty as far as greeting me was concerned and he turned away to field questions from constituents, skilfully avoiding Mrs Elton, who was determined to question whether an annual expenditure of £60,000 on a top grade chauffeured motor was a sensible use of taxpayer's money, given the fact that she had three children and wasn't even eligible for free school lunches. I could only admire his conversational skill, and his unfazed expression when one of our fathers, usually exceptionally polite and well spoken, pointed out that as far as he was concerned the prime minister was a fucking liar.

Then it was time for the whistle. Children who had only collected half a dozen stickers rushed to get a few more, and the road show moved on. Harriet seemed pleased, and promised to come again soon, but I wasn't sure that Gordon, or our parents, had gained very much from the visit. In assembly, I asked the children what questions he and his aides had asked. 'What's your favourite subject?' seemed to be the favourite. I trusted they'd all said 'Gardening, but we don't have quite enough money to finish the school garden...' Only Tommy had managed a longer conversation, but then, Tommy would. The main thrust of it seemed to consist of the Chancellor pointing out very firmly that, no, the party worker standing alongside him wasn't his girlfriend....

CHAPTER 16
TROUBLING TEACHERS

'Queen Victoria sat on the English thorn for over sixty years.'
Mirabelle, aged 9

The vast majority teachers love their job and the young people they work with, whose lives they can often dramatically influence. Teaching primary aged children can be intensely rewarding, and during the course of a school year the class becomes your family. You care deeply for the children, and you share their hopes, aspirations and fears as well as their enthusiasm and joy when everything is going well. You meet their parents and you understand how their families work. You are responsible for increasing their knowledge and experience of the world, their handling of relationships, and their developing personalities. It is a massive responsibility... something the best teachers understand almost by instinct.

Generally, when a new headteacher joins a school, the teachers will watch him or her very carefully. Just as the new head wants to make sure the teachers are up to speed and working well, so the teachers will want to satisfy themselves that the head knows what he is doing, that he has a vision for the school, and that he is a caring and reasonable person to work for. If he isn't, or if they don't agree with the direction in which the school is being taken, or if teachers feel they have been at the school for a reasonable period and that now might be a good time for a change, they will usually freshen their careers by moving elsewhere or seeking promotion. This can be a good thing, because a school can only grow effectively if the teaching staff is fully in tune with the headteacher's ideas and educational philosophy.

From the start of my headship, I wanted to make sure that I selected new teachers carefully, but as my school wasn't a new one I also inherited its staff. Some were exceptionally capable, some less so. In any school, several teachers will need nurturing and support, others with greater experience can usually be left to their own devices, and a few can prove quite a drain on a headteacher's energy. I found out very quickly who fell into which category. One teacher, for example, constantly sought my advice or approval, even on very minor matters.

Before I'd spent hardly any time in the school, she asked me whether I could shorten my assemblies by five minutes to give the children more time to negotiate the staircases on their way out to play. Later in the week I was asked to check whether the BBC had been broadcasting one of their school programmes two minutes earlier than usual, because her pre-set video recording had missed the first two minutes. Although I insisted it was almost certainly her recorder that had been set incorrectly, she was adamant that the Corporation was at fault. Two days later I was asked to phone the council to check whether they could alter the time sequence of the traffic lights near the swimming baths at two o'clock on Thursdays, because her class didn't have quite enough time to cross the road. After school, she checked whether I'd managed to have a talk with the council and somewhat frustrated by her requests I said that yes, I had, but they could only increase the pedestrian crossing time by nine seconds. The following week after swimming she appeared at my door again... not with a further request, but to inform me that the additional nine seconds had made all the difference. I was delighted, especially as I'd been far too busy to phone the council anyway....

When the first staff vacancy occurred at the school, I quickly discovered that newly qualified teachers were required to apply to the local education office for a job, not to the school itself. When a school phoned the office to say that it would shortly be needing a teacher, recruiting officers selected a candidate from the pool of interviewed applicants and then sent the teacher to the school for a suitability chat. In general, a school only took the very expensive option of advertising a vacancy if it was a senior position that held a curriculum responsibility, or a management position such as a deputy headship. Although this method of appointing teachers seems very odd today, local authorities had a far stronger hold on their schools forty years ago, taking responsibility for many aspects of school administration that are now the responsibility of the headteacher and the school governors.

In the seventies and early eighties, it was very difficult to recruit good young teachers who were willing to work in challenging schools or inner city areas, especially London, because a teacher's pay was poor and the cost of living in the big city extremely high. The recruiting people at the local education office could therefore be very disagreeable if you rejected one of their choices, because they'd expended considerable energy on trying to attract enough teachers to the borough. The greatest need was always in September. Teachers who were leaving their schools usually wanted to finish the school year, and they put off resigning until they were certain they had another job to go to. This meant there was often unprecedented demand for replacement staff just before the start of a new school year. Quite often, demand exceeded supply and the education office simply couldn't cope, which meant that headteachers could be on tenterhooks throughout their summer holidays, wondering whether they would be covering a class themselves in September until somebody suitable could be recruited.

Nevertheless, the system did work well at its best, and there was nothing so enjoyable as a newly trained, eager young teacher bouncing through the door in July, creating an instant rapport with you and your staff, especially if they said they were at a loose end for the last few weeks of term and would be happy to work alongside the teacher who was leaving. This was extremely satisfactory all round. The new teacher would get to know their new class, the extra help would be of enormous benefit to the class teacher in the last few busy weeks of term, and the youngster would have the bonus of being paid a salary during the Summer holiday.

But it was also possible for the system to go very wrong, and then it could create enormous difficulty, particularly if the teacher being sent to you wasn't the sort of person you considered suitable for your school. In their eagerness to gather a large enough pool of teachers to draw from, local authorities sometimes appointed teachers who would struggle to survive in London classrooms, and since the role of the authority was merely to fill vacancies, they didn't spend a great deal of time matching the personality of a teacher to the characteristics of a particular school. But headteachers can only work to the strengths of a school's teaching staff, and just one or two ineffective or disinterested teachers can make a massive dent in the ethos they are trying to create. I found this out very early in my headship, when a teacher had resigned unexpectedly because her husband had been appointed to a job abroad. I phoned the office, urgently requesting a teacher for the new term. Several days later, I phoned again, to check progress.

'I'm afraid we only have a couple I could send,' said the officer. 'One of them would be very suitable but she's got her leg in plaster at the moment and I think she'd have a problem with your stairs. The other lady's name is Celia. She's fifty eight, but she's very keen. I'll give you her number. See what you think.'

When I met Celia, she did indeed seem very fit for her age, but I soon realised there were two major problems. Firstly, she intended to travel up from Brighton every day because there were no suitable jobs near her home, although she was keen to earn the considerably larger salary that teaching in the inner city could offer. Secondly, she had spent her career teaching infant children, although when I met her she seemed sprightly and enthusiastic and very willing to try teaching my top class of Juniors, which was all I had to offer. The class had been extremely well taught during the first school term by the previous teacher, who'd now obtained promotion elsewhere, and although it contained some challenging children, they seemed settled and calm. Besides, I had no other option, because no other teacher was available, and I didn't want to start the new term by teaching the children myself. I simply had too much to do. I tried to convince myself that everything would be fine. Instinctively, I knew that it wouldn't.

On the first day, Celia arrived fifty minutes late, very flustered, carrying her large holdall of teaching aids. The train had been delayed, and then she'd caught the wrong bus from the Elephant and Castle. Apologising profusely, she refused to have a cup of tea and a rest, and hurried into the classroom. When I went in an hour later, the children had sensed her anxiety and were restless and talkative. Even children who were normally well behaved were getting out of their seats and wandering around the room wasting time.

By the end of the first week, the class was rapidly slipping out of control. Celia simply didn't have the personality or charisma of the previous teacher, and she lacked the skills necessary to keep older children interested and controlled. Having taught infants for most of her career, she was also taken aback by how quickly the children finished a piece of work, and she struggled to provide an adequate amount for them to do. Travelling was also proving a problem. If she left school early, she needed to carry heavy sets of exercise books home to mark in the evening. If she stayed at school to mark them, her bus and train journeys meant that she arrived home very late. And it was obvious that the behaviour of the children was getting her down.

After a second week of deterioration, I decided to offer some positive intervention. I sat her down with a mug of tea, looked carefully through her work plans for the following two weeks, and said that I'd teach the class for at least the next week and possibly longer, while she assisted and hopefully acquired some class management tips. Since I often taught classes for several days, particularly if a teacher was away or on a professional development course, the children would not think this strange. And since the class was learning about the Victorians... a period of history I was fascinated by... it would be easy to persuade them that I was merely coming in to assist Celia while they started to build models and make booklets about Victorian houses and jobs.

Everything went well. Even though it meant I was unavailable to see parents or take phone calls and had to take a lot of work home, the children worked exceptionally hard. By the end of the week they had learned a great deal about street criers, chimney sweeps, market traders, childhood diseases and the great divide between rich and poor. During the afternoons they split into groups and worked on constructing large Victorian houses by glueing shoeboxes together for the individual rooms. Then they designed and built miniature furniture to put in the rooms. Keen to see the work completed, I spent several sessions of the following week with the class and then I gradually retreated until, once again, Celia was on her own.

And then we were quickly back to square one. The children simply didn't respond well to her, partly because she was perpetually tired and short-tempered from her travelling and partly because she was simply too close to retirement to have the energy needed. Soon, the quality of work slipped again, and parents began to question what was going on. Although I defended Celia, it was clear something needed to be done.

Shortly afterwards, I attended a local headteachers' meeting to discuss the borough's continuing problem of recruiting enough suitable teachers. We knew there was little we could do, but it was important that we regularly made our voices heard. Chatting to the headteacher sitting next to me, I discovered that she'd just been sent a teacher for an infant class who'd never taught infants in her life, and that the teacher wasn't coping at all well. Since my colleague's school was only half a mile from mine, I had a sudden thought. Here might be the solution to my own problem. I hurriedly sought her out during the tea break.

'You have a teacher struggling with your infant class, and I've got a teacher who's only had experience with infants struggling with my eleven year olds,' I said. 'How do you fancy doing a swap?'

'Sounds great to me,' she said. 'Providing the two teachers agree, but I can't really see them refusing.'

And they didn't. But unfortunately, although Celia settled into her new situation well, I quickly discovered that I'd jumped from the frying pan into the fire. Jolene had indeed only taught older children... but much older children. She had been employed at a senior school in Adelaide, she enjoyed travelling, and she had decided to come to England for a few years to gain experience and try her hand at teaching older primary children.

At first, things seemed to go well. Each time I walked into Jolene's classroom, the children seemed attentive and well behaved, but after two weeks I realised I hadn't seen them do any painting, science experiments or any sort of practical work at all. I also noticed that Jolene had removed one of the overhead projectors from the Viewing Room and set it up in front of her classroom blackboard, which she'd painted white.

'I've got all my lessons and information for the children on acetate slides. I can just pop them on the projector,' she said. 'It makes it very easy for the children to copy all the information down.'

And indeed, that is all the children were doing. Copying sheets of information on history, science, geography and every other subject into their exercise books. Jolene rarely taught. The children merely copied. Furthermore, they were copying information from acetate slides that she'd obviously designed over previous years for older children. When I questioned her about it, she seemed very surprised that I found anything amiss.

'I'm filling them with good solid facts,' she said. 'I'll be giving them a week of tests soon and I think you'll find they are quite knowledgeable.'

Try as I could, it proved impossible to persuade Jolene that English primary education didn't work in this way. Soon, I began to worry that the children would be walking around the corridors staring upwards at a fixed angle from perpetually aching necks. Once again I said I would teach the class for a few days, while Jolene spent some time in other classrooms, watching other members of staff teach in the way I wanted. It made little difference. As soon as Jolene was back in her own classroom, she reverted to the overhead projector. The only bonus was that the children were extremely quiet, though whether from sheer boredom or Jolene's formal manner I wasn't sure.

Soon, parents began to complain again. Their children didn't want to come to school, and they couldn't understand why, because they'd always enjoyed school up to now. And why did this new teacher just make them copy stuff from slides all day long? Why couldn't I give them a teacher like Mrs Peters, who'd been so good with the class last year? Although, once again, it was important that I supported my teacher, I sympathised totally with their point of view. After the third complaint, I insisted that Jolene look closely at her timetable, and that she found appropriate time for activities other than writing. She accepted reluctantly, and though neither I nor the parents were very satisfied, we crawled through the next term and a half. I was bitterly disappointed that these children, now in their final year at my school, should be having such a miserable time.

As the school year drew towards a close, Jolene asked if she could have the top class again in September, but I said I intended shuffling staff around for the new school year, and I felt it would be better if she looked for a job at a local secondary school. She wasn't at all happy about this, but I pointed out that the only vacancy I would have in September was for a Reception class of very young children, and that I intended putting her with them if she didn't move. She took the hint and left at the end of term. I'm sure the children were as relieved as I was.

But even when you think you have found just the right person for a particular position, things can still go wrong. Early in my headship, I urgently needed a specialist part-time teacher to work with infant children who had learning difficulties, particularly with reading. Although I was managing to keep the number of children in my classes to less than twenty five, it is always hard for teachers of infant classes to cope adequately with the teaching of reading, and they tend to be dependent on regular parental support at the early stages. There was also a rapidly growing influx of immigrant children, many of whom had only a rudimentary understanding of English. Often, their parents spoke no English at all.

The education office had nobody suitable, and I decided to advertise in the local paper. This brought in five application papers. One was riddled with grammatical errors, another applicant had no experience of this sort of work but just thought it might be fun, and a third only wanted a job for a year. I interviewed the other two candidates, and Clare seemed the most suitable. She'd had much experience of teaching children with special needs, she'd worked in a school similar to ours, and she could start immediately. My only concern was that she seemed very thin, and I worried that she might find the job too stressful, as children who couldn't read or communicate could sometimes exhibit behavioural problems as well.

At first all seemed to be going well, although Clare kept herself to herself and rarely came into the staffroom at lunchtimes, stopping only to drink a glass of water when she did. I had never seen her eat anything on the premises, and assumed she brought her own sandwiches to eat in her room or off site in her own time, but I had no complaint about her work, which was professionally carried out and highly successful. Her tiny mezzanine classroom was bright and attractive to walk into, parents were pleased, and the children she taught made encouraging progress with the cleverly designed visual and aural reading aids she constructed. And then, after half a term, I began to worry, because she seemed to be becoming thinner by the day. When I spoke to her about it, she assured me there was nothing wrong and I carried on believing this until the morning a parent visited and asked to speak to me confidentially.

'I didn't know whether I should come to you or not,' she said hesitantly. 'Then my husband said I should. It's Mrs Branwood, you see. I was shopping at lunchtime yesterday and I saw her opposite the fast food place in the high street. She was picking up scraps of food from the gutter and eating them. Some of the other mothers have seen this too. I've put it all in a letter to you, but I thought it best to talk to you personally as well.'

The full horror dawned on me immediately. Clare was anorexic and obviously in a serious condition. It amazed me that her work hadn't suffered and that she'd had very little time away from school. I had no experience of this awful, debilitating condition, but I knew I had to talk to her immediately about it and I called her into my office after school. She listened quietly while I read out the letter the parent had written and then tearfully explained that she had been suffering from the condition for some time, but with help from her doctor and a specialist counsellor she had been managing to control it successfully until very recently.

I stressed that I wasn't unhappy with her work, but I couldn't possibly have a member of my staff wandering along the road during the lunch hour picking up scraps of food to eat. She nodded, thanked me, and left the room. After school I discussed the problem with Georgia, who agreed that there wasn't a great deal we could do, other than have regular talks with her about her health and wellbeing. We had no wish to lose her, because the children were undoubtedly benefiting from her teaching. A week later, I received a visit from Clare's mother, in a very distressed state.

'Clare doesn't know I've come,' she said. 'We've been so worried about her lately, but I think she'll pick up again. She's receiving good treatment. She's been through a difficult relationship with her partner, and I think that has contributed to her current state, but she's always been a poor eater right from when she was a young child. I wish I knew the cause of it. It's a dreadful worry for us.'

I explained that I'd been shocked by the visit from the parent, but that we wanted to do our best for Clare.

'That's my main reason for coming,' she said. 'She's had several jobs and this is the first school where she's been really happy. If there is anything I can do, or you have more concerns, please get in touch with me. I just hope you'll be willing to keep her on.'

Miraculously, Clare managed to keep her anorexia under control, and I attempted to involve her in as many school activities as possible so that she felt valued and involved. Although she gained little weight, she stayed with us for a further two years before deciding to move out of London. When she came to say goodbye on her final day I thanked her for all she had done.

'It's me who should be thanking you... and your lovely deputy,' she said. 'I don't know what the future will hold, but I'm optimistic. I've had such an enjoyable and rewarding time at this school.'

It's always a pleasure when a headteacher can make a

positive contribution to the wellbeing of a staff member, or make a dramatic improvement in the way they do their job, but occasionally, however hard you try, you fail to make any difference at all. Robyn Willbody was a teacher I inherited when I joined the school. She was approaching retirement, and I learned that she had undergone a very short period of training in the days when teachers were in such short supply virtually anyone would be accepted and the paper qualifications needed were minimal. Neat, slim and full of restless energy, Robyn looked ten years younger than she was, and always came to school with a scarf tied purposefully round her head to keep her hair in place. Her passion was art, and her flaw was her untidiness.

Although I could tolerate many things, classroom untidiness wasn't one of them. Perhaps my own need for tidiness stemmed from my father's lack of it. He was a photographer and although he lived in an age of austerity and make-do, he would seldom throw anything away, which was a source of endless frustration for my mother. I remember her opening his darkroom cupboard and being showered with hundreds of film spools falling from a box on a shelf. He was keeping them because 'they might come in handy one day.'

Most teachers are very organised beings, and well run primary classrooms are busy, colourful and exciting places, where everything has a place and the children help to keep it orderly and uncluttered. Robyn was the antithesis of this. The previous headteacher had discovered that she had very little class control, so he'd put her with Reception children, where he thought she would do the least damage. As I was getting to know my school, I visited Robyn several times, and although her classroom seemed to have more cardboard boxes, stashes of paper and modelling materials than any other room, I assumed this was because she did a lot of art work and model making with her very young charges, and that it would all be properly sorted out as the term progressed.

By half term, I had difficulty getting into her room. Although she only had twenty three small children, the classroom was in a constant state of clutter. Every cupboard was open because the doors wouldn't close on the piles of paper tipping from their shelves. Half made models filled every corner, piles of newsprint and old magazines were heaped on tables so that children had to find somewhere else to sit, boxes of junk lined the walls, unwashed paintpots and caked brushes filled the dirty sink, broken pencils littered the floor, and washing lines had been strung across the classroom to dry out the children's paintings. It was impossible to walk across the room without brushing against a wet painting. Moreover, clothes pegs were everywhere. They held the paintings to the washing lines, they kept bunches of newspaper together, they were clipped around pieces of writing the children had done, and they were clamped to every document on Robyn's desk. After narrowly avoiding being garrotted by a tight string line one morning, I asked her to come and see me after school, and I pointed out that children were hardly going to learn very much if the classroom around them was disorganised and chaotic. She seemed surprised, but very keen to please.

'I suppose I can be a bit untidy,' she said. 'That's the trouble, I just don't seem to notice. My husband is always nagging me about it. I'll come in at the beginning of the half term holiday and have a good tidy up.'

Well, that's wonderful, I thought. A quick word from me and the problem has been sorted. Unfortunately, my optimism was misplaced and after half term when I popped into the classroom again, expecting to see a major change, I found that everything had merely been shuffled around or stuffed into large carrier bags and left against the wall. Even the sink hadn't been cleared of its paint pots. I spoke to Robyn again.

'Oh, I thought I'd done quite a good job,' she said. 'I thought it was much tidier now. But I'll have another go if you like.'

I decided to leave things for a couple of weeks, and then visit her again, at the same time taking a long look at her teaching technique. On the morning of my observation visit, her planning indicated that she was spending the morning teaching shape. The idea was to familiarise the children with basic shapes and their attributes. I had never seen a lesson like it. Firstly, Robyn scurried round the room giving every child a large sheet of sugar paper. Then she hurried round again, handing each child a chunky plastic shape. Then she gave each child a thick coloured crayon and told them to draw round the shape and colour it in.

During the next forty five minutes, the children were given six different shapes and told to repeat the procedure. Finally, Robyn ran around collecting all the pieces of paper, put a couple of clothes pegs on them and dropped the pile in one of the overflowing cardboard boxes, presumably never to be seen again. I had never witnessed such a complete waste of time. The children had learned nothing, and had sat still while the teacher did all the running around. I suddenly understood why Robyn sometimes dozed off in my assemblies and staff meetings. The children had expended no energy at all, while Robyn had expended every ounce she had. Once again I asked her to come and see me.

This time I insisted that something had to be done about her classroom, and that her lesson planning had to be given to me in advance, every week. In that way, at least I could suggest all sorts of things she could do with the topics she had chosen. As usual, she nodded vigorously and seemed happy to comply, but within a week she seemed to have forgotten that I'd ever spoken to her. Her lessons continued to consist of much running round on her part, and little activity or real learning for the children. Moreover, the classroom was in such a state I couldn't stand it any more. Once again I discussed my concerns with Georgia.

'Well, there is an easy solution,' she said. 'Her classroom backs onto the playground. If it's okay with Danny we'll come in on Saturday morning and wheel one of the big rubbish bins outside her window. Then we'll go through the classroom and throw away everything we think she doesn't need.'

It seemed a good plan, especially as Robyn seemed incapable of sorting things out for herself. By the time we got to school on Saturday, Danny had already moved two bins into place. His cleaners had been complaining that the room was impossible to clean, and he was as anxious as we were to get the room sorted out. We began with the cupboards, and were astonished at what we found. Old magazines going back to the sixties, stock that had been ordered and forgotten about, packs of pencils and piles of exercise books browning round the edges, boxes of faded cloth for sewing lessons, and packets of unused bodkins. There were also sets of reading books for older children… presumably from a period when Reception children weren't using the room. But also, to our delight, we found boxes of unopened puzzles, reading aids and learning games packed at the back of the tallest cupboard. They would be ideal for the children and had presumably remained hidden because Robyn had been unable to reach the top shelf of the cupboard. For the next three hours we removed the rubbish, set out everything neatly, and made the classroom inviting and habitable.

'Well, I wonder what she'll say on Monday,' said Georgia. 'I don't know whether we'll improve her teaching, but at least we've improved the learning environment.'

On Monday morning there was a knock on my door, and Robyn popped her head around it, although I'd hardly anticipated what she was going to say. 'I think the cleaners must have done some extra cleaning in my room at the weekend. The trouble is, I can't find any of my bags of clothes pegs. I suppose you don't know where they've put them?'

Fortunately, just as the classroom junk level was beginning to build up again, Robyn decided that as her husband had recently retired, she would retire at the end of term too. I wasn't surprised. Times and teaching techniques were rapidly changing and parents were becoming much more demanding. Being a pleasant lady simply wasn't enough. But she'd been at the school a long time, and we gave her a rousing send off with a Summer evening boat trip along the Thames. Several of the teachers read out little speeches and at the end I fixed them all together with a handful of clothes pegs.

Sometimes, right from day one, you know things aren't going to work, and such was the case with Colin Sedgewood. Once again I found myself nearing the end of a Summer term with an impending September vacancy for a class of seven year olds. That term a new local inspector had recently been appointed to the borough and my school, plus twelve other primaries, came under his jurisdiction. Although I hadn't met him yet, he was aware that some of his schools had vacancies for the new term, and he obviously wanted to be seen doing something useful right from the start. Two weeks before the end of term he telephoned me. 'I've got just the teacher for you,' he said. 'First class chap. Exceptionally well qualified. Couple of degrees, science specialist, really knows his stuff. I interviewed him this afternoon and he was definitely the best of the bunch.'

'What about his teaching practices?' I asked. 'Did he do well on them? Is he personable? Has he got a sense of humour?'

'Didn't really consider all that. But his qualifications are immaculate. I don't think you can go wrong with this chap. I'd personally vouch for him.'

'Can you give me his number? Or get him to ring me? I really need him to visit at least once before the end of term.'

'I don't think that'll be possible. He was going abroad straight after the interview. But trust me... it'll be fine.'

Once again I had a sinking feeling that being fine was just what it wasn't going to be, especially when I discovered that my new inspector had headed the science department of a highly respected boy's grammar school in a leafy neighbourhood, and that he'd never been in a primary school in his life, apart from during his childhood in India. I couldn't help wondering why the authority had put him in charge of a dozen primary schools in the borough, as I was sure he'd have little knowledge of the primary curriculum or techniques for teaching very young children.

Unfortunately, barely a week had passed before Colin got into difficulty. He'd spent the Summer hiking abroad and his flight home had been delayed, which meant I wasn't able to speak to him in school until the last day of the holidays. He was immensely tall, impressively fit and tanned, with a rugged jaw and a fiercely determined expression. Unfortunately all this didn't sit too well with his high pitched voice, and I sensed that the children would quickly find this a source of amusement. I also discovered that his parents, although now divorced, had both been successful teachers and had urged their son to follow in their footsteps, something he didn't particularly want to do unless he taught science to secondary children. Since the borough had no more vacancies for science teachers in its handful of secondary schools, Colin had opted for primary, provided he could teach eleven year olds. All I had to offer was a class of lively seven year olds, but the inspector had sold my school well. He'd assured Colin that he'd be well supported, have a great time, and find plenty of opportunities to teach some science, especially as it now had high status in the primary curriculum. Colin had therefore reluctantly complied.

During the brief time I spent with him on the day before term started, I explained how I wanted him to organise and run his class. I gave him plenty of stock, talked about techniques for controlling behaviour and introduced him to as many staff members as I could. Then, promising to pop in several times during his first week, I had to leave him to it. At the end of the second day, he appeared at my door and I motioned him to sit down.

'I was wondering,' he said in his falsetto voice, 'whether there is any recompense for damage to a teacher's clothing during the course of a lesson?' It had been a long day, and I blinked questioningly at him. He motioned to the bottom of his light grey flannel trousers, where there appeared to be cartoon drawings in ink on both his turnups.

'It was done while the children were sitting around me on the carpet,' he said. 'I was holding a book up for them to look at. I don't know who it was and nobody owned up. I didn't feel them doing it but I'm jolly cross about it. They don't seem to listen when I'm talking.'

I tried to be reassuring. 'It's best to keep the children at a little distance until you get to know them. I'm afraid we've had that before… one of our school governors had a similar experience. I'm afraid we don't have a fund for buying you new trousers but we'll pay for them to be dry cleaned and see if that works. But it's down to you to prove yourself with the children. It'll take a while for you to really get to know them.'

A week later, I was faced with another problem. Colin had taken his class to the swimming baths for a lesson, accompanied by Sheila, his teaching assistant. After school she came to see me.

'I'm sorry to add to your woes,' she said, 'But I think the car salesman in the main road may be visiting you to complain. The thing is, Mr Sedgewood is very tall and he strides out at the front like a giant. The children have difficulty keeping up with him, and he never looks back to catch the stragglers. The naughties see a chance to muck about, and I caught three of them climbing on the cars in the showroom. The salesman shouted at Mr Sedgewood but he was too far down the road to hear. Then in the swimming baths he got soaked because Andrew jumped in just where Mr Sedgewood happened to be standing. And Andrew's no lightweight. I'm sure he did it on purpose. Mr Sedgewood will probably be demanding a new pair of trousers.' My heart sank. Even though Colin had only been teaching for a few days, it seemed common sense to keep a careful eye on a class if they were walking in the main road.

But things were to get much worse. Colin found it increasingly difficult to control his class, and as the noise volume rose, he simply raised his voice until it became a high pitched squeak. Eventually, he decided to abandon the children who weren't listening to him and just address his lesson to the few who were. If I put my head in the classroom, everything went quiet and the children gave the impression of working purposefully. As soon as I withdrew, the noise immediately returned. On one occasion, when I was showing prospective parents around the school, Colin's door flew open, a boy was pushed into the corridor, and Colin demanded to know why he had hurled the pot of pencils at Andrea. The parents rapidly discovered there were other schools in the neighbourhood they needed to consider.

Colin lasted just one year. The tipping point was reached while he was helping to supervise at the annual Summer musical on a hot, steamy July evening. Our tiny hall was packed with parents as usual, the play had just begun, and suddenly an inebriated woman at the end of the second row began to accuse another mother of trying to sleep with her partner. A quarrel broke out, the two women began poking each other, and then to the concern of the parents around them, a full scale scuffle broke out. I was on the other side of the hall and I quickly realised it would be impossible for me to reach them quickly, but Colin was supervising the doorway closest to their chairs. Hesitating for a moment and obviously concerned about the difficulties he might get himself into, Colin suddenly made up his mind that something needed to be done quickly. Partly urging, partly pulling, he managed to manoeuvre one of the parents out of the row and into the corridor, closely followed by the other mother who seemed intent on continuing the altercation. Then, as he made a strenuous effort to pull them apart, he received a kick in the groin from the younger mother. Extremely angry, he rose to his full six feet two inches, grabbed both of them forcibly, and ushered them down the stairs, saying that if they wanted to continue behaving like stupid teenagers they should do it in the playground. Amazingly, because the hall was in darkness and the cast were acting their hearts out under the lights, the children paused only momentarily before continuing with their lines. But Colin had had enough. The next morning, pointing out that he hadn't been employed as a bouncer, he handed in his notice and he left at the end of term. The last news we had of him came in the form of a postcard sent to his class from Africa, where it seemed he'd been chased across a plain by a rhinoceros.

But perhaps the strangest staffing incident in my headship occurred in my fourth year, when I was phoned by the borough education officer, and asked if I'd like a permanent teacher for free. This was hardly an offer I'd be likely to turn down, but I assumed there had to be a catch.

'No, there's no catch,' he said, 'but there is a bit more to it. This chap has got his teaching certificate and he's doing his probationary year at St. Andrew's Primary, but the trouble is he can't get on with the headteacher and she doesn't want him at her school any more. To be honest, he's pretty hopeless and if he fails his probationary year, which is highly likely, we'll have to ask him to leave. We've got to give him a chance though, and if you can have him for six months I'd be really grateful. You can use him as you want to. If he can't get on at your school I don't see much hope for him... he'll have had two chances and he'll have to go.'

'So what are his particular weaknesses?'

'I'm not sure where to start. I think the best thing is for me to bring him in to meet you, and we'll take it from there. His name's Malcolm Treet.'

Like Colin, Malcolm was an imposing character. Extremely tall with slightly hunched shoulders... presumably from the strain of reaching down to the children's level... the wire spectacles sitting on his almost perfectly round face gave him a permanently anxious look. My main concern at our first meeting was his scruffiness. His hair, stubbly beard and knee length knitted pullover all looked as if they would benefit from a good wash. I shook a limp hand and ushered him to a chair. The borough officer sat opposite him and spoke first.

'Now, Malcolm, we've gone over all this, but just so that Mike is fully in the picture let me explain once again. With Mike's agreement, I'm prepared to move you here for your second probationary six months, but this is the last chance for you to prove that you can do the job. One of our inspectors will be coming here a couple of times a month to see how things are going. He'll be looking carefully at your planning and he'll be watching you teach. When you were at St Andrews Mrs Keeton didn't think your planning was good enough, or that it was kept up to date, or that your class control was effective. You'll get lots of help here, but in the end it's up to you to improve. We can't do it for you.'

Malcolm said nothing. He smiled and nodded occasionally, seemingly grateful that he'd been offered another chance in a different school. I'd already made up my mind that I would take him. He wanted to teach Junior children and I'd decided to allocate him to Wanda, because she was meticulously organised, had excellent class control, and was very inventive with her teaching. Since she was also very successful with teaching practice students, I was sure that Malcolm couldn't fail to benefit from her skills. At first, I'd let him teach two days a week, closely observed by Wanda. Then, if she was happy, I would increase his teaching time to half a week, thus freeing Wanda to do additional work around the school. If things worked out, I felt this could be a winning situation all round. I also pointed out to Malcolm that he would need to come to school looking as if he'd taken some care over his appearance. Children, I said, notice these things very quickly.

As usual, my optimism knew no bounds, and after a month with Malcolm I wondered how on earth he had managed to obtain a teaching qualification. Although he was kind to the children, he seemed to have no idea of organising and running a classroom, and the children very quickly found they could constantly distract him by asking him questions about his particular interests, the most prominent one being ghosts and haunted houses. It seemed he had a library of books on the supernatural and was more than happy to bring them in to share with the children, telling them hair-raising stories of real life encounters. Although they thoroughly enjoyed his tales, parents began to ask Wanda who the funny man was, and why he talked about ghosts all the time. It didn't seem to occur to Malcolm that there was a curriculum to be taught.

When he did teach, he seemed unable to stop children calling out or wandering around the classroom… or doing something other than listening to what he had to say. Repeatedly, Wanda found it necessary to bring things under control, or take over a lesson, and she quickly realised she would be unable to leave the classroom for any length of time and leave him to it. Eventually, she was forced to use him as a minor classroom assistant, preparing paint pots and sharpening pencils. Once, when he came to my room asking if he could borrow my typewriter for typing up some lesson notes to show the inspector, I thought he'd had a change of heart. Then I discovered him in a corner of the staffroom using the typewriter to write an article for a real ale magazine, to which he was apparently a regular contributor. There seemed to be no hope, and after three months Wanda complained that her class was beginning to suffer and it wasn't fair on the children. I couldn't let this go on any longer and I phoned the borough officer the next day.

'Oh well, he's had his chances,' he said, 'and I'm really grateful for all the work you've put in. No wonder Mrs Keeton wasn't impressed. Let him finish the week and I'll have him back here on Monday. I don't know what I'm going to do with him. Put him in a corner with a reading book or something, well out of harm's way.'

Wanda's class was soon back to normal, the children were working conscientiously again, Malcolm was quickly forgotten, and three weeks later the school broke up for the Easter holiday. Then, on the Sunday before we returned to school, I received a telephone call from Daisy Silton, a young athletic Scottish teacher who'd gone for an Easter skiing holiday with a friend. She'd never had a day of sickness since she'd joined us three years previously, but her voice immediately indicated that she wouldn't be at school in the morning.

'I'm so sorry Mike,' she said. 'My skiing wasn't as good as I thought. I've hurt my back and I've broken my leg really badly. I'm afraid I'm going to be off for a while. Could be a month. But I've done all my plans for the next half term... I'll send them in tomorrow and you can give them to the supply teacher.'

I got up earlier than usual the next day, hoping I might be the first headteacher to phone the office that morning for a supply teacher. As usual, there was a negative response, and although the lady at the other end of the line was extremely sympathetic, she wasn't hopeful.

'I'll put you down as urgent,' she said. 'There are so many schools with vacancies at the moment, but supply teachers usually like a longer placement, so hopefully we can get somebody to you by tomorrow or Wednesday.'

Once again I abandoned any hope of doing my own work, and I hurriedly prepared some resources and activities for teaching Class 7. Although I always enjoyed teaching a class, it meant I was not on call to see visitors and parents, sort out problems, or deal with urgent organisational matters. By Friday morning, when a supply teacher still hadn't been found, I was approached by Mrs Benson, one of our parent governors, whose daughter was in Daisy's class..

'This is ridiculous,' she said. 'Samantha really loves being taught by you, but you shouldn't be doing two jobs. A few of us are going to the education office on Monday to find out what's happening.'

'I really appreciate your concern,' I said, 'But I don't think there's any point in going to the borough office. They just don't have any supply teachers.'

'Oh, we're not going to the office,' she said. 'We're going to County Hall. And we won't come back until we've got an answer.'

The parents were well prepared. On Monday morning, six mothers and a couple of dads assembled outside the school gates, complete with thermos flasks, sandwiches and placards. They'd also phoned the local press and a photographer was already taking pictures. By ten o'clock a woman from the education committee at County Hall was on the phone.

'What on earth is going on?' she demanded angrily. 'I've got a group of parents from your school here making a thorough nuisance of themselves.'

'And I've got a class of eight year olds who need teaching,' I snapped back. 'Perhaps you'd like to roll your sleeves up and come and give me a hand?'

'How dare you!' she retorted. 'It's your responsibility to organise the teaching in your school and that's what we expect you to do. I don't have time for this. I have meetings to attend.'

I hurried back to Class 7, annoyed and upset at the woman's attitude. And then, during playtime, I had a call from the BBC. They knew that London schools were having trouble finding cover teachers, they'd already interviewed the parents from my school, and could a small film crew come down and do a short item for that evening's local news? Still seething at the County Hall woman's attitude, I readily agreed. When the team arrived, I did a small piece to camera, outlining my predicament and explaining that although I loved teaching the children, my office work was steadily mounting up and it simply wouldn't be possible for me to carry on teaching the class for a whole month.

That evening, with considerable anticipation, I switched on the six o'clock news and waited for the local news bulletin. And suddenly, there was my little group of parents, saying how unsatisfactory it was that the education authority couldn't recruit enough supply teachers, how the education of their children was going to suffer, and how no headteacher should be expected to work all hours doing two jobs. Education officials were interviewed too, predictably stating that this was just a temporary problem, and that it had only occurred because schools had experienced such a high level of teacher sickness this term. And then came a statement I wasn't sure I'd heard correctly.

'Mr Kent needn't worry,' said an official. 'We have already managed to find him a supply teacher, and he's ready to start on Wednesday.'

Still in shock, I phoned the local office as soon as I arrived at school on Tuesday morning. 'I assume you saw the news item about my school,' I said. 'Is this really true? Have you actually found a supply teacher for me?'

'Yes, we have,' she said. 'His name is Malcolm Treet.'

CHAPTER 17
THE ROAR OF THE GREASEPAINT

Louis Pasteur was a very clever man who lived long ago. He found a cure for rabbis. Charlie, age 11

After twenty three years of working alongside me as my deputy head, Georgia reached the age of sixty and decided to retire. Although she would be enormously missed by everybody, and I would be particularly sorry to lose her, I could understand her reasoning. She was active and healthy, and wanted to have time for the activities she enjoyed outside school, which included spending much more time with her grandchildren. Although I was a similar age, I was still enjoying my job enormously, my wife was a highly successful Nursery teacher, and I wasn't quite ready to give it all up. After giving Georgia a magnificent send off, the search was on for somebody who could take her place.

Even though educational philosophy and practice were changing rapidly, I was determined that my school would stick to the original aims I'd had for it. I wanted children to experience as many different subjects and activities as possible, and to have the freedom to explore their individual talents and skills. I also felt that music, drama and the creative arts had an indispensable place at the heart of the primary school curriculum, in contrast to the view of the government, who were now demanding that primary schools concentrated their efforts on achieving high results in the basic skills, almost to the exclusion of everything else.

Parents in primary schools all over the country were becoming increasingly anxious, mainly because they didn't understand much of the data on their children that was being presented to them. This was resoundingly demonstrated to me when a member of my staff was asked if she could give a neighbour's daughter a little extra tuition. 'English and maths?' asked my teacher. 'No,' said the neighbour, 'could she do some art with you? She gets the other stuff at school all day long.'

Finding the right new deputy head was therefore going to be a challenge. I wanted somebody who would be thoroughly familiar with current practice, but also a person who was not merely content to string along with fashion to the exclusion of tried and tested methods the school had honed during my headship years. The new deputy would also need to be an outstanding class teacher who, like Georgia, could create an inspirational classroom as a model for newer teachers; I didn't approve of the fashionable notion that kept primary school deputies out of the classroom in order to wander around monitoring and checking up on everybody else. Finally, and particularly important, she would need to value music and the creative arts and consider them to have just as much curriculum importance as the basic skills.

Fifteen teachers responded to our advertisement, six were shortlisted and two, after interviewing the six, were our favourites. Once again, the governors weren't in harmony about which one to choose, but I knew who I wanted and after two hours of heavy discussion we appointed Claudette, a young New Zealand teacher who had settled in England and made her mark at a Catholic school. Her infectious enthusiasm had impressed me when she had visited our school, and again when I had spent an afternoon at her own school, watching her teach. She obviously had many talents, but the one that appealed to me very strongly was her ability with music, and with her help I now felt that it might be possible for me to realise a twenty year old dream... the creation of a full school orchestra.... something that is extremely rare in primary schools and virtually unknown in a challenging inner city one.

When I'd joined Comber Grove in the early eighties there hadn't been a great deal of music going on. A few boxes of percussion instruments in classrooms, and some occasional singing sessions in assembly. There was also a good crop of descant recorders, since Wanda had considerable ability on the instrument and together with Gerry on the piano, she'd taught the older children to play. Then one morning I discovered seven classical guitars in a stock room, presumably purchased by a teacher who had now left and they languished gathering dust in a corner. One of them was broken and one was far too large for a primary child. All of them needed restringing.

It was a start, though, and since I played guitar, I announced in assembly that I intended to form a small guitar group. Unsurprisingly, there was a great deal of interest, as children equate guitars with pop singers and instant celebrity status and I was soon giving up two lunchtimes a week to teach the group. Their enthusiasm prompted me to investigate further. I discovered that the music shop supplying local schools sold small classical guitars at a reasonable price and I asked whether there would be any discount if I ordered more than one instrument. When I said I wanted fifteen, the owner announced that he was my friend for life and he'd happily arrange further generous discounts if there were any other instruments I needed. Together with the guitars I already had, there were now enough for a whole class, and I decided to spend Wednesday afternoons teaching the seven to eight year olds, reasoning that it would be four years before they left the school and quite a few could be competent players by then.

Although I was enormously excited at the thought of so many children learning the guitar at once, the first lesson was a nightmare. Preparing the room carefully, I'd put chairs out carefully in rows and stood a guitar against each one. The children came in excitedly, chose a chair, picked up the guitar, and hammered away at the strings, mentally becoming fabulously wealthy pop idols. A guitar at the back seemed to be playing itself, until I realised it concealed George, the tiniest lad in the class. Cedric, in a loud voice, informed the group that his uncle played an electric guitar, which impressed everybody until Cedric said that a string had snapped and broken his uncle's thumb. I watched several children peep at their guitars cautiously, wondering whether it might have been more sensible to join the gardening club instead. Busola, a very boisterous girl with an incredibly deep voice, started to sing as she strummed. The child in the next seat grimaced and I called for silence. Everybody except Busola and her partner stopped.

Eventually, she caught my eye, and told her partner to shut up because sir was trying to talk.

The first trick with any new group is to make sure the children point their guitars in the same direction. This entails knowing left from right, which catches a few children on the hop. It's why I always put out the chairs for the first lesson myself, keeping several metres between them. When children are manoeuvring instruments which can be as tall as they are, tuning pegs can easily end up in somebody's nostril.

But at last we are all playing on the same wicket and I introduce the parts of the guitar. 'These are the strings,' I say, running my fingers across them, 'but please don't play them for a moment.' Immediately, somebody does. 'Sorry, sir,' Spencer apologises, 'It's me nerves. Me finger slipped.' I forgive him and then I tell the children I'm going to say a very rude word to describe a part of the guitar. They look up eagerly. 'This,' I say, 'is the belly.' They giggle and repeat the word softly. I introduce some science to the lesson, explaining why the sound hole is important. There is a clattering noise because Faye has dropped all the change from her dinner money inside her guitar. The other children are fascinated and wonder how I'm going to get it out. I explain that the best guitarists make it a rule never to carry dinner money around while they're on a gig.

The sunlight is strong, and tiny George discovers he can bounce light off his instrument and into Samantha's eyes. Science again. Other children try, until I explain that we're here to become Segovias, not Newtons. I explain how a note is produced and I say we're going to learn a note called 'E' first, because it's very easy to play. I demonstrate, and the children have a go. It's easy to spot the children who are going to be successful; the less able are having difficulty finding the right string, and a thumb to play it with. George gives up and bounces light again.

I ask them to play eight 'E's in a row, to my hand claps. I count them in, but several play before I stop counting. I try again. And again. I wonder how we're going to progress to the next stage, in which they have to use a left hand finger to hold a string against a fret. Then, the half hour has passed and the lesson is over. The children hang their guitars on the hooks and file out, pleased to be heading for stardom. After my first experience of teaching such a large group, I wonder if, after all, it was a good idea to teach so many children at once. But the weeks pass quickly and by Christmas, although we've lost a few children who've realised that playing the guitar isn't for them, the group can play a dozen simple tunes. They pluck the notes, I pick the chords, and they make an impressive debut in front of their parents at our Christmas concert.

Spurred on by this, I encouraged Wanda to join her recorder groups with the guitars for some of our sessions, and we added tuned percussion. Before long, using Gerry's talents on the piano and Georgia's enthusiasm for singing, we'd formed an Infant and a Junior choir. There was no difficulty in getting girls to join... but many older boys were extremely reluctant. Singing was uncool, and not something they particularly wanted to do. I decided the only way round this was to give every boy a short audition, and if they could sing 'Twinkle Twinkle Little Star' in tune, they were compulsorily admitted to the choir. When they discovered that singing was actually a lot more fun than they'd thought, and that even with my cracked voice I was not only willing to run the choir, but have a go at singing myself, we were well on the road to success.

But we'd still only achieved what most primary schools achieve. Now I wanted something more challenging, and I bought six second hand brass instruments from my helpful music shop. I couldn't teach brass... but I knew a man who could. Joe, a professional orchestral player who worked with schools as a sideline, had taught brass at the primary where I'd been deputy head, and he agreed to join me for a morning a week. For a while, some extraordinary noises floated under the door of the music room, but by Easter his little band was playing a creditable version of 'When The Saints Go Marching In.'

The importance of music for primary children was becoming increasingly recognised at my school, the children were allowed to take their instruments home to practise, and no charge was made to parents for the cost of their children's tuition, a fact that impressed them very much. Many bought their children musical instruments for Christmas or birthdays. The staff, too, were becoming intrigued by the steady growth of music within the school, and the children's apparent ability to master whatever instrument we decided to introduce. New teachers joining the school were routinely asked if they could offer anything musically. One said that she could play the ukulele and within months an Infant ukulele band had been formed.

And then, on the first day of a Spring term, my friendly shopkeeper phoned and said that he had a batch of violins for sale. They were manufacturer's rejects with slight defects, but I could have the lot for a song.. and he knew somebody who had a spare hour or two on Thursday mornings to come and teach us how to play them. I wasn't sure if this was a bridge too far; when children were learning to play the guitar they could be told which fret on the fingerboard to place their finger behind. Violins had no frets. Not a problem, said my new violin teacher, we simply needed to put tiny slivers of masking tape on the fingerboard, and there were lots of simple tunes the children could play on a violin with just a handful of notes.

We'd also added tenor recorders to our stock of descants, and since a recorder is a relatively easy instrument to learn many of my teachers were willing to have a go, even if, like me, they couldn't read music. The children handled the tenors well, so I had a further thought... why not buy a few clarinets... or would they prove too difficult for our children? Wanda, who could play every variety of recorder, felt that it would be worth taking a chance, especially as children are always anxious to prove they can tackle anything, however difficult it might seem.

I bought five, found a charismatic teacher... and before long they could play 'Jingle Bells'... a stunningly effective jazzed up version. The only difficulty with adding so much music to the curriculum was the danger of children spending too much time out of class, particularly if they played more than one instrument and sang in the choir as well. However, the staff now seemed really excited by the musical progress we were making, and by constructing the timetable with great care we avoided any major clashes.

As the years passed we added more and more instruments. Six cellos, tuned percussion instruments, a timpani, a full drum kit, some flutes and some keyboards. It was then that I realised we now had all the components for a real school orchestra, a logical conclusion to everything we had introduced.

Although I didn't have the skill to put one together, my new deputy head did, and she set to work with a passion, spending several Saturday afternoons trawling the music shops for suitably simplified scores. Once she'd settled on three pieces of music for the term, she arranged for the separate parts to be taught by our visiting instrumental teachers until she felt all the groups were ready to play together. We decided that orchestral practice would take place in the school hall at eight o'clock in the morning, as this would not disrupt any lessons and ensure commitment from the children, although as it was a privilege to be in the orchestra it was rare for a child not to turn up.

Unsurprisingly, the first rehearsals were difficult. The violins and cellos went out of tune very quickly, impatient children would give an annoying blast on their trombones, a percussionist would mislay one of his sticks. Getting the instrumental balance right was also a problem. If a couple of flutes were away, the woodwind contribution was too light and didn't seem to work. If all the cellists turned up, the lower string section seemed a little heavy. But just as the children practised and persevered, so Claudette became adept at arranging and conducting. Week by week, the sound began to change, until one morning just before Christmas everything suddenly seemed to gel. Every child knew that something magical had happened and that thirty five dedicated young instrumentalists had successfully played a full orchestral version of 'What Shall We Do With The Drunken Sailor'. Yes, there had been the occasional dodgy note, and yes, there had been a slight hesitation here and there, but to me it was as thrilling as the last night of the Proms, especially when Claudette announced that by the end of the next term my school orchestra would be playing small pieces by composers such as Mozart and Handel. It was an enormously exciting time, and when the orchestra was invited to play their first gig at an educational conference I couldn't have been a prouder headteacher. 'I'll never, ever, forget today', whispered a little violinist happily on the coach as we were travelling home after wowing our audience. 'Neither will I, Chloe', I said, 'Neither will I'.

As our reputation for music began to grow steadily, so did our reputation for drama. Young children love acting and performing, whether for the benefit of their peers or their parents, and I was determined that we should give them every opportunity to do so. The highlights of our dramatic activity soon became the Christmas Concert and the Summer Musical. At Christmas each class was asked to produce a short concert item for a programme of seasonal songs, carols, poetry and plays. These would be strung together into a ninety minute performance for parents and visitors. As there wouldn't be enough room to seat all the classes in the hall as well as the parents, the children entertained each other at the dress rehearsal, and that also gave the class teachers an opportunity to fine tune anything that hadn't gone quite right before the performances given to the parents. But because Christmas is essentially a religious festival, I soon discovered that parents of differing religions could cause unexpected obstructions.

'I'd like Cheryl withdrawn from Christmas activities', Mrs Stebbin announces. 'We don't celebrate it, you see.' I steer Mrs Stebbin into my room. 'You must remember that we teach the children tolerance of everybody's beliefs', I say. 'The curriculum covers many religions, Christianity being one of them.' She nods. 'Yes, of course, I understand that. I'm a tolerant person myself. But I still want Cheryl put in another classroom when her teacher's talking about Christmas.'

I explain that this isn't at all practical. All the classes are working on Christmas activities and their concert items, so perhaps Cheryl should be kept at home for a few days. Mrs Stebbin reluctantly agrees, although Cheryl herself is obviously far from happy about it.

By the time we get to parent number four, I'm a trifle irritated. 'I don't want Femi in the Christmas concert,' says Mrs Amit two days before the show. 'It's against our religion.' Femi has been rehearsing enthusiastically, and apart from the little Nativity item being performed by the Reception classes the concert isn't religious. I explain that Femi will be bitterly disappointed, and after heavy bargaining Mrs Amit reluctantly compromises. 'Well, perhaps she could just hold the curtain... so long as she doesn't look directly at the manger.' I am so astonished I don't know what to say.

Mrs Okinde doesn't want her child in the concert either. 'I'm afraid we don't like Jeremiah drinking at the poisoned well,' she says mysteriously. 'But hang on,' I say. 'Jeremiah's just bought a ticket for the Christmas disco.' 'Yes,' she says. 'He can go to the disco and the parties, but he can't join in the concert. It's against our religion.' It's quite obvious that Jeremiah, always adept at twisting his mother around his little finger, has been assessing our Christmas agenda and selecting the items he fancies most. I tell his mother, firmly, that if you're in for one part of our Christmas activity, you're in for the rest as well.

By the time all the rehearsing has been done and we reach the week of the Christmas concert, there is always the worry about what might go wrong. Will the music player pack up, or skip a track? Will the scenery collapse? Will a mobile phone ring, because if it does, the owner is bound to be sitting in the middle of the hall where nobody can prevent them having a loud conversation.

The children, of course, are always eager to give their best possible performance, but as the years went by I found that we rarely got through a concert without something unintentionally amusing happening, whether it was the Angel Gabriel telling one of the shepherds in no uncertain terms to get his bleedin' foot off her wing, or Baby Jesus falling ignominiously out of the delicately constructed manger. The Angel Gabriel, unfortunately, caused concern on a number of occasions. Making an extremely impressive swooping entrance at one performance, Darrell's wings became caught in the wooden structure of the stable. As he moved position, his costume and wings remained firmly on the stable and he greeted the baby Jesus clad only in vest and underpants. Horrified, he hurriedly sought refuge behind the ox and ass.

Jason, on the other hand, wouldn't leave the stage. His teacher knew he had talent, but she had struggled to convince him that he was right for the main role in her little class play. Then, as he experienced the thrill of performing for his mum and other assorted relations who'd turned up to watch his maiden performance, he decided this was more enjoyable than he'd imagined and he refused to get off the stage, repeating his song ad nauseum and ignoring his teacher's increasingly curt insistence that his time was up. Finally, she climbed on stage, grabbed his arm, and led him firmly off, while he waved enthusiastically at his adoring relatives, and they waved back.

Sometimes, it's the props that seem to have a life of their own. Santa's toybox was a prime example. Beautifully constructed from wood and sturdy corrugated cardboard by the teacher, it took centre stage ready for the chief elf to open, whereupon Santa's toys would come out and perform their actions on the stage, all in time to a cleverly syncopated piece of music. When the time came for the lid to be lifted, chief elf Alfie seemed to be struggling. 'Open the lid, Alfie,' urged his teacher from the wings, 'open the lid!' Six year old Alfie fiddled and then struggled frantically. 'Open the lid, Alfie!' implored his teacher again. 'I'm trying, I'm trying,' Alfie announced loudly and irritably. 'but the bloody lid's stuck!'

The Summer Musical, unlike the Christmas show, involved the cream of the school's acting talent. In my early years of headship, I'd used commercially available musicals, and then one year, after we'd been stung by a publisher's particularly greedy performance charges, I decided it might be fun to write one myself, especially as Gerry was very keen to write the music and had shown a real talent for composing songs that children enjoyed singing. We decided on a musical version of The Tinder Box, it was hugely successful, and from that year on part of my summer holiday was regularly given over to writing the following year's show. I wrote for a large cast... around eighty children... and there would also be parts for dancers, singers and brief walk-on parts for children who were desperate to tread the boards but unsure of their acting ability.

Children would be chosen by audition, there was no age limit. and often it was difficult to decide who to use. The children's enthusiasm was extraordinary; when I needed a witch for Hansel and Gretel, I had so many clever, individual interpretations I decided to let the cast decide by voting. On another occasion, when I needed five comic legionnaires, the children auditioning were so amusing I rapidly doubled the number to ten. Often, a very young child who had only two lines to speak would go on to be the star of the show in later years as their talent blossomed to full maturity. Year after year the quality and standard of the show increased, until it was an eagerly anticipated event on the school calendar.

But this gave rise to a massive problem. The hall that we'd made into our little theatre was relatively small, every child in the cast wanted their parents and relatives to attend, and it was impossible to pack them all in. Admission had to be strictly by ticket, and parents rather than relatives had to be given top priority... causing particular difficulty the year a talented infant had been chosen for a major part and her mother had insisted on bringing both her current boyfriends, plus a six pack of lager to celebrate Brenda's performance.

Unfortunately, our little theatre wasn't very comfortable, but there was little we could do about that. To admit the maximum number of parents it was necessary to seat them on children's chairs, and for the larger parents this wasn't easy. The heat didn't help, either; the hall was on the top floor of the school, the weather during the last fortnight of term was invariably piping hot, and the combination of a large number of bodies in close proximity and the strength of the stage lights made it a considerable feat of endurance, although the wonderful performances of the children tended to mitigate the negatives. On one particularly hot July night, a parent in the audience fainted from the heat, and I feared for the two children hidden inside a dense cloth costume playing the front and back ends of a cow. Amazingly, the heat didn't affect them at all... they were too busy lapping up the audience's laughter. Nevertheless, as I introduced the performance each year after that, I taught the audience how to make effective little fans out of their programmes and encouraged them to wave them energetically.

I soon learned that I needed to be strict with audiences, too. Despite my newsletter saying parents shouldn't bring their babies to the show, a handful always did because there was nobody to look after them at home and I waited, tentatively, for the babies to start crying. It would always be during a quiet scene, and the mother would be right in the middle of a row, causing the child to howl loudly for the two or three minutes it took for the mother to extricate herself from the hall.

But babies weren't the greatest headache; the parents themselves, often simply through their enthusiasm, could cause unintentional disruption. Photography was the worse culprit. It is entirely natural that parents would want to take photographs of their children in a show and for some years parents were happy to comply with my request that they should wait until the end of the performance, when I would assemble the whole cast on the stage for them to take as many pictures as they wanted. But as the years passed and parents, in common with the rest of society, felt they had the right to do whatever they wanted, things became in danger of getting out of hand. The arrival of the video camera, a truly massive instrument in its formative days, meant that mum and dad would arrive in the hall kitted out like a small film crew intent on shooting the whole production, never mind the apparatus obstructing the view of half the row behind them. Fortunately, as technology strode forward and made pieces of recording apparatus ever smaller, this problem soon disappeared. Nowadays a tiny mobile phone can record large chunks of a school play, the parent merely having to hold the camera up in the air. Since most parents now do this, I suspect many of them end up with recordings of other people's hands holding mobiles. During one of our concerts, a parent filmed her daughter's performance and then immediately played it back at full volume.

Attending a cinema, theatre or music concert today is no guarantee that you're going to watch the performance in peace. People walk into a film with cartons of popcorn, sweets and various hot snacks and eat them noisily throughout a show. People chatter, fall asleep, or switch their mobiles on in the dark, and these annoying habits have increased steadily in recent years. Audiences attending school concerts are no different, but at least teachers can insist that parents don't settle into their seats with mountains of food, even if it is virtually impossible to stop some of them chattering in the dark. I've never understood why parents feel it necessary to talk to each other during a show, particularly when small children are trying to make themselves heard on stage.

Although I'm naturally keen for an audience to show an appreciation of all the hard work that has gone into producing a concert, it seems we have become so conditioned by vacuous American game shows that parents seem unable to simply clap any more. They whoop. They watch the performance given by their child's class and then they clap and cheer. And whoop. They usually stand up to do this, waving their hands or punching the air repeatedly as they whoop. It can be heavy going when there's a whooping after every song or dance. And even worse when they sit down again and miss their seat.

But all these little difficulties can never take away the sheer joy of putting on a show. Children adore performing, teachers are incredibly talented at creating entertaining concert items and parents love watching their offspring rise to the occasion. For many children, starring in a show can be a real highlight of their time at primary school… and one they will never forget. And even though we crammed so many talented performers and their parents into our little theatre hall year after year there was only ever one serious accident. It happened when Tony was playing an evil magician, and emoting wonderfully well until, in the darkness between scenes, he decided to give the scene shifters a hand. There was a cry of 'Mind me foot!', a loud thump, and for the rest of the performance the magician had a pronounced limp which grew steadily worse during the evening. After the show, I suggested that his mum might want pop him to the local hospital, just in case. The following morning, she told me that Tony wouldn't be back for a while because he'd broken his foot and it was in plaster.

'I'm amazed we got him there. Me and his dad had to carry him home,' she said. 'Mind you,' she added proudly, 'he was bloody good in his part, wasn't he?'

CHAPTER 18
WINDING DOWN

My Grandad is very old. He told me he could remember the Dead Sea when it was only feeling ill. Alan, age 10.

Before 2010, it was mandatory to retire from teaching once you'd reached the age of sixty five. Teaching a large group of lively youngsters is an enormously demanding job, and it is understandable that class teachers would find the job too difficult to cope with after that age. For senior managers, the position is rather different; although keeping a school running efficiently can be extremely stressful, it does not compare with the challenge of keeping thirty children constantly occupied and interested. By the time I reached retirement age, several factors made me want to carry on for a while. I was still thoroughly enjoying the job and had no wish to leave, the staff were continually pressing me to do 'just one more year', the school was extremely successful and a pleasure to run, and the cap on retirement age had just been lifted. I decided I could probably carry on for at least three years. Health is essential for teaching and managing a school effectively, and I'd been very fortunate. In my entire career I'd had hardly any time off work and even when I reached sixty eight I still felt fit and capable.

And then things suddenly changed. I'd been for a long walk at the seaside with my wife and was proud of the distance we'd managed. The only downside was a nagging pain in my left knee, but like every other ache I'd experienced, I was sure it would disappear in a day or two. It didn't, and several weeks later the other knee began to hurt too. After suffering for another month, the doctor sent me for an x-ray, and I was diagnosed with arthritis in both knees. Although I could take pills that would manage the pain, I knew it was going to be difficult to climb all the stairs and get around the three floors of my school every day, and the thought of not visiting every classroom regularly was depressing. It also meant that if a problem developed in a classroom on the top floor while I was on the bottom floor, it would take me an age to get there. Undoubtedly, travelling up and down the flights of stairs daily for thirty years had taken their toll, and although I gritted my teeth and carried on for another six months, I knew the time was approaching when I would have to end the career I had loved. After thinking long and hard, I told the staff that I had decided to retire at Christmas.

But health wasn't the only reason for my decision. I was becoming increasingly concerned about governmental interference in every aspect of school life and the constant, enforced changes in primary education practice... changes that seemed the very antithesis of what, to me, primary education should have been all about.

When I had taken up the headship of my school three decades previously, the emphasis had been on a free-flowing curriculum, with children's individual needs being given a high priority. There was a requirement that children should not only achieve to the best of their ability in the basic skills, but also receive a fully rounded education from an introduction to a vast range of practical subjects and activities. Now, much of that thinking had disappeared, the national curriculum had become increasingly rigid, and the emphasis was on target setting, data analysis and an insistence that children should progress in every lesson. Children were being pressured to reach academic levels that often weren't appropriate for their abilities. They certainly weren't appropriate for children with special learning needs, and yet similar high academic levels were being demanded of these children too.

Increasingly in primary schools, practical subjects and the arts were being abandoned in the final two years of a child's primary education, with insistence on the two core subjects taking precedence. This was leading to boredom for the children, tedious rote exercises for the teacher to administer, and a stifling of creativity for both. Schools were becoming clones of each other, with teachers being pressed to abandon anything creative in order to determine specific targets and achievement levels for the children they taught, all of which would be monitored by the school's senior management team.

Alongside these changes, performance pay was replacing the annual incremental pay scale, creating fear and mistrust amongst teaching staff. If a certain cohort of children didn't achieve as highly as the teacher would have liked, it didn't mean she wasn't working flat out to improve them. It merely meant that some children were more able than others, just as it has always been.

Governments of either hue were no longer viewing teachers as professionals and letting them get on with things. Successive secretaries of state, with their banks of civil servants who had no experience of teaching or understanding of what it entailed were increasingly interfering, stating what they felt schools should be teaching the children, and at what age. At one time, a teacher's personality, individuality and teaching style was key; now, teachers were becoming automatons, tracking children's progress on their classroom computers, gathering and assessing progress data, and submitting all this information to the school's centralised databank, which would in turn submit information regularly to the government's education department. From this wealth of data, the government would churn out statistics, pie charts and line graphs to show how the school was performing compared with every other school in the country, attempting to convince the public that this often flawed information was useful.

Though I found myself becoming increasingly alarmed by what was happening, I couldn't deny the changing educational world, and stopping it was akin to Canute holding back the waves. All I could do was keep it at bay in my own school. I had resisted the worst of the changes for a long time, and the fact that our most recent Ofsted inspections reflected the individuality of our school... recognising that although our school didn't necessarily correlate with what was required on the inspectors' tick charts we still achieved excellent test results and gave children a holistic educational experience... was at least of some compensation. It was also heartening that having challenged the competency of an Ofsted team a decade ago, our subsequent Ofsted inspections always included an HMI, sent along to make sure the inspectors were carrying out their job properly.

To be a successful experience for a young person, education must be enjoyable, a fact that isn't always recognised by those in charge of our schools. During my final year of headship, our local educational psychologist asked if he could spend a couple of days with us. He couldn't understand why he received no requests from us for help with challenging children, and yet in the other schools under his supervision, all similar to ours, he was besieged with requests for help and advice from teachers stressed to the point of illness by children who couldn't be controlled in the classroom. He discovered that the answer was very simple; in an environment where talented, capable teachers are given the freedom and encouragement to develop their own individual teaching skills, and where the richest possible curriculum is offered, even the most difficult child will thrive, especially if parents are encouraged to be fully involved with their children's education too.

The staff were saddened by my decision to retire, but they knew I had gone on for as long as my health would allow. And having made my decision, everything I did in my final few weeks assumed a special significance, as I realised I would be doing it for the last time. Clearing my room in preparation for the new headteacher was like moving house. I was amazed at how much stuff I'd accumulated, and all of it held interesting memories. Although I've never been a hoarder, my largest cupboard seemed to contain a history of education from the previous thirty years in documentation from the Department of Education. As successive secretaries of state had been determined to make their mark, so fresh documents and tool kits had been churned out by their armies of civil servants, virtually all of them now redundant and forgotten, and fit only for a museum.

The bottom half of the cupboard contained apparatus and chemicals I'd used for science assemblies. Years ago I could set light to magnesium ribbon, fire a carbonated rocket across the hall, show how a potassium ball skoots on the surface of water. Now it almost seemed mandatory to issue hard hats and protective clothing if I merely wanted to show children how to connect a piece of wire to a battery.

The walls of my office had always been decorated with pictures and photographs, a fact that always fascinated the children who came to show me their work. As I took them down, I found a photo of our first violin group, taken long before our school orchestra was formed, playing with frozen fingers to an appreciative audience at Southwark's Globe theatre at Christmas. What an exciting musical road the school had travelled since then. There were also pictures of many school events and snaps of staff past and present.. people fired with a passion for primary education and who had been such a pleasure to work with.

Another wall was covered with letters from past pupils, teachers, visitors. Many of the letters had faded, but all expressed joy and gratitude for what they'd experienced at our school. Some of the writers were now headteachers themselves, influenced by what they'd found here and determined to create a similar ethos in their own schools. As I emptied my bookcase, I looked through the books I'd read to the children over the years. Children may be tech savvy now, I thought, but they still thrilled to the tale of Baba Yaga the iron toothed witch, or the amazing tablecloth that prepares a feast on demand, or the old woman who tries to marry off her daughters to Jack Frost. Looking through the pile of books that I selected a story from when I read to the Nursery children every Thursday morning, I realised just how much I would miss that session, and the pleasure of watching the children's faces when I acted in character and spoke in funny voices.

Beneath the bookcase was the box of tools I used every week to mend the Nursery children's scooters, or their trucks, or the mini kitchen units that needed putting together when they arrived flat-packed from the manufacturers. I found myself hoping that the new headteacher would be keen on DIY too. In a dusty corner lay a magic kit I'd forgotten about. My first assemblies after Christmas always contained a few conjuring tricks and the children loved them. Mind reading and astounding card tricks for the Juniors, strings of silk handkerchiefs produced from an empty hat for the infants. And then, on a corner shelf with trophies gathering some dust, I found the tiny hand-crafted basket, beautifully mounted in a glass frame and given to me by a Maori teacher who'd taught with us for two years. Translated, the inscription read 'Truly, Comber Grove Is The Basket Of Inspiration.'

I knew my final week would be hard, but I hadn't realised just how hard. Christmas is a delightful time to spend with children and I had enjoyed thirty of them. My final week began with our concerts, a colourful kaleidoscope of seasonal music, poetry and carols. As usual, it was of an exceptionally high standard, and the hall was packed with parents. At the end of the concert, one of our parent governors stood up and gave a little speech, thanking me for everything I had done for his children and for those of everybody in the hall. 'It isn't just the wonderful education,' he said. 'It's the affection you have for every one of them, and that they also have for you.' It was a deeply touching moment, the more so because it was unexpected.

As the week moved on, many parents past and present arrived with gifts, cards and letters. Mrs Rollings had written two sides of A4, remembering all the experiences her four children had enjoyed at the school. Mrs Anderson reminded me of all the letters I had written when she and her family were in desperate need of rehousing. Ms Azizi tells me that if I hadn't been so helpful when she was having difficulty settling her daughter, she doesn't know what she would have done. Each day, teachers wandered into my room for a chat... just as they had always done... but knowing, sadly, that this was for the last time. My mind wandered back through the years... and the many times when I had comforted tearful staff members who were having teaching or personal problems, or shared abundant laughter, or discussed educational ideas with a passionate enthusiasm.

And then the final day. Knowing that I'd always placed music at the heart of the school, Claudette had been secretly organising a special concert of songs and instrumental playing from every year group. All our part-time music teachers had come along for the concert too, and all played a piece of music they had chosen especially for the occasion. I sat at the back of the hall, desperately trying to control my emotions as I listened to the children singing and playing their hearts out. Then, I was called to the front, and children from each class presented me with gifts and memories that I could take into retirement. Giving a brief speech at the end to thank everybody, and to sum up my feelings about the school, was the hardest thing I have ever done. Then on to an Italian meal in the evening with my wonderful staff, and a hug with every one of them. 'You must have been a pretty good boss,' the manager said as I left, 'A lot of them were tearful as they went out.' The next day, Saturday, I went into school to collect the remaining gifts, and I wandered slowly around my school for the last time. Then, and only then, I let the tears flow.

And what of the future for primary schools like mine? The educational landscape has altered beyond belief, and no doubt that change will accelerate. Technological invention continues at a frighteningly rapid pace, to the extent that we may soon be asking what the purpose of education actually is. Young people can now access information on anything, anywhere, from the internet, and every two years, the amount of information on it doubles. There is almost nothing we can't find on it, and it has changed our lives irreversibly, so is there any point in a teacher imparting knowledge, rather than directing youngsters to a piece of equipment that will find it?

In my own school, I watched information technology progress from one large clunky desktop computer with a handful of memory, to a dedicated ICT room, then to an electronic whiteboard in every classroom and finally to groups of classroom laptops. Within a year of my leaving, primary schools were buying small, individual tablets for children, all able to be linked wirelessly to the internet, and the price was dropping dramatically. It surely won't be too long before children are wearing a tiny device with a massive information storage facility and no doubt the time will also come when a tiny pod can be injected into the body, containing access to everything anyone could possibly need to know.

Technology has also changed almost every aspect of the curriculum, from measuring bodily functions and performance in physical education, to learning a musical instrument. These days, if I want to, I can create an entire symphony at home using immensely sophisticated software, or edit a digital movie I have filmed using software that is almost as clever as the professionals use. I can publish my own book, I can landscape my own garden, I can create a home cinema with sound and visual quality to rival the very best in town, and I can learn virtually any skill that I care to think of. And as today's children grow up who knows what wonders they will be enjoying.

But humans still have a basic need to interact with each other, and this will continue to be a vital role for schools to play. Children joining a Nursery class learn to share, develop social skills, collaborate with their peers, harvest their natural skills, try a range of interesting activities and listen to the wisdom of adults. If education works as it should, these attributes will be honed as they move through their primary years and further refined through secondary and possibly further education. Friendships for life will be made, and however sophisticated social media may become, nothing will ever alter the value of personal interaction with people who are truly loved and appreciated.

Throughout my years as a London headteacher, however swift and dramatic the pace of change around me became, I never altered my view of what a primary school should be. I saw it as my extended family, a place where young people could grow and thrive in the company of teachers for whom teaching and being with young people was a passion, not a job. From premises officer to administration officer, from teaching assistant to catering manager, everybody was held in the same esteem and valued for the part they had to play. And this, I believe, is how the best primary schools still function today.

Headship was, and is, an immensely demanding job. It can often be exhilarating, it is always demanding, and at times it can be immensely frustrating and worrying. But looking back over my thirty years, I wouldn't have missed a moment of it.